Using Microsoft Publisher 97
Quick Start to Publisher Perfection!

The Publisher screen

New to Publisher? This handy quick-reference card fills you in on all the basic features on the screen.

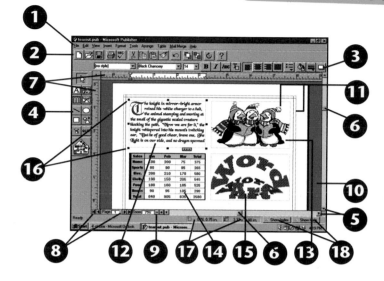

1 Menu bar

Give Publisher your orders from here.

2 Standard toolbar

The commands you'll use most often: Cut, Paste, Save, Print, the all-important Undo, Send to Front, Send to Back, Help, and more. See inside for details.

3 Formatting toolbar

Depending on what kind of object you're working with, you'll see various buttons here that can help you format text and tables, change colors, and otherwise dress up your publication.

4 Publisher toolbar

Use these buttons to draw text, tables, graphics, and WordArt frames, access the PageWizards and Design Gallery, insert objects from other programs and add boxes, circles, lines, and custom shapes.

5 Scroll arrows

Click to scroll up and down the page you're working on.

6 Scroll box

Drag the box for fine adjustments to the positioning of your page; click on either side of it to move a whole screen.

7 Rulers

Move these up and down or across the screen to help you precisely position text frames, tables, graphics, or WordArt.

8 Page selection

Use these buttons to move to the next page, the previous page, the first page, or the last page of your publication, or click on the text box to directly enter the page you want to go to.

9 Zoom

Click these buttons to zoom in or out from the page, or click on the text box to select what percentage of full-size you want to view the page at.

10 Scratch area

Use this area as a virtual tabletop on which to place text frames, tables, graphics, and WordArt until you're ready to precisely position them in your publication.

11 Layout guides

Layout guides mark the margins you've established for your page and any columns you want to indicate.

12 Text frame

Text frames hold text: the meat and potatoes of your publication.

13 Graphics frame

Graphics frames contain the artwork that brings your publication to life.

14 Table

To present some information properly, just put it in table form.

15 WordArt

When plain text just won't cut it, WordArt lets you create text with extra flair—thanks to plenty of built-in special effects.

16 Selection handles

When you select an object, these little black handles appear around it. Grab them and drag them to change the shape and size of the object.

17 Status bar

This bar shows you, on the left, the precise position of your mouse arrow on the page, and, on the right, the dimensions of the currently selected object.

18 Show Index/Help

Click Show Help to bring up the built-in Help files; click Show Index if you need help getting around Help!

® 201 W. 103rd Street • Indianapolis, IN 46290 • (317) 581-3500
Copyright © 1995 Que Corporation

Publisher shortcuts

Menus and mouse-clicking are a terrific way to move around Publisher and get things done, but sometimes it takes just a little too much menu-opening and mouse-clicking—especially when you're in a hurry. Here are a few keyboard shortcuts you might find useful.

Navigating text frames and tables

If You Want To...	Press This...
Move to the start of a text frame	Ctrl + Home
Move to the end of a text frame	Ctrl + End
Move to the next connected text frame	Ctrl + Shift + Enter

Highlighting text

If You Want To...	Press This...
Highlight the entire story	F8
Highlight to the end of a line	Shift + End
Highlight to the start of a line	Shift + Home
Highlight to the end of a paragraph	Ctrl + Shift + ↓
Highlight to the start of a paragraph	Ctrl + Shift + ↑
Highlight to the end of the text frame	Ctrl + Shift + End
Highlight to the start of the text frame	Ctrl + Shift + Home

Changing and positioning objects

If You Want To...	Press This...
Add a drop shadow	Ctrl + D
Make transparent or opaque	Ctrl + T
Bring to front	F6
Send to back	Shift + F6
Nudge left	Alt + ←
Nudge right	Alt + →
Nudge up	Alt + ↑
Nudge down	Alt + ↓

Opening, printing, and saving

If You Want To...	Press This...
Create a new publication	Ctrl + N
Print	Ctrl + P
Save	Ctrl + S

Formatting text

If You Want To...	Press This...
Bold	Ctrl + B
Italicize	Ctrl + I
Underline	Ctrl + U
Decrease space between letters	Ctrl + Shift + [
Increase space between letters	Ctrl + Shift +]
Increase font size by one point	Ctrl +]
Decrease the font size by one point	Ctrl + [
Center	Ctrl + E
Justify	Ctrl + J
Align left	Ctrl + L
Align right	Ctrl + R
Check spelling	F7

Adding and viewing pages

If You Want To...	Press This...
Add a page after the current page	Ctrl + Shift + N
Move between current view and actual size view	F9
Move between background and foreground pages	Ctrl + M
Go to page...	F5
Show or hide boundaries and guides	Ctrl + O

Working with Web pages

If You Want To...	Press This...
Add a Hyperlink	Ctrl + K
Preview Your Web Site	Ctrl + Shift + B

Using

Microsoft®
Publisher™ 97

Using

Microsoft® Publisher™ 97

Edward C. Willett

Using Microsoft Publisher 97

Library of Congress Catalog No.: 97-65542

ISBN: 0-7897-1220-2

99 98 97   6 5 4 3 2 1

Interpretation of the printing code: the rightmost double-digit number is the year of the book's printing; the rightmost single-digit number, the number of the book's printing. For example, a printing code of 97-1 shows that the first printing of the book occurred in 1997.

Screen reproductions in this book were created using Collage Plus from Inner Media, Inc., Hollis, NH.

Composed in *ITC Century*, *ITC Highlander*, and *MCPdigital* by Que Corporation.

This book is dedicated to Margaret Anne...
and so am I.

About the Author

 **Edward Willett** is a freelance writer in Regina, Saskatchewan, Canada. Born in New Mexico, he moved to Weyburn, Saskatchewan from Texas as a child but returned to the U.S. for college. He graduated from Harding University in Searcy, Arkansas with a degree in journalism. Edward was a newspaper reporter, photographer, cartoonist, and eventually, editor for the weekly *Weyburn Review* for nine years; then, for five years, he worked as the communications officer for the Saskatchewan Science Centre. Working at the Science Centre led directly to the weekly science column he now writes for several Canadian newspapers. He's also a regular guest on radio and TV programs to talk about science.

In addition to writing about science, Edward writes everything from plays and TV scripts to science fiction and fantasy: his first young adult fantasy novel, *Soulworm*, has just been published by Royal Fireworks Press. He's also a singer and actor who has performed in numerous plays, musicals, and operas across Saskatchewan.

We'd like to hear from you!

As part of our continuing effort to produce books of the highest possible quality, Que would like to hear your comments. To stay competitive, we *really* want you, as a computer book reader and user, to let us know what you like or dislike most about this book or other Que products.

You can mail comments, ideas, or suggestions for improving future editions to the address below, or send us a fax at (317) 581-4663. For the online inclined, Macmillan Computer Publishing has a forum on CompuServe (type **GO QUEBOOKS** at any prompt) through which our staff and authors are available for questions and comments. The address of our Internet site is **http://www.mcp.com** (World Wide Web).

In addition to exploring our forum, please feel free to contact me personally to discuss your opinions of this book: on America Online, I'm at **HWolin**, and I'm **hwolin@que.mcp.com** on the Internet.

Thanks in advance—your comments will help us to continue publishing the best books available on computer topics in today's market.

Henly Wolin
Product Development Specialist
Que Corporation
201 W. 103rd Street
Indianapolis, Indiana 46290
USA

 NOTE **Although we cannot provide general technical support, we're** happy to help you resolve problems you encounter related to our books, disks, or other products. If you need such assistance, please contact our Tech Support department at 800-545-5914 ext. 3833.

To order other Que or Macmillan Computer Publishing books or products, please call our Customer Service department at 800-835-3202 ext. 666.

Contents at a Glance

Table of Contents

Part II: Working with Words

5 Before You Add Text, You Have to Add Text Frames

6 Adding and Editing Text: The Basics

7 Formatting Characters and Paragraphs: The Basics

8 Making Text Stand Out: Special Formatting

Part III: Adding Graphics and Tables

9 Adding Graphics

10 Adjusting Graphics

11 Let's Table That

Part IV: Special Effects

12 On the Border

13 Getting Creative with Shapes

Part V: Putting It Together

16 Fine-Tuning Your Layout

17 Mail Merge

Part VI: Reference

A Installing Microsoft Publisher 97   321

Introduction

I started using Microsoft Publisher with version 2.0—and I haven't missed an upgrade since.

At the time, I had just become a full-time freelance writer, and I needed a powerful, but inexpensive, desktop publishing program, one which would give me the ability to do professional work for which I might get paid, without costing so much my already much-strained bank account would implode. Publisher proved just the ticket, and although I had used supposedly higher-end DTP programs before moving to Publisher, I found Publisher could do everything I asked of it—and then some.

The newest version, Publisher 97, expands those already remarkable capabilities even further.

What's new in Publisher 97?

Each upgrade has brought new features to Publisher, and this latest version, Publisher 97, is no different. Although it looks very similar to Microsoft Publisher for Windows 95, the previous version, it has new bells and whistles (such as the ability to preview typefaces before applying them to text), new PageWizards—and three really powerful new features, outlined here.

Create Web pages using Publisher 97!

By far the biggest improvement in Publisher 97, as far as I'm concerned, is that you can now use it to design Web pages.

I've had a home page on the World Wide Web for some time now, and I also maintain a site for another organization. I created them basically by typing HTML code into a word processor. It worked, but it was difficult to visualize the final product—and difficult to fully engage any creative impulses I had, since they tended to drown in the waves of gray code.

As I typed, I thought more than once, "Boy, I wish I could do this in Publisher." So imagine my delight when Publisher 97 appeared, complete with Web site design capabilities!

Now you can create a great-looking Web site in a fraction of the time it once took, using the same tool you use to create newsletters, flyers, and brochures. In fact, you can even easily turn existing newsletters, flyers, and brochures into Web pages using Publisher.

For the experienced Publisher user, this means creating Web pages is now a snap; and newcomers to Publisher will find they've purchased a powerful Web-design tool as well as a powerful desktop publishing program.

Publisher's Web-page design capabilities are explored in detail in Chapter 19, "Paperless Publishing: Design Your Own Web Site!"

To check out two sites created using Publisher, point your browser to my home page at **http://www.wbm.ca/users/ewillett** or to the Web site I maintain for the Regina Lyric Light Opera Society, at **http://www. regina.ism.ca/orgs/rllos/**.

Get online support for Publisher from the Web!

Not only can you design Web pages using Publisher, you can now (assuming you have Internet access and a World Wide Web browser) access extra Clip Art, templates, help, and more, via the Web, at the click of a button. There's a Microsoft Publisher home page maintained by Microsoft, and Clip Gallery Live, pages upon pages of additional Clip Art that Publisher's built-in Clip Gallery can call up as easily as it can the Clip Art that came with the program.

Create ready-to-mail documents with mail merge!

The other major addition to Publisher 97 is mail-merging capability. Now you can create a mailing list in Publisher itself, or import one from another program and use it to create mailing labels, personalized letters, ready-to-mail brochures, and more! For details on Publisher's new mail-merging capabilities, see Chapter 17, "Mail Merge."

All the tools you need

Even before the improvements to this version of Publisher, it was a powerful desktop publishing program, and all that power is still at your command.

That power is important, because the purpose of publishing anything is to communicate—and it's easy to get drowned out by the noise of all the other people trying to communicate at the same time. A journalist by training, I have a huge respect for the printed word. But there's something else you learn in the newspaper business: almost as important as the words themselves are the way they look on the page. You have to entice your readers, draw them in, capture them with a first glance, make them welcome. If you want a reader to look at your publication before he turns on the TV, your publication had better look good. That's even more necessary on the World Wide Web, where a million other pages are just a restless mouse-click away.

So join me for a step-by-step exploration of Microsoft Publisher 97. We'll explore every aspect of this terrific program—and have some fun along the way. And when we're done, you'll know exactly what you need to use Publisher to its full potential—and keep those restless readers away from the TV.

What makes this book different?

Before we begin our journey into the heart of Publisher, you should first know a little bit about this book you hold in your hands.

Using Microsoft Publisher 97 guides you through the features of Publisher in the same order you are likely to use them: from text to graphics to tables; to embellishments to make your publication sparkle; to a final check of the layout and printing.

How do I use this book?

That's up to you; but however you choose to use it, you'll find that it works.

If you're just looking for quick help on a particular topic, turn to the Table of Contents at the front of the book first. There's a good chance you'll find it there. If you don't, turn to the Index at the back for more detailed help.

If you're a browser, flip through the book and take a look at the start of each chapter. You'll find a short list of the topics covered, plus a summary statement of what the chapter's about.

There are also large, clear headings throughout the book that divide chapters into sections. Browse until you see a section heading that interests you, and plunge in.

Finally, you might even want to read the whole thing from beginning to end. I wrote *Using Microsoft Publisher 97* with that possibility in mind, so each chapter flows logically into the next. It might not be the latest Stephen King thriller, but if you're interested in getting the most out of Publisher, you won't be bored.

How this book is put together

A desktop publishing document is made up of many elements. So is a desktop publishing program like Publisher—and so, too, is this book. In fact, it's divided into the following six parts:

Part I: Getting Started

If you let it, Publisher will take you by the hand and practically design your publication for you. After a quick tour of the Publisher workspace and tools, and available help, you learn about all the different types of publications the PageWizards have up their sleeves, from newsletters to paper airplanes. Visit the Design Gallery and find out how its selection of snazzy design elements can perk up your publication.

If you'd rather do it yourself, find out how to start and how to customize Publisher's tools to suit your needs. Explore a few more basic Publisher principles, and then move on to....

Part II: Working with Words

A picture may be worth a thousand words, but for really effective communication, most people still find words pretty useful. Find out how to put words into your publication, format them, edit them, and bring them in from and export them to other programs. Have fun with fonts!

Part III: Adding Graphics and Tables

If you just wanted to use text, you'd have stuck with your word processor, right? Find out how to add the perfect pictures to your publication, whether they come from the built-in Clip Gallery, a diskette, a CD, or the World Wide

Web. Learn how to relocate graphics, resize them, recolor them, and rotate them. Move on to try your hand at tables: find out how to build one, how to fill one, how to decorate one, and how to bring one in from Excel or another program.

Part IV: Special Effects

The tools to make your publication shine just keep on coming. Add borders, shadows, and fills to any sort of Publisher object. Draw lines, boxes, ovals, star bursts, and more. Twist, stretch, flip, and color text with WordArt. And if that's still not enough, learn to add just about anything you can create on the computer to your document via OLE (Object Linking and Embedding).

There are so many ways to tweak your publication that you might have to force yourself to quit playing with shapes and text and drawings and get back to "work." (That's something I noticed right away when I started learning desktop publishing, but which seldom gets mentioned: it's a heck of a lot of fun!)

Part V: Putting It Together

Text frames, picture frames, tables, WordArt, and more: what happens when they all end up on the same Publisher page together? Can they peacefully coexist?

You bet they can—with a little help from this part of the book. Learn how to control frames even if you have to lasso them with a mouse. Line them up and give them a nudge if they step out of line. Group them the way you want them. Keep that text flowing. And finally, check your layout: use your own eyes first, then let Publisher loan you a second pair. Then take the Big Step: print your document, or prepare it for an outside printing service—or publish it to the World Wide Web.

Part VI: Reference

But wait! I don't even have it installed yet!

If this is the case, the Appendix show you what kind of equipment you need to run Publisher and what it takes to install it. You'll find clear, step-by-step instructions and answers to your common installation questions. And, of course, the book ends with a complete Index, so you can find any topic in a flash.

Special book elements

This book contains a number of special elements and conventions to help you find information quickly—or skip stuff you don't want to read right now. (I won't be hurt; I promise!)

TIP **Tips either point out information often overlooked in the** documentation, or help you use your software more efficiently, like pointing out a shortcut. Some tips help you solve or avoid problems.

CAUTION **Cautions alert you to potentially hazardous consequences of a** procedure or practice, ranging from the relatively mild (your publication will look really ugly if you do this) to the potentially catastrophic (if you do this, you'll never see your precious data again!).

Q&A *What are Q&A notes?*

Cast in the form of questions and answers, these notes provide you with advice on ways to avoid or solve common problems.

 Plain English, please!

These notes explain the meanings of technical terms or computer jargon in language you can easily understand.

Throughout this book, I use a comma to separate the parts of a pull-down menu command. For example, to start a new document, you choose File, New. That means "Pull down the File menu, and choose New from the list."

And if you see two keys separated by a plus sign, such as Ctrl+X, that means to press and hold the first key, press the second key, then release both keys.

Sidebars are interesting nuggets of information

Sidebars provide interesting, nonessential reading, side-alley trips you can take when you're not at the computer or when you just want some relief from "doing stuff." Here you might find more technical details, funny stories, personal anecdotes, or interesting background information.

Part I: Getting Started

1

Introducing Microsoft Publisher 97

● **In this chapter:**

- **Launching Publisher 97**

- **What are all those things on my screen?**

- **Playing it safe: saving your work**

- **Opening and closing publications**

I studied art in college and, at the unanimous recommendation of my teachers, promptly became a writer instead. But even the artistically challenged can create great-looking publications using Publisher 97. . . . . ▶

So, you've installed Microsoft Publisher 97 and you're ready for action! (If you haven't installed it yet, refer to the Appendix and come back here when you're done. I'll wait.) Follow me, and let's plunge into Publisher together.

A first look at Microsoft Publisher 97

The very first thing you see when you start Publisher for the first time is a special "Welcome to Microsoft Publisher" screen! This opens an 11-page Introduction to Publisher. You can read this now to get a quick overview of the program, or you can click Cancel and read it at any time in the future by choosing Help, Introduction to Publisher.

Once you click Cancel, and every subsequent time you open Publisher, you see the dialog box in Figure 1.1, which includes the invitation to "Select the type of publication you want to create, and then click OK."

Fig. 1.1
Whenever you start Publisher 97 (after the very first time), this dialog box is the first thing you see.

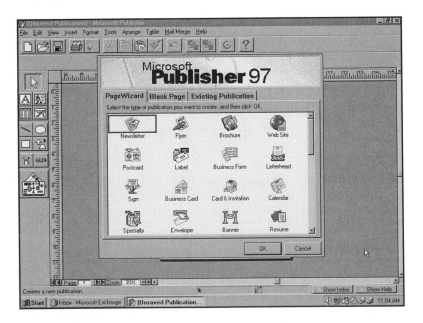

The three tabs you can click are PageWizard, Blank Page, and Existing Publication. We'll talk about PageWizards in Chapter 3 and opening existing publications later in this chapter; for now, click the Blank Page tab. This brings up another dialog box, which we'll look at in detail in Chapter 4; for now, just click OK. This accepts the default selection, Full Page; Publisher will set up a blank page as in Figure 1.2.

Fig. 1.2
Publisher awaits your creative input!

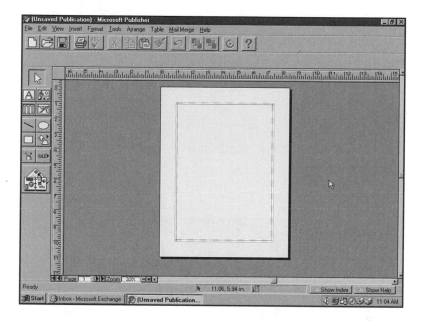

At the click of your mouse, these buttons help you create artwork, add fancy designs around your words, or insert a picture.

Status bar	Tells you where you are in your publication; helps you move from place to place and page to page, and zoom in on areas you want to work on in detail.
Status line	Keeps you informed as to the size of various elements of your publication, and also contains handy Help buttons so you can get quick advice while you work.
Formatting toolbar	Contains the buttons you click to change the way your text or graphics look, from colors to alignment to whether they appear right-side up or upside down.
Rulers	Help you line objects up on the page and judge their size. A thin line always indicates your mouse pointer's position.

The Publisher toolbar

This may look a bit intimidating at first—there are an awful lot of buttons and text all over the place—but with a little practice, Publisher's controls will become second nature. Follow me now on a guided tour through the forest of buttons.

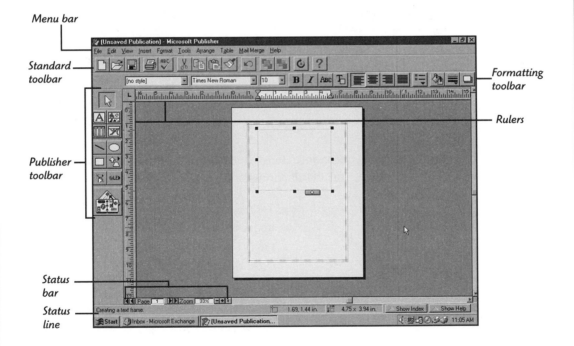

Menu bar

Standard toolbar

Publisher toolbar

Status bar

Status line

Formatting toolbar

Rulers

Standard toolbar	Controls functions you use frequently, like printing and saving your work.
Menu bar	Click any of these words, and a menu will drop down, offering you the commands you need to perfect your publication.

Meet the Standard toolbar: Easy access to common tasks

You'll normally find two toolbars in Publisher: the Standard toolbar and the Publisher toolbar. When you work with text or graphics, you'll also have access to the Formatting toolbar. We'll look at the Publisher toolbar in Chapter 5, "Before You Add Text, You Have to Add Text Frames," and the various formatting toolbars as we talk about the different objects you can create in Publisher.

The Standard toolbar is probably already familiar to you from other Windows software. Its buttons give you one-click access to many of the most common tasks (see Figure 1.3).

Standard toolbar

Fig. 1.3
Although many of the Standard toolbar's buttons are the same as those found in other Windows software, there are a few unique to Publisher.

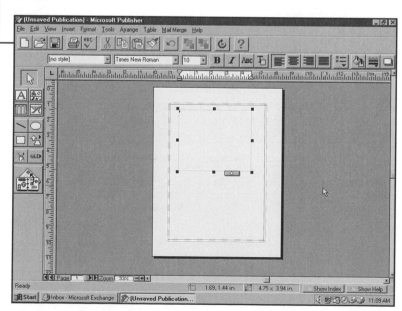

Button	Name	What it does
	New	Opens a new publication.
	Open	Opens an existing publication.
	Save	Saves the current publication.
	Print	Prints the current publication.
	Spelling	Checks the spelling of text in the publication.
	Cut	Removes the selected item from your publication and places it on the Clipboard.
	Copy	Makes a copy of the selected item and places it on the Clipboard.
	Paste	Places the contents of the Clipboard where your pointer is when you select the Paste button.
	Format Painter	Takes the formatting of one item and applies it to another item.
	Undo/Redo	Reverses your last action.
	Bring to Front	Brings an object in the background to the foreground.
	Send to Back	Places a foreground object in the background.

Button	Name	What it does
↻	Rotate	Rotates a graphic element.
?	Help	Opens the Help window.

Finding your way around your publication

Moving around your publication in Publisher is a little different from moving around a document in a word processor. For example, Page Up and Page Down don't move you between pages in Publisher: they just move the page you're working on up and down. Publisher provides you with several special controls for getting from place to place in your publication, and locates them conveniently in the status bar (see Figure 1.4).

Fig. 1.4
Like the cockpit of an airplane, the status bar contains all the controls you need to move from place to place.

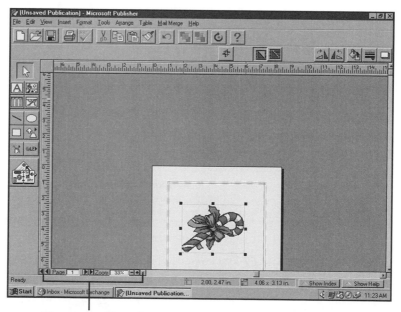

All controls on Status bar

Button	Name	What it does
First Page	First Page	Moves to the first page of your publication.
Previous Page	Previous Page	Moves to the page before the current page.
Page 1	Change Pages	Lets you choose the specific page you want to move to.
Next Page	Next Page	Moves to the page after the current page.
Last Page	Last Page	Moves to the last page of your publication.
Zoom 33%	Select Zoom Mode	Lets you select how big the page will appear on your screen, based on a percentage of the page size.
Zoom Out	Zoom Out	Makes the page appear smaller incrementally.
Zoom In	Zoom In	Makes the page appear larger incrementally.
Left Horizontal Scroll	Left Horizontal Scroll Bar Arrow	Moves the display toward the left.
Right Horizontal Scroll	Right Horizontal Scroll Bar Arrow	Moves the display toward the right.

TIP **The F9 key toggles you between whatever the current zoom** percentage is and a full-sized view. This allows you to work on something in extreme close-up and then "step back" to see the overall effect more easily.

The Status line: More tools and information

Just below the status bar is the status line, which provides information about the elements of your publication, and also holds handy Help buttons (see Figure 1.5).

Fig. 1.5

The Status line tells you the size and position of selected objects.

In the center of the status line are the Object Position box and the Object Size box.

- When you select an object, its position is indicated in the Object Position box. The left number is how far from the zero on the horizontal ruler the object is located, and the right number is how far from the zero on the vertical ruler the object is located. A positive number indicates the frame is to the right or below the zero; a negative number indicates it's to the left or above. (The zero on both rulers defaults to the upper left corner of the page.) When no object is selected, the Object Position box indicates the position of your mouse pointer.

- The Object Size box tells you the size of the selected object. The left number is the width, and the right number is the height.

66 *Plain English, please!*

Selecting an object means choosing it to work on. To select an object, click it. This changes the object's frame to a dark line with squares appearing on all sides and on the corners. The squares are *selection handles.* 99

The right side of the status line holds buttons for Publisher Help. For more information on Help, see Chapter 2, "Calling for Help!"

Playing it safe: Saving your work

If you ever plan to use your publication again, you naturally have to save it. But don't wait until you finish! All it takes is a flicker in the power supply or an accidental brush of the reset button, and your hours of work will have been in vain.

Fortunately, Publisher not only makes it easy for you to save, it will even remind you when you haven't!

 TIP

How often should you save? Whenever the amount of work you've done has reached the point where you don't want to do it again—which, for me, means every time I've placed a new graphic, or finished formatting a text frame, or written a new paragraph. It only takes a second to save, but it takes a long time to do something for the second time, especially when you're trying to do it while muttering curses under your breath.

You can save a publication by:

- Clicking the Save button on the Standard toolbar.
- Choosing <u>F</u>ile, <u>S</u>ave.
- Pressing Ctrl+S.

I get caught up in my work and forget to save

What do you do to remind yourself of something that needs to be done? Some people tie a string around their finger. Some people leave sticky notes all over the place. I've tried both and I still forget.

Fortunately, you don't need either to remind you to save your Publisher publication. Publisher does the reminding for you with a little nag—um, reminder box (see Figure 1.6)—that comes up every 15 minutes.

 CAUTION

This reminder is ONLY a reminder; it is NOT an automatic save feature like you can find in some other applications. If you click Yes, Publisher saves the file. If not, it doesn't.

Fig. 1.6
Publisher reminds you that you haven't saved your work for a while.

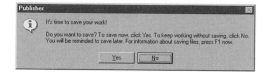

If 15 minutes seems like a long time to wait between saves (it does to me), you might want to shorten the time between reminders. (You may also find the reminders so annoying—also like me—that you want to get rid of them entirely.)

1 Choose Tools, Options to open the Options dialog box; then click the Editing and User Assistance tab. You'll find the Remind to save publications check box at the bottom (see Figure 1.7).

Fig. 1.7
Use the Options dialog box to adjust how frequently Publisher reminds you to save, or to turn off the reminders altogether.

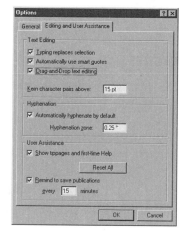

2 To adjust the time between save publication reminders, specify the time period you want between reminders in the every box.

3 To disable the save publication reminders, remove the check in the Remind to save publications check box.

Back up for extra safety!

When you save a publication for the first time, or when you choose File, Save As, you're given the option of also creating a backup copy of your publication. If you create a backup, Publisher saves a second copy of your publication every time you save the original copy. This doubles the disk space required to save your publication, but it also adds one more level of protection from unforeseen disasters!

To create a backup, just check the Backup check box in the Save or Save As dialog box (see Figure 1.8).

Other Save options

Take another look at Figure 1.8, and you'll see there are other check boxes besides Backup in the Save dialog box.

- Save All Text as File—When you click this check box, selected text, or all text, if none is selected, contained in your Publisher publication will be saved as a text file. Choose the format you want (that is, Word-Perfect 5.1, Word 6.0, Rich Text Format, and so on) from the Save as type list box, which only becomes active when you check this check box.

- Save Preview—When you select this check box, Publisher saves a thumbnail sketch of your publication, which will appear the next time you browse among your publications. Previews can help you find the right publication from among many with similar or cryptic names.

- Template—A template is a blueprint you use to create a new publication in the style of an old one. Templates are stored in their own directory. If you create a design you're particularly proud of, and plan to use again—say, for an ongoing newsletter—it's a good idea to save it as a template.

Opening and closing publications

You don't always want to start a new publication when you first launch Publisher; sometimes, you want to work on an old one or print another copy of it.

Opening a publication when Publisher first launches

As you'll recall, when you first launched Publisher, you had three options to choose from. To open an existing publication, choose the Existing Publication tab (what else?) from that opening dialog box (see Figure 1.9).

Fig. 1.9
Choose the publication you want to open from this dialog box.

From here, you can choose from one of your <u>M</u>ost recently used files, in the upper left corner. Below that are listed other files in the same directory as the last file you opened. Finally, you can click the button in the lower left corner to browse your computer for the publication you want. (As you can see, this is where it's handy to have saved a preview of your publication.)

Closing a publication

Closing a publication means you remove it from your workspace, clearing your screen to make room for the next publication you want to work on. Closing isn't the same as exiting, which means leaving Publisher completely.

To close a publication, choose <u>F</u>ile, <u>C</u>lose Publication. If you made any changes to the publication since opening it, Publisher asks you if you want to save those changes before closing.

One at a time, please

Unlike some applications, which allow you to work on several documents at once and move among them, Publisher will only allow you to have one publication open at a time. That means that if you want to work on a new publication, you have to close the old one.

If you try to open a new publication when one is already open, Publisher automatically closes the one that's open. But don't worry; it will give you the chance to save any changes you might have made to it.

 TIP   **If you really need to work on two publications at once—usually** because you want to cut and paste between them—then all you have to do is launch a second copy of Publisher and open the second publication in it. You can easily toggle between the two by pressing Alt+Tab or clicking their respective buttons on the Windows 95 taskbar.

Planning your publication

Now that you've had a quick tour of some Publisher basics, you're probably eager to launch into designing your own publication—but not so fast!

You can avoid a lot of the bad design that plagues the world of desktop publishing by following one simple rule: plan ahead.

Before they paint a masterpiece, most artists spend a lot of time thinking about it and sketching out how they think it will look. That's a good rule for desktop publishers, too.

First, know your goal. Do you want to sell things? Promote an event? Educate the public? Lay out an agenda? This will helps you determine the overall look of the publication.

Every publication has its own tone: aggressive, seductive, intriguing, funny. Your goal and your audience help you determine which tone is right for your publication.

Next, ask yourself more specific questions.

1   What font should I use?

2   What kind of artwork do I want to include, and how much of it?

3   Do I want colors? How many? Which ones?

4   What size should my publication be?

5   How should it be folded?

Keeping your answers in mind, sketch out your publication. Indicate where you'll put text and graphics, where you'll want a table or a drawing, what you want to leave blank.

Always keep in mind that your goal is to *communicate*. Don't get so carried away with fancy design ideas that you obscure the message you're trying to get across.

With sketch in hand, you'll find it's really easy to create a publication that does what you want it to do. But remember, the sketch is just the beginning—don't be a slave to it. Go ahead and make any improvements that suggest themselves during the design process.

After all, desktop publishing makes it easy to make changes. That's one of its greatest strengths; it allows you to fine-tune your design to achieve the maximum impact.

2

Calling for Help!

● In this chapter:

- ● Quick demos

- ● Built-in help of all sorts

- ● Technical support

- ● The Microsoft Publisher Web site

Whether you need help doing something for the first time or advanced help for tricky situations, Publisher provides a way to find it!. . . . . ●>

My girlfriend tells me it's a guy thing: I don't like to ask for help. That includes asking somebody else for ideas for the weekly science column I write, asking someone how to accomplish a particular task, and especially (of course) asking for directions. (Personally, I think it's a survival trait going back millions of years: a fear that if you show weakness, younger males will drive you out of the tribe and steal your mate.)

Fortunately, my allergy to asking for help doesn't apply to getting help by reading, so I never have a problem with using the help features that come with computer programs…and Publisher, as it happens, has some really good ones!

Help at your finger tips

Publisher is a very easy program to use and learn, but you're still occasionally going to have questions about a specific procedure. For those occasions, Publisher provides an enormous amount of built-in help, available at the click of a button.

Click for a quick demo!

For many concepts and functions, Publisher provides a Quick Demo. To access a list of available demos, choose <u>H</u>elp, Quick <u>D</u>emos. Choose the demo you want from the list and click OK.

When the first page of the demo appears, it indicates the number of pages in the demo and provides buttons for moving from page to page. Figure 2.1 shows the first page of the Rotating demo.

 TIP **In addition to demos on various functions, Publisher offers two** more general demos. Choose <u>H</u>elp, <u>I</u>ntroduction to Publisher. This gives you two choices: Introduction to Publisher and What's new in Publisher? Introduction to Publisher is a good place to start if you've never used Publisher before; it introduces some of the basic concepts and tools. If you are familiar with previous versions of Publisher, take a look at What's new in Publisher, which points out some of the new features in Publisher 97.

Fig. 2.1
Demos combine words
and diagrams to show
you how to use a
particular Publisher
function.

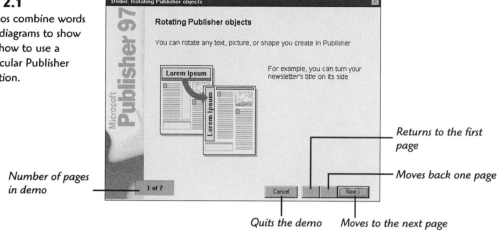

*Returns to the first
page*

Moves back one page

*Number of pages
in demo*

Quits the demo   *Moves to the next page*

More help: Show Help and Show Index

In Chapter 1, "Introducing Microsoft Publisher 97," I pointed out the Show Help and Show Index buttons on the status line. These buttons are the easiest way to access Publisher's built-in help.

Clicking the Show Help button (or choosing Help, Microsoft Publisher Help Topics) for the first time in a Publisher session brings up the Help window (see Figure 2.2), which asks you "What do you want to create or work on?" When you select one of the available types of publications, Help then asks you additional questions to focus in on your specific area of interest, eventually presenting you with a "How to" tab that details how to accomplish a particular task. The Contents button takes you back to the first listing of topics about the type of publication you've indicated you're working on, and you can always print out a particular topic by clicking Print.

For complete access to all Help topics, not just those related to a specific type of publication, click the Show Index button, which makes the Help Index appear. When you select a topic in the index, information on that topic appears in the Help window to the right of the index (see Figure 2.3). Notice that the buttons on the status line now read Hide Index and Hide Help: clicking them again will close the Help windows.

Fig. 2.2
When you click Show Help, Help asks you a series of questions designed to focus in on your specific concern.

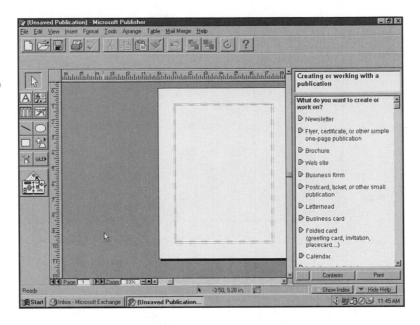

Fig. 2.3
The Help Index is a handy way to access all the help Publisher has to offer.

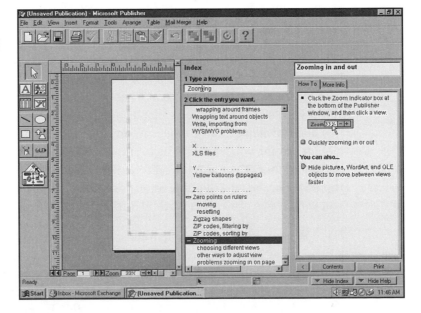

To adjust the size of the text in the Help and Help Index windows, choose Help, Help Text Size, and then your choice: Smaller, Normal, or Bigger.

TIP **Some people like to learn all the keyboard shortcuts they can so** they don't have to push the mouse around all day. For those people, Publisher provides a shortcut (though not a keyboard shortcut, oddly enough!) to the Help section on keyboard shortcuts. Just choose Help, Keyboard shortcuts. Happy memorizing!

What's This?

That isn't a question; it's a feature. You can find it in most dialog boxes. Just place your mouse pointer over a button or text, and click the right mouse button. A little box opens with the message What's This? displayed (see Figure 2.4). You can either click the little box again or type **W** to bring up a message box containing a description of the item (see Figure 2.5).

Fig. 2.4
Point at any item in a dialog box you're interested in, and right-click to bring up the What's This? message box.

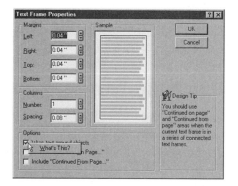

Another way to get the same help is to first click the ? in the upper right corner of the dialog box. This adds a question mark to your mouse pointer. Place the pointer over the item you want more information on and click once.

TIP **Sometimes, when you click What's This?, you get a message that** says "No Help topic is associated with this item." That doesn't necessarily mean there's no answer to your question. Instead of What's This?, try using the Help Index instead. The help available in the regular Help files is more detailed than that accessible through What's This?.

Fig. 2.5
Clicking What's This?, or clicking the question mark in the upper right corner of the window and then clicking an item in a dialog box brings up a description of the item.

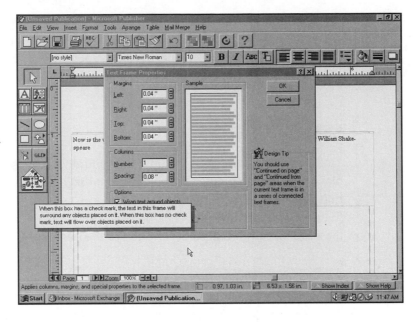

There's a first time for everything

The first time you use certain features in Publisher, Publisher explains the feature and offers detailed explanations and help if you want it (see Figure 2.6). If not, just click Continue.

Fig. 2.6
This typical first–time Help dialog box offers additional information about Text Styles.

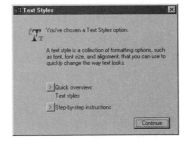

As well, the first time you attempt certain actions, such as resizing an object, Publisher offers you helpful tips in a bright-yellow speech balloon like you might see in a comic strip (see Figure 2.7). For some reason known only to Microsoft, these tips aren't called tips, though; they're called **tippages**.

Fig. 2.7
Publisher also offers
first-time help and
useful hints with
"tippages" such as
these.

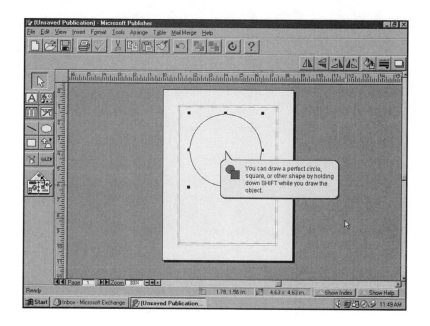

> **TIP** If you like the first-time tips you received, but you're afraid you'll
> forget them by the second time you use those particular functions, you can
> reset Publisher to offer the tips again: Choose Tools, Options. Then click the
> Editing and User Assistance tab, and click the Reset All button in the User
> Assistance area at the bottom of the tab.

Technical support

Microsoft offers complete technical support, but the best way to access it
depends on where you live. For information about technical support, go to
your Microsoft Publisher folder (usually in your Windows 95 Program Files
folder), and open a Windows Help file called MSPUBPSS. This provides
complete details on Microsoft Technical Support and how to reach it.

The Microsoft Publisher Web site

If you have Internet access, you have a whole new way to access information
about Publisher. Choose Help, Microsoft Publisher Web Site. If your computer is configured to automatically link you to the Internet through shortcuts, this will activate your Web browser. Log on as usual, and in a moment,
you'll see the Microsoft Publisher Web site (see Figure 2.8).

Fig. 2.8

The Microsoft Publisher Web site (http://www.microsoft.com/publisher/) offers information, new clip art, technical support, and more for Publisher 97 (and earlier versions).

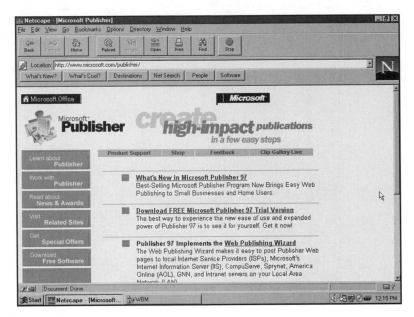

From this page, you can explore many other pages about Microsoft Publisher, offering everything from free publication templates to extra clip art (more on that in Chapter 9, "Adding Graphics"). You can also link directly to Microsoft Product Support, which offers a wizard to guide you to (with luck) an online answer to your question, or at least a link to other places to find more information.

Of course, the very best source of Publisher help is this book—so keep it close at hand at all times! Maybe you should even buy a second copy (you know, just to be safe).

3

Create a Publication Pronto with Publisher PageWizards

● **In this chapter:**

● **PageWizards cut design time in half!**

● **Take the brochure PageWizard for a test drive**

● **The Design Gallery: Guggenheim at your fingertips**

● **Adding your own designs to the Gallery**

Creating polished, professional documents is remarkably easy, when you let Publisher do half the work for you! . . . . ▸

Working with any unfamiliar software, no matter how user-friendly, can sometimes feel like plunging into the Amazon jungle. The going is hard, it's easy to get lost, and there are potential pitfalls everywhere for the weary and unwary traveler.

If you were an explorer in such a situation, you'd hire a local guide; so why not do the same in Publisher? There's a very experienced guide, called the PageWizard, just a mouse-click away. And it works for free!

Cut your design time in half with PageWizard

A PageWizard is a program within Publisher that builds a sample publication that you can then add your own content to. Best of all, many of the PageWizards ask you questions as you use them so that the finished publication more closely matches your needs.

Accessing PageWizard is easy. Whenever you launch Publisher, it's available from the opening screen (see Figure 3.1); if Publisher is already open, choose File, Create New Publication to bring up the same screen. If it's not already selected, click the PageWizard tab; then choose the type of publication you'd like help with and click OK.

As you can see, there are PageWizards for everything from newsletters and labels to business cards and résumés—even PageWizards for origami and paper airplanes!

 TIP   **Don't worry if the exact type of publication you're working on** isn't listed; just pick one that's close. Nothing PageWizards create is written in stone: you can modify it to your heart's content to suit your own needs.

Fig. 3.1
There are PageWizards for many different types of publications available at the click of a mouse from this opening screen.

Take the brochure PageWizard for a test drive

The best way to see how a PageWizard works is to try one. I'm going to use the brochure PageWizard as an example; if you like, you can follow along with your own copy of Publisher.

Once I've chosen the brochure PageWizard, the first thing I see is the screen in Figure 3.2. Here I have to choose what style of publication I want.

Fig. 3.2
Each PageWizard offers you a variety of styles to choose from. As you click each one, the preview at left changes, so you have some idea of what the design will look like.

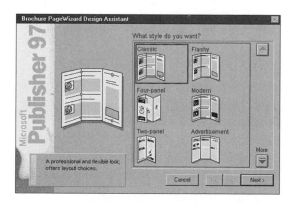

Although many PageWizards allow you to fine-tune the publication they design by making certain layout choices, not all do. Among the brochure styles, for example, only the Classic, Flashy, and Modern styles offer you any choices. The written description of the style underneath the preview always includes the phrase "offers layout choices" if the style you chose lets you fine-tune it.

Since I want layout choices, I've chosen the Classic style of brochure and clicked Next, which brings up the dialog box in Figure 3.3. Here's my first layout choice: whether I want my brochure to fold from side to side or from top to bottom. I choose a side fold.

Fig. 3.3
There's a big difference in layout between a brochure that folds side to side and one that folds top to bottom, but with PageWizard, the only work you have to do is choose one or the other.

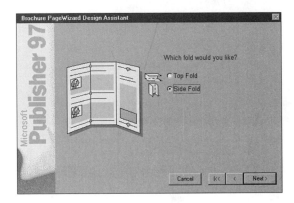

Now I'm asked if I'd like a picture on the front (see Figure 3.4). I like lots of artwork in my publications, so I choose Yes.

 CAUTION **Using a PageWizard doesn't relieve you of the responsibility to** plan ahead. It doesn't do you much good to use a PageWizard to design a brochure with lots of artwork in it if you don't already know what kind of artwork you want to insert! Remember that PageWizard is only setting up the design of your publication: content is still your responsibility.

Fig. 3.4
PageWizard even looks after the task of deciding where your artwork should go.

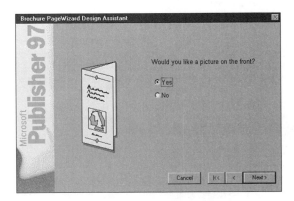

The next question (see Figure 3.5) also relates to the amount of artwork in my brochure, asking if I want it to have lots of text, lots of pictures, or both. I choose "A lot of pictures."

Fig. 3.5
Notice how the preview of your brochure changes as you click each radio button so you have a clear idea of what effect your decision will have on the finished design.

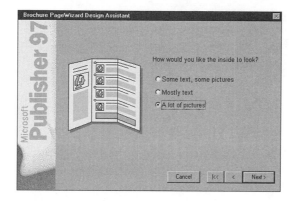

Brochures are promotional items, which don't accomplish much unless they're distributed. The next question PageWizard asks (see Figure 3.6) is whether I plan to mail my brochure or just hand it out. I intend to mail it, so PageWizard will include a place in the design for my return address and a stamp.

Fig. 3.6
Sometimes PageWizards include small text boxes to make sure you understand what your choice will add to the publication.

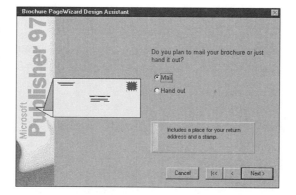

Brochures can be complicated to design because you have to remember where each panel you're working on will appear when the finished product is folded. PageWizard thoughtfully includes an informational screen that makes sure I understand this (see Figure 3.7).

When I click Next this time, PageWizard informs me that I've answered all the questions, so I click Create It and then sit back while PageWizard does in a few seconds what would have taken me hours, and creates the layout for brochure. All I have to do is add the actual text and pictures I want to use, and possibly tweak the design here and there. (See Chapter 6 for information on adding text and Chapter 9 for information on adding pictures.)

Fig. 3.7

Sometimes, PageWizards present specialized information you need to success- fully complete your new publication.

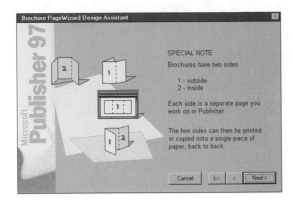

When PageWizard finishes its work, I'm rewarded with a checkered flag (see Figure 3.8) and one last choice: do I want step-by-step help for adding my own text and pictures? Good help is hard to find, so of course, I choose Yes and then click OK. (After you work in Publisher for a while, you might decide you don't need step-by-step help any more. Just select No instead, and click OK.)

Fig. 3.8

Here's one choice that's always available: step-by-step help as I add my own text and pictures to my PageWizard-designed publication.

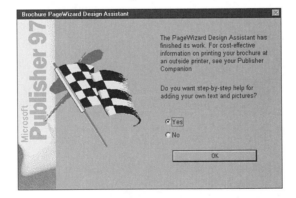

This brings up Publisher Help, which asks you, "What do you want to do?" (see Figure 3.9). As you polish up your publication, help on any topic is right there at your elbow. (For more information on using Publisher Help, see Chapter 2.) Notice that the topics presented are specific to the type of publication PageWizard has just created, so that, in this case, one of the options is, "Set up my brochure for mass mailing." If you were working on a banner instead, that option wouldn't appear.

Fig. 3.9
Publisher proffers help
that's both prolific and
specific as you finalize
your publication.

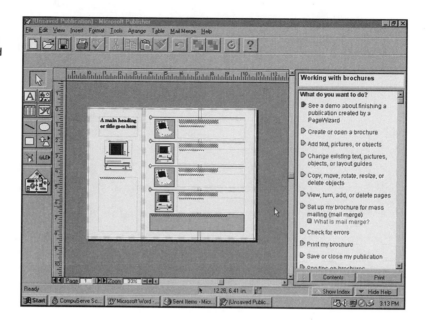

There's a template for almost any project

Now that you've seen how the brochure PageWizard works, take a look at some of the others. Whether you need to design a newsletter, a flyer, a business card, a banner, or a sign, there's a PageWizard to help. And if you want to take up origami, the ancient Japanese art of paper folding...well, there's a PageWizard to help you do that, too!

TIP **Make sure you check out the Paper Airplane PageWizard. Among** the "layout choices" you're offered is AM/FM Radio. Click it and see what sort of message Publisher give you. Who says those guys at Microsoft don't have a sense of humor?

Add special elements to a publication you already started

Even after you have your publication underway, PageWizard stands ready to help. Four special PageWizards for calendars, ads, coupons, and logos are always at your beck and call.

To call up these special PageWizards, click the PageWizard button on the Publisher toolbar, and choose the one you want.

For example, to add a calendar:

1 Click the PageWizard icon; then click Calendar on the PageWizard menu.

2 Place your pointer on the page where you want the left top edge of the calendar to appear. Then drag to the right and down until you have the size you think fits best (you can always change it later).

3 When you release the mouse button, the Calendar PageWizard appears (see Figure 3.10).

Fig. 3.10
Inserting a calendar into any publication is a simple operation with the help of a PageWizard.

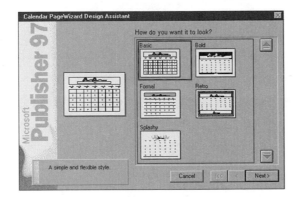

4 Just as with the other PageWizards, you have several styles to choose from. Choose the style you want, and then click Next. Continue to make layout choices until the calendar is complete and Publisher inserts it in your publication (see Figure 3.11).

Fig. 3.11
Poof! A completed
calendar appears in
your publication.

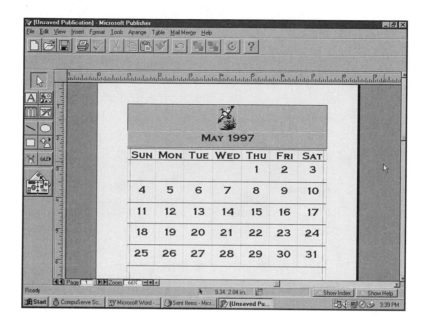

Design Gallery: Guggenheim at your fingertips

The Design Gallery is a collection of objects that add pizzazz to your publication. There are fancy headlines, handsome titles, attractive ornaments, even buttons and dividers for World Wide Web pages (see Chapter 19, "Paperless Publishing: Design Your Own Web Site!").

To visit the Gallery, click the Design Gallery icon on the Publisher toolbar. Scroll through the many possibilities available, and then choose the type of object you want to insert in your publication (see Figure 3.12).

Fig. 3.12
Ornaments such as
these are just some of
the dozens of attractive
elements you can find
in the Design Gallery.

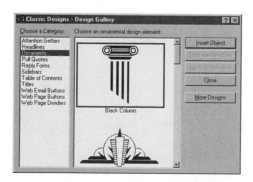

Click More Designs to see a menu of different types of Design Gallery objects. Like the design options presented by the PageWizards, the Design Gallery objects have been divided into styles: Classic, Modern, Jazzy, and Plain. Each of these styles affects the overall "mood" of your publication. For example, notice how different the Modern ornaments in Figure 3.13 are from the Classic ornaments in Figure 3.12.

Fig. 3.13

Just as an art museum divides its collection into Romantic, Baroque, Renaissance, and other styles, so Design Gallery divides its collection into Classic, Jazzy, Modern, and Plain.

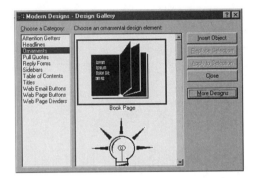

TIP   **Using only one "mood" of design element in your publication** can help ensure a greater sense of unity in the layout. But there's nothing to keep you from experimenting, either, so if you really think a Classic headline goes great with a Jazzy sidebar, go for it! In the end, you're the final judge of whether your publication's design is successful or not.

Inserting elements from the Gallery

To insert an object from the Design Gallery, just highlight it and double-click it (or choose Insert Object). The Design Gallery dialog box closes and the object appears in your workspace. Drag it to any position you want in the publication.

Add your own masterpieces to the Gallery

Typically, any publication you work on will contain several design elements. Some of them may be straight from the Design Gallery; others may be Design Gallery objects that you modified; still others may be objects that you created from scratch.

You can store these elements as a design set that is always available when you work on that same publication—and which you can also access from other publications, so that you could use, say, that perfect title bar you created for your newsletter on your letterhead, too. It's like opening a new wing at an art museum dedicated to displaying only your works.

To demonstrate, I'll start a new design set using an element already in the Design Gallery:

1 Open the Design Gallery by clicking its icon.

2 Choose a category and a design element. I've chosen Blueprint from the Titles category of the Classic Designs set (see Figure 3.14).

Fig. 3.14
I've chosen this element to begin my new design set.

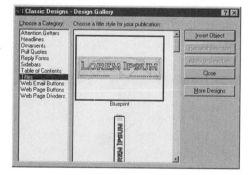

3 Insert the design element into your publication, and then make sure it's selected.

4 Open the Design Gallery and choose More Designs. The menu now has two new choices:

- Designs for Your Current Publication

- Add Selection to Design Gallery

5 Choose Add Selection to Design Gallery. Publisher asks if you want to start a new design set; since that's the whole point of this exercise, answer Yes. The Adding an Object dialog box appears (see Figure 3.15).

6 Type a name for the element in the Object Name text box and choose a Category to place it in. Choose OK.

Fig. 3.15
You can add objects to a new design set that you form for a specific publication.

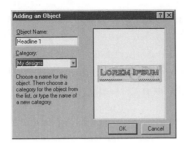

7 The Create New Category dialog box opens. Type a description of this new category in the Type a Description text box (where else?), and choose OK.

8 The Design Gallery now has a new category for your publication (see Figure 3.16). You can return to the other design sets by selecting More Designs.

Fig. 3.16
Once you select a name for your design set, it's always available in the Design Gallery.

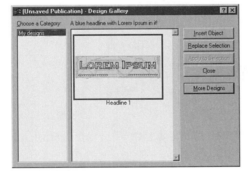

Using your new design set in other publications

The design set you just created is specific to the publication you had open while you created it, so it's not ordinarily available when you open another publication. But it's still easy to access, because it's saved along with your publication.

To use the design set from a saved publication in a new publication:

1 Open the Design Gallery by clicking the icon.

2 Click More Designs.

3 Choose Other Designs.

4 This opens Windows 95's standard file-browsing dialog box. Just find the publication you had open when you created the design set you want to access, and double-click it, or click OK. The design set from the saved publication will open, allowing you to place any elements you like from it in your new publication.

 TIP **Just because a design element comes straight out of the Design** Gallery doesn't mean you can't change it. Once it's in your publication, you can use all of the tools and procedures outlined in the rest of this book to alter it as much as you like. Then, once you have it just the way you want it, save it in the Design Gallery. That way, you can preserve all your work, and it's always ready for you to use again in some other publication.

Doing It Yourself

● **In this chapter:**

- **I'm ready to start a new publication**

- **How can I customize the way things look while I work?**

- **How do I use the tools in Publisher?**

- **What do I need to know about back-grounds and foregrounds?**

- **I need to add more pages**

It's time to get to work and create a publication. Publisher provides plenty of help and lots of tools to make your work easier . . . . ＞

Okay, you've been introduced to Publisher and you've seen how PageWizards go about creating publications. But sometimes, you have to do it yourself—so now it's time for some hands-on work.

Now we'll start a publication and go over some of the basic functions and tools Publisher makes available to you.

Starting a new publication

As we discussed in Chapter 1, whenever you start Publisher, you'll land in the right place to start a new publication. If you already have Publisher open, choose File, Create New Publication. Either way, the same opening screen appears, offering three tabs you can choose from: PageWizard, Blank Page, or Existing Publication. Since we're not going to rely on PageWizard's help this time around, click the Blank Page tab (see Figure 4.1). From the options presented, select the type of publication you want to work on.

Fig. 4.1
The first step in creating a new publication is to tell Publisher what sort of workspace you require.

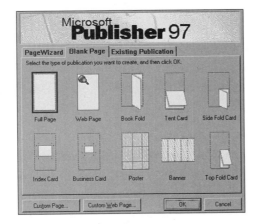

Page setup

If none of these layouts appear to be exactly what you're looking for, you can create a custom layout by clicking Custom Page to bring up the Page Setup dialog box (see Figure 4.2). Some of the things you can control here are:

- The size of the paper

- The orientation of the paper

- The size of the printed area of the paper

Fig. 4.2
Use the Page Setup
dialog box to change
the paper size you're
working on and modify
the layout scheme.

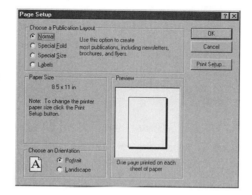

 TIP **If you later decide you chose the wrong size of page to work on—**
say you want to put your publication on legal-sized paper instead of letter-
sized—you don't have to start over. The Page Setup dialog box is available at
any time by choosing File, Page Setup.

First, determine the paper size

Obviously, you don't want to be working on an 11"×17" layout when
you're printing on 8 1/2"×11" paper, so it's important to be sure you have
the right-sized paper. The dialog box indicates what size paper your layout
is currently designed for under Paper Size. If you want to limit your design
to the sizes of paper your printer can use, you can change the paper size by
clicking Print Setup and choosing a paper size from the Size pull-down
menu in the Print Setup dialog box. This will automatically change the
paper size in the Page Setup dialog box, as well.

If you want to print on any other size of paper, click Special Size to bring up
the dialog box in Figure 4.3. You can choose a standard size, such as Index
Card (5" × 3"), from the pull-down menu under Choose a Publication Size.
You can also create a custom-sized layout as I've done in Figure 4.3, by
choosing Custom from the Choose a Publication Size menu and then entering
the dimensions you want in the Width and Height boxes.

Fig. 4.3

If you just can't bear to work with ordinary paper, Page Setup lets you create a page of any size.

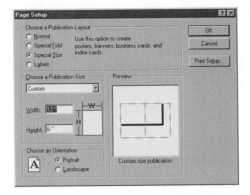

Notice in the Preview box that whenever you set up a page that's larger than the size of the paper your printer is set up to use, gray lines overlap the black lines that indicate the shape of your page. These gray lines show you how Publisher will "tile" your printout, printing parts of it on separate sheets of paper. For more information on tiling, see Chapter 18, "Printing: Putting Your Baby to Bed."

You can tell your printer to print in either Portrait (where the long side of the paper is the vertical axis) or Landscape (where the long side is the horizontal axis) by choosing the appropriate button under Choose an Orientation in Page Setup.

Second, decide how you want the publication folded

Many types of publications—brochures and tent cards, for example—require folding once they're printed. Clicking the Special Fold button gives you four options: Book Fold, Tent Card, Side-Fold Card, and Top-Fold Card. Again, the Preview box shows you exactly how each works (see Figure 4.4).

It's important to get this right, and to know exactly what information has to go on each segment of a folded publication—and how that information should be oriented. If you get your publication to a printer or service bureau and find out that, for example, the greetings from the CEO are upside down when the publication is folded, a lot of time and money will be wasted.

Fig. 4.4
If your publication requires folding, Publisher gives you four built-in options to choose from.

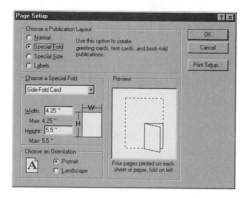

 **CAUTION** **If you choose Special Fold, Publisher automatically adjusts your** page size to whatever size you've told your printer to use in Print Setup. In Figure 4.4, notice that the folds are based on a paper size of 8 1/2"×11", the size of paper my printer is loaded with, even though in Figure 4.3, I set the paper size at 12"×6". You can apply the folds to publications smaller than the printer's paper size by adjusting the Width and Height (again, see Figure 4.4), but if your custom paper size is larger in any dimension than that in the printer, you'll have to figure out the folds yourself.

A word about labels

There's one other button in the Page Setup window besides Normal, Special Size, and Special Fold: Labels. Choose this button if you want to print a set of mailing labels; then choose the size of labels you want from the proffered list.

Once you set your paper size and the folding scheme you want, click OK. Publisher displays a blank page, ready for you to begin your publication on.

Arrange your layout guides

The first thing you'll notice about your blank page is that it isn't really blank: it has pink and blue lines forming a frame around it. These are layout guides. They only display on the screen; they don't print.

What are they good for? Well...

- They ensure headlines, headers, the bottom lines on pages, and all other elements in the publication line up at the same place on every page.

- They help you place graphic elements properly, so they're not just a little bit out of place (which can be as annoying to your reader as a crooked picture on a wall).

- If you change margins, the layout guides make sure those changes apply to every page of your publication.

On a standard-sized page, Publisher places the layout guides by default an inch from the edges in all directions. That's seldom exactly what you need for your publication; fortunately, they're easy to adjust.

Choose Arrange, Layout Guides to open the Layout Guides dialog box (see Figure 4.5). Here you are offered several choices to help you place the layout guides just where you want them.

Mirrored guides

At the bottom of the Preview area of the Layout Guides dialog box is the Create Two Backgrounds With Mirrored Guides check box. This is important when your publication has facing pages, because you need to mirror the margins, not duplicate them.

Publication size

There's a difference between paper size and publication size. For example, if you are printing a newsletter on paper that is 8.5"×11", keep text and graphics at least a quarter of an inch away from the edges of the paper, both because most printers can't print right up to the edge of the paper and because it looks better.

If you're printing something much, much smaller than your page size, like business cards, the difference between page size and publication size is even more noticeable. In that case, you'll probably arrange several copies of your final design on each page, then cut the paper after printing to make the individual cards.

At the opposite extreme, a 12-foot banner is obviously much larger than any kind of paper you're likely to find for your printer, so pieces of it have to be printed on several sheets of paper, which you can then paste together.

Fig. 4.5

Use the Layout Guides dialog box to place the guides where they can best help you lay out your page with precision.

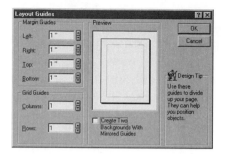

To understand this, picture two facing pages in a book with left margins of a half-inch and right margins of three-quarters of an inch. That would look very odd. In the more usual arrangement, the left page would have those margins, while the right page would reverse those margins, so that in both cases, there would be half an inch between the edge of the text and the edge of the outside page, and the distance from text to gutter would also be the same on each page.

If you check the Create Two Backgrounds With Mirrored Guides check box, Publisher automatically takes care of this mirroring of facing pages.

 Plain English, please!

Facing pages are two pages that are side by side when a publication that folds down the middle is open. If page numbering starts with the first, outside page—which has no facing page of its own—then the page on the left is always an even-numbered page, and the page on the right is always odd-numbered.

The space between the pages, where the fold or binding is, is called the **gutter**. You should always plan your gutter width to accommodate any binding devices (staples, three-ring punch holes, and so on).

Margin guides

In the Layout Guides dialog box, you can also set margins for the Left, Right, Top, and Bottom of the page layout. If you check the Create Two Backgrounds With Mirrored Guides box, the margins you can set are labelled a little differently: Inside (the margin next to the gutter), Outside (the one next to the edge of the page), Top, and Bottom.

Grid guides

In addition to margin guides, you can add grid guides for columns and rows. Enter the number of columns you want in the Columns box, and Publisher will place grid guides that vertically divide the space inside the margins into that number of equal-sized columns. Similarly, enter the number of rows you want in the Rows box, and grid guides will appear that horizontally divide the layout space into that number of rows.

To see how all these guides work together, take a look at Figure 4.6. Here, I've set up two facing pages with mirrored margins, two columns and three rows. Click OK and the new guides appear on your page.

Fig. 4.6

In Publisher, you can easily adjust margin sizes and guides for rows and columns.

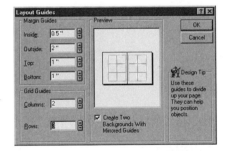

TIP   **Sometimes, while you want rows and columns, you don't want** them all the same width. Maybe your layout calls for two columns, one twice as wide as the other, on each page.

To make that adjustment, set up a column grid guide as previously demonstrated; then close the Layout Guides dialog box. Choose View, Go to Background. Place your mouse pointer over the layout guide you want to move, and hold down the Shift key. The mouse pointer changes to a new shape (see Figure 4.7), with the word "adjust" below it. Now, still holding down the Shift key, you can move the layout guide to wherever you want it. Return to the foreground by choosing View, Go to Foreground.

I'll talk more about the differences between the background and foreground, and what you can do in each, later in this chapter.

Fig. 4.7
When you adjust a layout guide, its original position remains clearly marked while you move it, so you can move it back if you change your mind before releasing the mouse button.

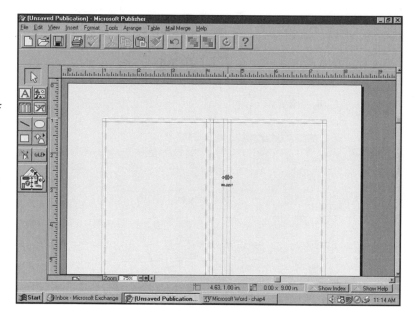

What display options do you want?

The way the workspace looks as you create your publication is important, because you need to be comfortable in it to do your best work.

As well, there are some aspects of your work that need specific parameters. For example, if you work in inches but the project (and the printer) requires points, you need to change the way you work.

To set display options, choose Tools, Options. The Options dialog box opens (see Figure 4.8).

The first option available is Start with page. If for some reason, you want to see some page other than the first one when you open a publication, place the page number in the Start with page box. Otherwise, leave it as is.

How can I measure the objects on my page?

The second option is Measurement units. As previously noted, sometimes you have to learn to think and work in measurement units other than inches. Publisher gives you four choices:

- Inches

- Centimeters

- Picas

- Points

Fig. 4.8
Use the Options dialog
box to design a set of
working conditions
you're comfortable
with. You can specify
the way everything in
your Publisher work-
space looks and works.

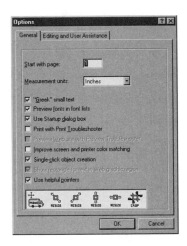

❝❝ *Plain English, please!*

Inches and centimeters are, of course, standard units of measurement. Picas
and points are used exclusively by printers.

A point is equal to about 1/72 of an inch. It's normally used to measure the
height of a particular typeface. The standard Courier type that comes out of
a typical dot-matrix printer is 12 points high.

A pica is 12 points. Because points are so small, if you choose to use them,
the ruler on your screen will indicate picas (otherwise, you probably
wouldn't see the individual markings).

An outside printer or service bureau might ask for the specifications of your
publication in picas or points, so it's important to understand them! ❞❞

Greeking small text

Next, you can choose to *greek* small text. To greek text, in Publisher's terms, is to make it appear on your screen as a gray bar, rather than displaying each character (see Figure 4.9). If you activate this option (the default setting), text smaller than a certain size on the screen will be greeked. (Just what that "certain size" is depends on how close in you've zoomed.) This can speed up your display considerably if you have a lot of small text. (Note that greeked text becomes legible if you enlarge your view of it, so if you really need to read it, just use the Zoom control to move in until it's legible.)

Fig. 4.9
I didn't really design this newsletter with a series of gray bars running through the columns. There's actually text there, but because it's so small at this scale of display, it's been greeked.

Points versus CPI

Points, when used to measure typefaces, are only a measure of the height of a character, not a measure of width or the number of characters you can fit in an inch. Dot-matrix printers and other printing standards occasionally refer to CPI (characters per inch). The 12-point Courier typeface I mentioned earlier, for instance, is measured at 10 CPI.

There's no real relationship between point size and CPI, however; a really wide 12-point typeface might fit only a couple of characters into an inch, even though each character is exactly the same height as the 12-point Courier characters. Similarly, when you make a typeface bold, you'll sometimes find it's become too wide to fit into the space it fit into before—but the height doesn't change. That's why professional printers never use CPI; they only talk about typeface sizes in points or picas. Widths are two variable to be of any use.

Other helpful options

Most of the other options available to you are designed to make life with Publisher a little easier, especially when you first start using it. They include:

- **Preview fonts in font list**—This option, new to Publisher 97, shows you the name of the font in the font list in the font itself. In other words, the words Times New Roman appear in Times New Roman, Courier appears in Courier, and so on. If you have as many fonts installed as I do (I can't bear to remove any), this can greatly speed the process of finding just the right one.

- **Use Startup dialog box**—If you select this, every time you start Publisher you'll see the opening screen that offers you the choice of PageWizard, Blank Page, or Open Existing Publication. If you remove the check from this box, Publisher automatically opens a blank page when launched.

- **Print with Print Troubleshooter**—If you select this, whenever you print a publication, Publisher opens a Help window that asks you if the print job was successful. If not, a series of follow-up questions may lead you to a solution to your printing problem.

- **Improve screen and printer color matching**—Sometimes, the colors on your screen and the colors emerging from your color printer aren't a very close match. Clicking here may help improve that. However, not all color printers support color matching, so this choice isn't always available. If your printer does support color matching, it may offer you additional options. Check your printer documentation.

- **Single-click object creation**—This is an extremely useful option. When selected, you can insert a shape, a graphic frame, a text frame, or a WordArt frame simply by clicking the appropriate icon in the Publisher toolbar, and then clicking once on the page where you want the object to appear. Then you can adjust its size and other characteristics as usual.

- **Use helpful pointers**—With this selected, the various special pointers that appear when you crop, resize or otherwise adjust objects in Publisher both change shape and come with a small text label, so you know exactly what it is you're about to do. If you do not select this, the pointer changes shape, but no text appears.

There are two other options here that are only active if you work on a Web page. I'll explain them in detail in Chapter 19, "Paperless Publishing: Design Your Own Web Site!"

Editing and user assistance

The Options dialog box has a second tab called Editing and User Assistance. Click this tab to bring up more options you can control (see Figure 4.10).

Fig. 4.10
This tab of the Options dialog box controls hyphenation, how editing works, and how much help Publisher gives you as you work.

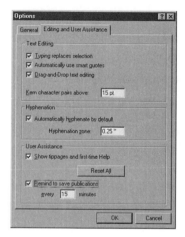

We looked at the bottom section of this tab in Chapter 2, "Calling for Help!" There are six other controls:

- **Typing replaces selection**—By default, when you enter text at a point that has existing text, the new text replaces the old text. If you prefer that new text simply push existing text along in front of it, deselect this option.

- **Automatically use smart quotes**—Smart quotes are quotation marks that curve in toward the phrase they enclose. On the standard computer keyboard, there's only one key with quotation marks, and you use exactly the same marks for the beginning and end of a phrase. However, most professionally published documents use smart quotes. If you select this option, Publisher automatically changes the quotation marks in any text you insert.

- **Drag-and-Drop text editing**—This option lets you highlight a block of text and then drag it to a new position. If you disable this choice you have to move text by selecting it, cutting it, and then pasting it where you want it. (I find Drag-and-Drop text editing annoying—I'm always dragging bits of text around when I don't want to—so I always disable this option.)

- **Kern character pairs above**—Here you can specify a size (in points) above which Publisher will kern certain pairs of characters. This means that Publisher adjusts the spacing between those characters so they look better together.

66 *Plain English, please!*

Kerning is a typographical term that means spacing between characters depends on their shapes. For example, if you type WA, kerning pushes the left side of the A closer to (and under the right side of the W). When characters get larger, especially in headlines, the extra white space that would otherwise result becomes very noticeable. Kerning makes your publication look more professional. 99

- **Automatically hyphenate by default**—If you let Publisher hyphenate automatically, you'll find you have fewer gaps between words (if your text is justified) or at the end of lines (if it isn't). On the other hand, you'll have words split in the middle at the end of lines, which can make your text harder to read. This choice depends on your personal preference and such details of your publication as column width and vocabulary.

- **Hyphenation zone**—This is the minimum width of a gap required to force hyphenation. If you make this zone smaller, there will be smaller gaps, but more words will be hyphenated. Making the zone larger increases the size of the gaps but decreases the number of hyphenated words.

In the background

We've already paid a short visit to the background to move layout guides around. But before you really plunge into adding objects to your new publication (which is what the next section of this book focuses on), it's important that you understand the difference between the background and the foreground—and what the background is good for.

What goes on in the background?

The best way to think of a background is the same way you might think of a distinctive watermark on a sheet of paper. You can write, draw, or type on the paper, but none of that effects the watermark: it's always there and it's on every sheet.

Similarly, in Publisher, the background is where you place anything you want to appear on every page of your publication, no matter what text and graphics you add in the foreground (your usual workspace).

Background items can include a logo, decorative elements, headers and footers, or page numbers. Actually, background items can include anything, because anything you can create in the foreground you can also create in the background.

Getting to the background and back again

To move to the background, choose View, Go to Background. To move back to the foreground, choose View, Go to Foreground. Or you can press Ctrl+M to toggle between the two.

Most of the time, it's not very hard to tell whether you're on the foreground or the background, unless you have a blank page. Figure 4.11 shows the foreground of a blank page and Figure 4.12 shows the background of the same page.

The difference is on the status bar. When you work in the foreground, you see the page buttons and a page number indicator box, to the left of the Zoom button. When you work in the background, the background page icon replaces the page controls. If you ever forget whether you're in the foreground or background, just glance at the status bar and you'll know.

Hiding the background

You can order any page in the foreground to ignore the background, so that the items on the background don't appear on that page in the finished publication. This can be handy if, for example, you only want the background objects to appear on the left-hand pages, or the background includes headers, footers, and page numbers that you don't want to appear on your title page.

Fig. 4.11
The foreground of a blank page.

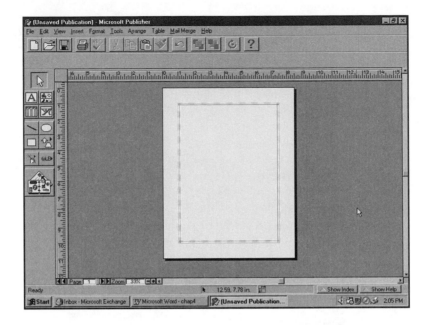

Fig. 4.12
The background of a blank page. (No, honestly, it really is a different figure!)

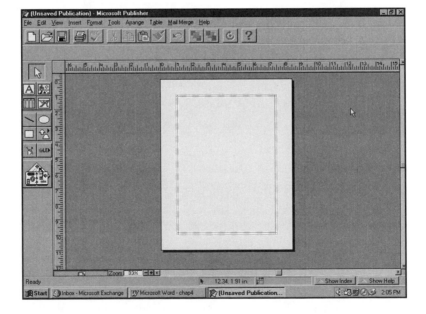

To order any page to ignore the background, go to the page in question and choose <u>V</u>iew, Igno<u>r</u>e Background.

You have a choice on the View menu of viewing a single page or a two-page spread. If you're viewing a two-page spread, when you choose <u>V</u>iew, Igno<u>r</u>e Background, you'll see a dialog box with two check boxes, one to tell the Left Page to ignore the background and one to tell the Right Page to ignore it. Choose one or both.

 TIP **Sometimes, you only want to prevent one object in the back-** ground from printing on a particular page, and you'd still like other background objects to appear. There's a simple trick to make that happen: in the foreground, create a non-printing object—usually a rectangle with no border, filled with solid white—and place it so it hides the object in the background you don't want visible. You can also make a single background object invisible on all pages, without deleting it, by placing a non-printing object over it in the background. For more information on drawing rectangles and other shapes, see Part III, "Adding Graphics and Tables."

Adding and deleting pages

None of your decisions in Publisher are ever carved in stone. You can always change things—even something as major as the number of pages in your publications!

Inserting pages

It has happened more than once: I'm working on a four-page newsletter. It's tight, but I think I can fit everything in. And then I get a frantic call; there's some vital information that absolutely must get into the newsletter. Not only that, but it must go on a particular page of the newsletter—a page I've already formatted.

Do I panic? I do not. (Do I grumble? Of course I do. But that has nothing to do with Publisher!) All I do is add pages to the newsletter to make room for the new content.

Here's how:

1 Choose Insert, Page, which opens the Insert Page dialog box.

2 Specify the Number of New Pages you want to add.

3 Specify whether you want the new page(s) inserted Before or After the current page.

4 In the Options area, choose one of the following:

- Insert Blank Pages
- Create One Text Frame on Each Page (the new page will have a single text frame that extends to the margins)
- Duplicate All Objects On Page Number (insert the number of the page you want to clone)

5 When you finish, click OK.

Adding pages

Sometimes, you don't have any idea how long a publication is going to be before you begin it. All you know is that the page you're working on is full, and you still have lots of things you want to add.

Don't worry; this one's easy. To simply tack a new page onto the end of your publication, click the Next Page button on the status bar while you're on the current final page. Up pops a message asking if you want to insert a new page (see Figure 4.13). Just click OK, and your new page is added automatically.

Fig. 4.13
Use the Insert Page
dialog box to add
pages to your
publication.

TIP **When you create a newsletter or brochure that will be folded,**
you have to have an even number of pages (otherwise you end up with one
blank one). This means that you can't just add a single page; you have to
add two.

Sometimes, you only have enough material for one. If you don't want to
redesign the whole publication (and you probably don't), you might want
to do what I do: fill most of that final page with a large, eye-catching
graphic. "Holiday greetings" (there's always a holiday coming up) are always
a good choice. Make sure that any recurring items that are on the other
pages are also on that extra page, though, so it looks like you planned for it
all along. Only you and your computer need ever know the truth.

Deleting a page

To delete a page, choose Edit, Delete Page, and then confirm that's what you
really want to do when Publisher asks you (see Figure 4.14).

Fig. 4.14
If you're at the end of
your publication and
you try to move to the
next page, Publisher
will make sure there's
a next page for you
to move to.

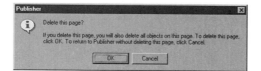

Part II: Working with Words

Before You Add Text, You Have to Add Text Frames

● **In this chapter:**

● **How my words look is just as important as what they say**

● **Setting up text frames**

● **Flowing text from frame to frame**

● **Connecting and disconnecting text frames**

At the heart of most publications is the text, but Publisher isn't a word processor; you can't just start typing. First you have to decide where you want your text to go. . . . . ➤

Now you have a blank publication staring you in the face. (If you don't, refer back to Chapter 4 and set one up.) You're itching to get some words onto that white page and start designing your publication. You start typing…and nothing happens.

Don't worry, nothing's wrong with your program. You just have to remember that Publisher isn't a word processor. Text is only one element, among many elements, you include in most of the publications you design. You have to have some idea of where you want it to go and prepare a space for it, before you add it to your publication. That prepared space is a **frame**.

What are frames, and how do they work?

Every element in your publication is contained by one of these "frames," and it's really the frames you manipulate to put together your publication. Building a publication is sort of like decorating a wall with pictures. You get a friend (or several friends) to hold the pictures up at various places on the wall while you stand back and look. You may experiment with several different placements before finally hanging the pictures. When you create a publication, Publisher is your picture-holding friend. You supply it with the frames holding your text, graphics, and other elements and tell it where to put them. When you're satisfied with the result, you print it.

All frames look the same when they're first created, and there are certain tools you can use with all of them. To experiment with these tools, you need to create a frame.

To insert any sort of frame, click the proper button on the Publisher toolbar, to the left of the page (see Figure 5.1).

Fig. 5.1
You use the Publisher toolbar to create all the various items that go into making a finished publication.

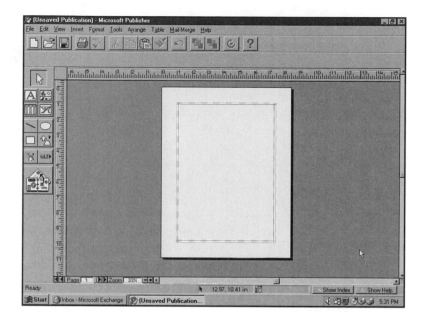

Button	Name	What it does
	Pointer	Returns your pointer to its normal shape after you use the other buttons on the Publisher toolbar.
	Text Frame	Inserts a text frame.
	Table Frame	Inserts a table frame.
	Line	Allows you to draw a line.
	Box	Allows you to draw a rectangle.
	PageWizards	Helps you insert a calendar, ad, coupon, or logo. (See Chapter 3, "Create a Publication Pronto with Publisher PageWizards.")

continues

continued

Button	Name	What it does
	Picture	Inserts a picture frame.
	WordArt	Inserts a WordArt frame.
	Oval	Allows you to draw a circle or oval.
	Custom Shapes	Inserts starbursts, pentagons, and other special shapes.
	Insert Object	Inserts an object created by another program, such as an Excel spreadsheet, into your Publisher publication.
	Design Gallery	Lets you choose from an array of custom-designed elements to add flair to your publication. (See Chapter 3.)

Inserting a text frame

 To insert a text frame, click the Text Frame button on the Publisher toolbar. Move your pointer to the page, positioning it on the place where you want to insert the text frame. Then you can do one of the following:

- Click the mouse pointer on the page to have a text frame appear instantly; or

- Place the mouse pointer on a corner of the area where you want the text frame to be and click and drag diagonally. When the frame is approximately the size you need, release the mouse button.

Either way, you'll see a frame like the one in Figure 5.2.

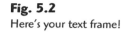

Fig. 5.2
Here's your text frame!

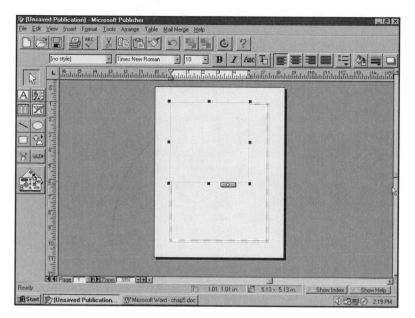

Resizing a frame

Notice the small squares around the frame's perimeter. These **handles** appear whenever you select a frame by clicking it.

If you place your mouse pointer on one of the handles, the pointer changes to a double-headed arrow (see Figure 5.3). You can drag the handle to change the size of the frame.

If you move your pointer to one of the corner handles, it becomes a double-headed arrow that points at an angle. When you drag the mouse, the two sides that intersect at the corner move simultaneously.

TIP **No matter how careful you are, resizing a frame from the corner** can change the frame's proportions. You can avoid this by using special keys while you're dragging:

- To keep the proportions of the frame, hold down the Shift key as you drag the corner handle. Don't let go of the Shift key until after you release the mouse button.

- To keep the center of the frame in place, hold down the Ctrl key as you drag. Don't let go of the Ctrl key until you release the mouse button.

- To do both, hold both keys while you drag.

Fig. 5.3
Use the handles to change the size of a frame.

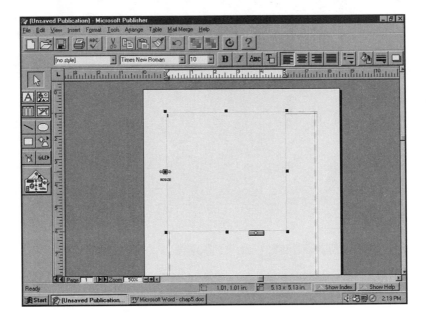

Moving a frame

If you put your mouse pointer on the edge of a text frame anywhere but on a selection handle, the pointer turns into a moving van (see Figure 5.4). Drag the mouse to move the frame (and its contents) anywhere on the page.

With graphic and other types of frames, your mouse pointer turns to a moving van whenever you point it anywhere inside the frame. With text frames, however, your mouse pointer controls the cursor used for editing text inside the frame, so you have to aim at the edge to move the frame as a whole.

Fig. 5.4
When the moving van shows up, you can move your whole frame around the page.

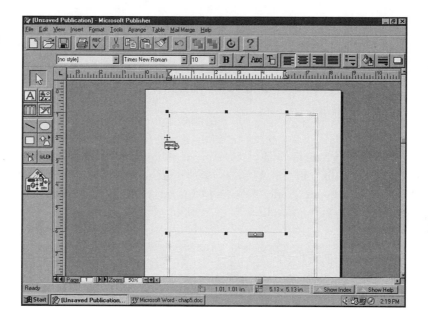

Deleting frames

To delete most frames, just select them and press the Delete key. If you didn't mean to do it, after you finish screaming "Arrrgh!", immediately click the Undo button on the Standard toolbar.

Q&A *I entered text into my text frame, and then changed my mind and decided to delete the whole frame. But when I pressed Delete, nothing happened. What gives?*

You can only delete a text frame by pressing Delete if it has no text in it. To delete a text frame into which text has already been entered, you must press Ctrl+Delete. That's because the Delete key is also used to edit the text within the frame, and Publisher assumes that's what you're trying to do when you press it.

Flowing text from frame to frame

You can connect text frames to each other, forming a link that's like a pipeline leading from one pool of words to another. This is useful because it allows you to begin a story in one frame and have it move automatically to another frame when the first one is full. A good example would be a story that begins on the front page of a newsletter and then jumps to another page.

As you edit the story, its length may change, which means the point in the text where the story jumps to the next frame will also change. With the frames *linked*, the text in the second frame adjusts automatically.

If you enter more text into a text frame than will fit, Publisher hides the excess in the overflow area. You can't see this overflow area, but Publisher tells you something is in it by changing the Connect button at the bottom of the text frame. Normally this button displays a small diamond, but when text is in the overflow area, it displays three dots (see Figure 5.5).

Fig. 5.5
Three dots on the Connect button tell you there's more to the text in this frame than appears.

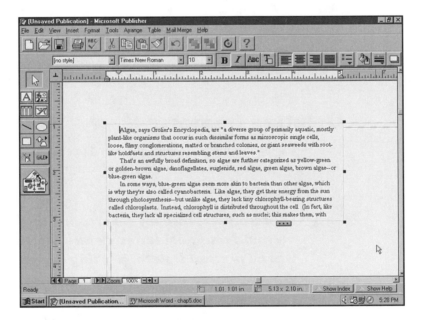

Making the connection

To connect text frames, you need a frame with too much text in it and a new, empty frame. Click the Connect button on the overflowing frame, move to the empty frame, and click again.

When you click the Connect button, the mouse pointer turns into a pitcher (see Figure 5.6). You're supposed to think of the pitcher as being filled with excess text, which you then "pour" into an empty frame. (Isn't that cute?)

Fig. 5.6
With a click of the mouse, this little pitcher...

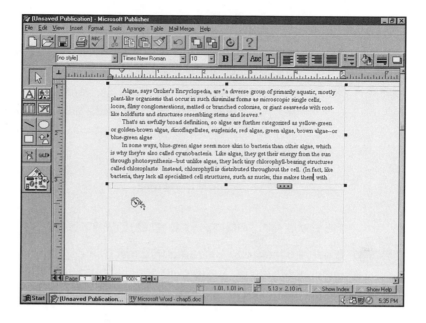

Fig. 5.7
...pours the next part of this fascinating article on blue-green algae into a new text frame.

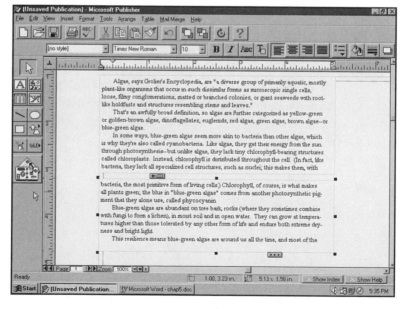

If all the text still doesn't fit (as in these figures), the second frame will also display three dots on its Connect button. Repeat the process with as many connected frames as you need to accommodate the text.

Q&A *I have overflow text but I don't want to connect it to a new text frame. How can I solve the problem without cutting some of my text?*

Just enlarge the frame until all the text fits. If that makes the frame too large, try formatting the text differently; choose a different font that doesn't take up as much space, use a different size of font, or reduce the space between lines. For information on how to format text, see Chapters 7, "Formatting Characters and Paragraphs: The Basics," and 8, "Making Text Stand Out: Special Formatting."

Moving from frame to frame

 If a text frame connects to another text frame, a navigation button appears, either at the top of the frame or at the bottom (or both, if the frame is in the middle of a chain of frames). Click this button—it has a box and an arrow pointing left (if it's at the top) or right (if it's at the bottom) to immediately go to the previous or next frame.

Disconnecting frames

 If the text in one frame connects to a following frame, the Connect button looks like a section of a chain-link fence. Click it to disconnect the frame from the following frame. This will empty all the text out of the following frame and return it to that cute little pitcher, which you can then use to pour the excess text into another text frame.

Adding and Editing Text: The Basics

● **In this chapter:**

- **Type text directly into Publisher**

- **Bring in text from other documents and programs**

- **Now I want to make it perfect! How do I edit text?**

- **Let Publisher check your spelling!**

- **Search and replace text automatically**

You can add text to your Publisher document by typing it in, copying it from another publication, or importing it. Publisher can do a lot of things for you automatically, but you still have to write the words! . . . . ➤

Once you create a text frame, you come to the hard part: writing the text to go in it. Fortunately, Publisher offers several different methods for putting text into your publication. Unfortunately, there's no help for the words themselves. That's your job.

Type it in

A text frame is like a miniature word processor that you turn on by selecting the frame. In addition to bringing up the handles we talked about in the last chapter, selecting the frame also activates a flashing cursor. Start typing, and that's where your words will appear.

Some people like to type in text and then format it; others prefer to set up all the formatting before they start typing. I'm only going to talk about entering text in this chapter without discussing formatting. If you want to know about formatting before you even begin typing, refer to Chapters 7, "Formatting Characters and Paragraphs: The Basics," and 8, "Making Text Stand Out: Special Formatting."

 TIP   **As your fingers fly over the keyboard (or hunt and peck),** remember to play it safe: save your work early and often.

Copy it from other documents

Maybe you wrote something a few months ago that would work perfectly in the publication you're working on now. Does that mean you have to retype it?

Of course not! You can place text you've already written in Publisher and save a lot of time and energy. There are several ways to go about it, depending on how you originally created the text you want to use.

Get text from other Publisher publications

Perhaps you want to use text you created in another Publisher publication. Maybe you want to create a shorter version of a larger, more complex publication (or the other way around).

Unfortunately, you can't just open the other publication and grab the text you need. Publisher only lets you work on one publication at a time.

The easiest way to grab one chunk of text, then, is to close the current publication and open the publication that has the text you want to use.

1 Save the current publication.

2 Choose File, Close Publication.

3 Choose File, Open Existing Publication. This opens the Publisher 97 start-up window with the Existing Publications tab displayed (see Figure 6.1). You can choose a file from the Most recently used files list or from the list of files in the default publication directory. Be aware, though, that the list of Most recently used files may include files that aren't Publisher files, such as Word documents you recently imported into Publisher.

Fig. 6.1
This window displays recently used publications and those in the default directory, to help you find the one that contains text so wonderful you want to use it again.

If the publication you want isn't listed, click the Click here to open a publication not listed above button to bring up the Open Publication dialog box (see Figure 6.2). By selecting Publisher Files in the Files of type drop-down list, you can ensure that only Publisher files will appear as you browse through your various folders.

Fig. 6.2
The Open Publication dialog box lets you browse all your drives for the Publisher file you want.

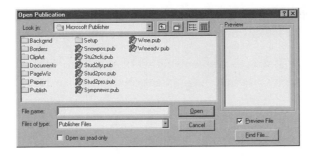

4   When the publication opens, move to the text frame that has the text you need and zoom in so you can read it.

5   Use your mouse to drag across all the text you need, highlighting it (see Figure 6.3).

Fig. 6.3
To select text inside a text frame, just drag the cursor across it.

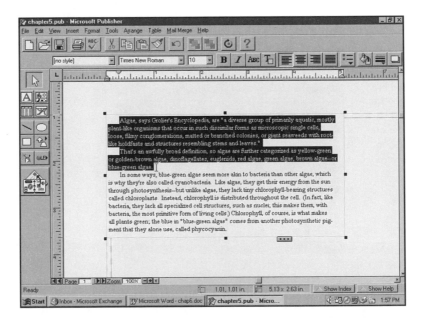

6   Click the Copy button (or click the right mouse button and choose Copy Text from the shortcut menu). This places the selected text in the Clipboard.

7   Now close the publication and open the publication that needs the text. The selected text will stay safely saved in the Clipboard until you cut or copy something else.

8 When the publication opens, select the text frame that will receive the text; then click the Paste button (or right-click and choose Paste from the shortcut menu). The text you copied from the other publication appears in the frame.

TIP **If you want to copy all the text in a text frame from one** publication to another, you don't have to create a blank frame first; you can copy the entire frame. Follow the previous steps, but instead of highlighting text and then clicking the Copy button, click the Copy button as soon as you selected the text frame you want to copy. Move back to the new publication and click Paste, and the copied text frame appears, exactly the same size as the original, with all formatting intact. You can then adjust the size and formatting to fit the new publication.

Things can get a little more complicated if you need several different text selections from another publication. You may find yourself opening and closing and opening and closing publications until you can't remember exactly which story you want to copy to what.

Fortunately, there's an easier way:

1 Minimize Publisher.

2 Click Start, Programs and double-click the Publisher icon. This will open a second copy of Publisher. (Hey, Windows 95 is a multitasking operating system! Take advantage of it!)

3 Open the publication that has the text you need.

4 Copy the first section of the text you want.

5 Move back to the other copy of Publisher by clicking its button on the toolbar or pressing Alt+Tab, and Paste the text where you need it.

6 Return to the other copy of Publisher and repeat steps 4 and 5 as needed.

Import text from other programs

There are two ways to place text from other programs into your Publisher publication. You can copy it just as you did from another Publisher publication (provided it's a program that allows you to interact with the Clipboard), or if the text is saved as a word processor file, you can import it.

Publisher 97 can import files of the following types:

- Microsoft Word for Windows, versions 2.0, 6.0, and 7.0.

- Microsoft Works for Windows version 3.0 and Windows 95 word-processing files (those with a .WPS extension).

- Microsoft Write for Windows version 3.1 and Windows 95.

- WordPerfect for MS-DOS or Windows versions 5.0, 5.1, and 6.0.

- Plain text.

- Rich Text Format (files with an .RTF extension).

If you don't use one of the word processors listed, there's no problem: almost all word processors provide a way to save a file as plain text (sometimes called ASCII or DOS Text) or in Rich Text Format.

To import one of these files:

1 In Publisher, create a text frame or select an existing text frame to hold the new text.

2 Choose Insert, Text File. The Insert Text File dialog box appears (see Figure 6.4).

Fig. 6.4

If you've written an article in your favorite word processor you'd now like to add to your Publisher publi-cation, use Insert, Text File to get it.

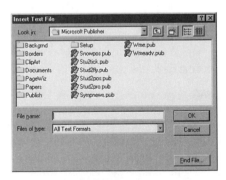

3 Type the file path and file name in the File name box, or browse your system until it appears. You can use the Files of type pull-down menu to choose which types of word-processing files you want to see listed.

4 If you're not sure exactly where the file you want is hiding, choose Find File. This opens the Find File dialog box in Figure 6.5. You can tell Publisher to find all files of a particular type or to find a specific file, and where on your system to search.

Fig. 6.5
The Find File dialog box can help you locate any text file on your system. Here I've conducted a search for Word 6.0 and 7.0 documents.

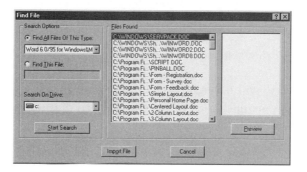

5 Once you locate the file you want, double-click it, and it appears in the selected text box in your publication.

OLE

There's one other way to add text to your publication, called OLE (Object Linking and Embedding). An OLE text object appears in a special frame that, when selected, activates the editing tools of the program it was created in. As well, OLE objects can be linked to other programs so that changes made to a text file in, say, Word, can be automatically made to that same file in a Publisher publication. For details on OLE, see Chapter 15, "OLE: Objects Created in Other Applications."

Editing text

It's a rare writer who comes up with perfect prose on the first try. Most of us have to heavily revise and polish our words, sometimes to make them clearer, sometimes just to make them fit the amount of space available.

Moving, copying, and deleting text

After you highlight text by holding down the left mouse button and dragging the cursor across it (refer back to Figure 6.3), it's easy to move, copy, or delete it.

To move text from one place to another within your publication:

1 Highlight the text.

2 Click the Cut button, or click the right mouse button and choose Cut Text from the shortcut menu.

3 Click the new location.

4 Click the Paste button, or right-click and choose Paste Text.

To copy text without removing it from its original location, follow the same procedure, but click the Copy button instead of the Cut button in the second step.

To delete text, highlight it, and press Delete; choose <u>E</u>dit, De<u>l</u>ete Text; or right-click and choose Delete Text.

CAUTION

Remember, unlike cut text, deleted text is NOT placed in the Clipboard. If you accidentally delete something, the only way to get it back is to immediately click Undo, or choose <u>E</u>dit, <u>U</u>ndo Text Editing. If you perform any other action first, the text is gone forever.

Use Copy Text to save keystrokes

It's quite likely that in your publication you have several repetitive elements. Maybe you have a title at the beginning of every frame with certain formatting; maybe all your frames contain numbered lists.

You can save a lot of work by setting up the first frame of that type and then copying it throughout the publication wherever you want similar frames to appear. You'll probably have to change some text in each frame, but the rest of the formatting and configuration will already be done for you.

Remember that once you copy text to the Clipboard, it stays there until you cut or copy something else. That means you can take a repeating selection, copy it once, and paste it all over the place as many times as you want.

Check your spelling!

There's nothing more embarrassing than having a publication go out into the world with a word spelled incorrectly. Publisher can help you avoid this humiliation by checking your spelling for you.

1 Select the frame you want to spell check.

2 Click the Spelling button, or choose Tools, Check Spelling.

3 When a word appears in your text that is not in the Publisher dictionary, the Check Spelling dialog box appears (see Figure 6.6).

Fig. 6.6
The Check Spelling dialog box helps you correct your mistakes, like this very common one.

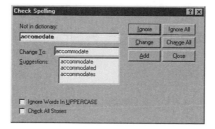

If there are no errors, nothing happens (you'd think Publisher would at least congratulate you on having spelled everything correctly, but no dice). You're just back in your text frame.

There are a number of options in the Check Spelling dialog box:

- If the dialog box offers suggestions, highlight the correct one and choose Change. If you know the same word is in the frame more than once and you want to correct every instance of it, choose Change All.

- If you know a word is correct but the spell checker questions it (usually this happens with proper names or technical jargon), choose Ignore. To make sure the spell checker doesn't stop at the next instance of that word, choose Ignore All.

- If the spell checker stops at some terminology or phrase or proper name that you know you'll use frequently, choose Add. This puts that text into the dictionary so the next time it comes up, Publisher won't consider this a mistake.

- To tell the spell checker to ignore text that is in uppercase, select the Ignore Words in <u>U</u>PPERCASE check box. This is useful if your story contains a lot of acronyms such as NASA, IRS, FBI, and M&M.

- To have the spell checker move throughout your document and check all of your text, instead of just the selected text frame, select the Ch<u>e</u>ck All Stories check box. (A story, in Publisher's terms, is all the text in a text frame or linked chain of text frames.)

CAUTION **The spell checker only looks at text and tables. If you spelled** something wrong using WordArt, it won't see it.

Making changes with Replace

If there's a word or phrase you used several times that you want to change, you can use the Replace command, which will find every instance of usage for you. This is useful if, for example, you find out you spelled someone's name wrong throughout your publication, or you want to send the very same "personal" message ("You, Mr. John Brown, may have already won!") to someone else ("You, Mr. John Smith, may have already won!").

To replace text:

1 Select the frame you want to search.

2 Choose <u>E</u>dit, <u>R</u>eplace to open the Replace dialog box (see Figure 6.7).

Fig. 6.7
Using the Replace dialog box, you can make wholesale changes to words or phrases throughout a text frame.

3 Enter the word or phrase that needs changing in the Fi<u>n</u>d What text box.

4 Enter the new word or phrase in the Replace With text box.

5 Click Find Next to locate the next occurrence of the current word or phrase. Publisher highlights it and you can choose Replace to change it.

Using the options available in the Replace dialog box can make your changes easier and more accurate.

- If you don't want to stop at each occurrence of the text to confirm the change, choose Replace All.

- If you only want to replace whole words and not parts of words, select Match Whole Word Only.

- If you want to replace the word or phrase with the exact upper- and lowercase characters you entered in the Replace With text box, select Match Case. In Figure 6.7, I checked this box because I only want to change occurrences of the proper name Brown with Smith, not other occurrences of the word brown, as in, "First prize is a brown Cadillac!" Without this box checked, Replace would change that sentence to, "First prize is a Smith Cadillac!"

Replace starts searching the story from the location of the cursor. If the cursor is in the middle of the story, Replace will search to the end and then ask if you want to continue searching from the beginning of the story. Choose Yes or No as required.

Don't have an itchy trigger finger!

As powerful as the Replace function is, it can be dangerous if you don't use it correctly. Always save your publication before replacing. If things get messed up, you can close the publication and open it again with everything the way it was before you ran the Replace command. (Undo can also help; it will undo the last Replace command you gave, but it won't be much help if you've done several ill-considered replacements in a row.)

The big danger comes from not thinking of all the possible ramifications. For example, suppose you decide it would be less egotistical if you replaced all occurrences of "I" with "We." You could end up with a document full of gibberish. That last sentence, for instance, would turn into, "You could end up wweth a document full of gwebberwesh." Usually, you can avoid this danger if you select the Match Whole Word Only check box.

Using Word to edit stories

If you have Microsoft Word version 6.0 or later installed on your computer, you can edit your Publisher text in it, and take advantage of its much larger selection of text-editing tools, such as Word Count, AutoCorrect, and grammar checking.

1 Select the frame you want to edit.

2 Choose Edit, Edit Story in Microsoft Word (or right-click and choose Edit Story in Microsoft Word from the context menu). This launches Word, which appears on your screen with your text loaded and ready to work on.

3 Edit your text as necessary.

4 To close the Word document and move the edited text back to your Publisher text frame, choose File, Close and Return from the Word menu bar.

Formatting Characters and Paragraphs: The Basics

● **In this chapter:**

● **Two ways to format**

● **Introducing the Text Formatting toolbar**

● **Having fun with fonts**

● **Alignments, tabs, margins, and more!**

Just adding text to your publication isn't enough—you have to make it look good, too! Publisher provides plenty of tools for that purpose. . . . . ▶

As a writer, I hate to say this, but in desktop publishing, mere prose, no matter how cogent, concise, witty, or whimsical, isn't enough. Not only must your words sparkle, so must their appearance—which brings us to the topic of formatting.

Two ways to format

There are two ways to format text in Publisher. You can either change your text frame's defaults so that Publisher properly formats your text as you add it, or you can enter the text and then format it. You use the same tools either way.

- To change the default formatting of a text frame, select the text frame either before you place any text in it, or if it already contains text, without highlighting any text.

- To change the formatting of specific text, select the frame, and then highlight the text you want to change.

Q&A *I changed the default formatting of a text frame that already contains text, and the text didn't change. Why not?*

Changing the default formatting of a text frame only affects text that you enter after you make the change. For example, if you type a paragraph into a text frame in the default font of Times Roman, and then change the frame's default font to Arial, the paragraph you already typed in won't change, but the next word you type in will be in the new font.

The Text Formatting toolbar

Whenever you select a text frame, you activate the Text Formatting toolbar (see Figure 7.1).

Fig. 7.1
The Text Formatting toolbar makes it easy to tweak your text to perfection.

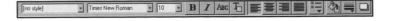

Button	Name	What you can do with it
[no style]	Style list box	Format text the way you want it; then save it as a style so you can easily apply it to more text in the future.
Times New Roman	Font list box	Choose a font (typeface).
10	Font Size list box	Make your text larger or smaller.
B	Bold	Make your text thicker and darker.
I	Italic	Make your text lean to the right.
ABC	Small Capitals	Make lowercase letters versions of uppercase letters.
T	Font Color	Pick the color for your text.
	Left	Line up text against the left margin, leaving a ragged right margin.
	Center	Center each line of text.
	Right	Line up text against the right margin, leaving the left margin uneven.
	Justify	Line up text evenly against both margins.
	Bulleted or Numbered List	Create a list with each item marked with a bullet or number.
	Object Color	Pick the color you want to appear behind your text.
	Border	Add a border to your text frame with a thickness and color you choose.
	Add/Remove Shadow	Add a shadow to the border around your text frame.

Having fun with fonts

The first thing to do when formatting text is to choose a font. I've already mentioned fonts several times—so maybe it's about time I defined the word!

A font is a complete set of characters drawn in the same style. We know what each letter of the alphabet looks like. But if I write out the alphabet, and you write out the alphabet, the way we form the letters will be noticeably different. They're similar enough to be recognizable and readable (actually, I'm not entirely sure about that, given how bad my handwriting is, but we'll make that assumption), but quite different in the details.

That's the way it is with fonts. Someone designed each letter of the typeface in which the main text of this book is set. Someone else designed each letter of the text used in the section headings. Like the alphabets written by you and me, they're different, but equally legible. Each design is given a name such as Highlander or ITC Century. Fonts are also distinguished by their size, measured in points.

 Plain English, please!

A point is a basic unit of measurement used by printers. A point is equal to 0.013837 of an inch, which is rather an awkward number to work with. ("Let's see, so 12-point type would be how tall? That's 12 times 0.013837... two times seven is 14...carry the one...times three is...umm, can I get back to you next week?") It's easier to think of a point as about 1/72 of an inch. (72 times 0.013837 is only 0.996264, but that's close enough for the non-obsessive.)

Point size refers to the distance between the top of the font's ascenders (the top of a lowercase "d," for instance) and the bottom of the font's descenders (such as the bottom of a lowercase "p").

When printing was done using cast metal (the word "font" is from the French word fonte, which means "casting,") most printers made do with a rather limited selection of fonts. The desktop publisher doesn't have that problem: her problem is more likely too many fonts than too few.

Computers add another level of complexity to the discussion of fonts by introducing new divisions of fonts: screen fonts, printer fonts, and TrueType fonts.

Screen fonts

Screen fonts are fonts that display on your computer screen. Most of the time, information on how to print screen fonts is stored in the computer, so you can print the fonts you see on the screen. Some fonts, however, are only intended to be seen on the screen. The fonts used by programs in dialog boxes and menus, for example, often aren't intended to be printed.

Printer fonts

Printer fonts are the fonts installed in your printer. Most printers come with a number of these fonts. Some might have screen fonts to accompany them, but some may not.

 **CAUTION** **If you use a printer font in a Publisher publication that doesn't** have an accompanying screen font, Publisher chooses a similar font for the screen display: however, your printed publication might look quite different due to differences in letter size and spacing between the printer font and the screen font. This can cause serious layout problems, so be careful.

TrueType: Two! Two! Two fonts in one!

Publisher recommends that you only use TrueType fonts in your publications. TrueType fonts contain both screen and printer information, so they look exactly the same on paper as they do on the screen.

Your computer probably already has several TrueType fonts installed. Publisher comes with many new TrueType fonts, a few of which are shown in Figure 7.2.

 Q&A *What's the difference between a font and a typeface?*

As printers use the two terms, a **typeface** includes all sizes of letters and numbers drawn in the same style, whereas a **font** is all the letters and numbers in one size within the typeface. But that's a throwback to when typefaces were cast in metal and you only had so many fonts, or sizes, of a particular typeface to work with. Computers make it so easy to change sizes that font and typeface have become synonymous.

Fig. 7.2
These are just some of the many new fonts supplied with Publisher 97 that can help you set the ideal mood for your publication.

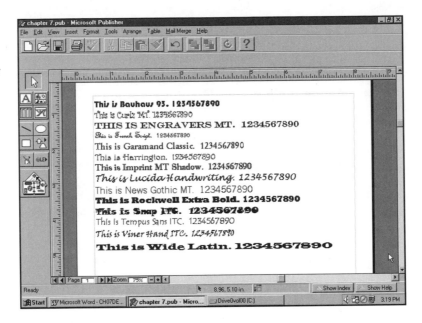

Choose your weapon, er, font

So you have all the fonts supplied with Publisher, and maybe hundreds more already on your computer. Choosing the right font can be a paralyzing decision. How do you decide which font to use where?

Personality contest

Every font has its own personality. Using a font gives your publication that same personality. The goal, then, is to find a font whose personality matches that of your publication.

Take another look at the Publisher fonts in Figure 7.2. Harrington has a light, frothy, 1890s feel to it. It might be perfect if you're preparing a brochure about your company's new brand of sarsaparilla ice cream, and you want to conjure up images of 19th-century Fourth of July celebrations, band shells, parasols, and tandem bicycles. But it would give your publication a very odd flavor if you're creating a brochure about your company's new line of road-building equipment: for that you might want something heavier, solid, no-nonsense, such as Rockwell Extra Bold.

TIP **Some fonts, such as Engravers MT, don't have lowercase letters.**
Stay away from these fonts for extended sections of text. Although they're
great for headlines and titles (which is why they're sometimes called display
fonts), they're difficult and tiring to read after more than a few words (see
Figure 7.3).

Fig. 7.3
With Engravers MT,
and other fonts in all
uppercase letters, it's
hard to tell where
words and sentences
begin and end.

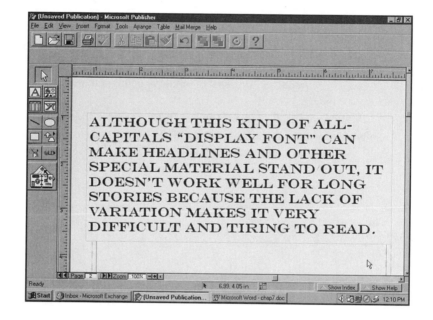

Size matters

Point size is like the volume control on a public address system: crank it up
too much and the reader feels like you're shouting at her; turn it too low and
your voice becomes a whisper that is easily ignored.

Text that's too small looks dull and uninviting and is as fatiguing to read as
text in all uppercase letters. Publisher lets you set the size of fonts at anything from 0.5 to 999.5 points, but the main text of your publications will
usually be in the 9- to 12-point range.

I don't like this font. How do I change it?

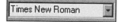

The font Publisher automatically applies to a new text frame is Times New
Roman. If you want something different, select the text frame and highlight
the text you want to change. Then click the arrow to the right of the Font list

box, which displays all the fonts installed in your system and, to make it even easier to pick out the best one, displays each font's name in that font (see Figure 7.4). Click on the font you want. The change is made instantly to any highlighted text. The highlighted text remains highlighted: you can preview it and decide if you want to keep the new font, revert to the original font, or try another font.

TIP   **If you want to highlight the entire story, choose Edit, Highlight** Entire Story; right-click and choose Highlight Entire Story; or, easiest of all, press Ctrl+A. This highlights not only all the text that is in the text frame you selected, but all the text in any linked frames.

Remember, if you only select the text frame but haven't highlighted any text, the new font will only be applied to new text you enter into the text frame, not to the text already there.

Fig. 7.4

To make it easier for you to choose the best font, Publisher 97 displays the name of each font in that font. This pull-down list shows fonts installed on my computer; your list may be quite different.

TIP   **You can also navigate through the font list by typing directly into** the Font list box. Highlight the current font name and begin typing in the name of the font you want. Suppose you want to find News Gothic MT. As you type the **N**, you move down the list to the start of the font names beginning with N. Type the **e**, and you move to the fonts that begin with Ne, and so on. You can type in the whole font name and press Enter, if you want, or use your mouse to highlight the font you want as soon as it appears in the list. If you know the name of the font you want, this can be faster than scrolling through the menu, especially if you have several dozen fonts installed.

One size does not fit all

Changing point size is exactly the same as changing fonts, except, of course, you use the Size list box. Select your text, highlight the point size you want from the Size drop-down list, click once, and voilà! Your text changes size.

Q&A ***When I open the Size list box, only certain numbers appear. There's no 21-point option, for instance. Why not?***

The point sizes displayed are those most commonly used in traditional printing. When type was made of cast metal, a printer might have complete sets of a typeface in, say, 5-, 6-, 7-, 8-, 9-, 10-, 12-, 14-, 18-, 24-, 30-, 36- and 60-point sizes. It would have been enormously expensive and bulky to maintain a complete set of type in every single point size, but a series like this gave adequate flexibility. Computers have made it possible to print text in any point size, but the convention of listing only the most common sizes continues. (It shortens the list Publisher has to display, too.)

If the point-size you want is not displayed, click in the Size list box and type the size you want. Press Enter when you finish.

Basic formatting

Once you settle on a font style and size, there are still many formatting options available to help you achieve exactly the look you want. The three available to you right off the Text Formatting toolbar are bold, italic, and small caps.

Be bold!

Making a font bold thickens and darkens characters, which can help them stand out from surrounding nonbold text. To make text bold in Publisher, highlight the text you want to change and click the Bold button on the formatting toolbar.

This is an example of bold text.

To return bold text to normal, highlight the text and click the Bold button again.

Italicizing text

Italic text slants to the right and takes on a cursive look—more like handwriting and less like printing. (Italic also means "relating to ancient Italy," and that's no coincidence: italic text gets its name from an Italian Renaissance script in which all the letters slanted to the right.) Italics are often used to set off the titles of books and magazines, for foreign words, and to add emphasis.

This is an example of italic text.

To put text in italics, highlight it and click the Italic button. To return italic text to normal, highlight it and click the Italic button again.

You can activate the Bold and Italic buttons at the same time.

This text is both bold and italic.

Isn't a small cap a diminutive hat?

Take a look at the font in Figure 7.5. This is Copperplate Gothic Light, and you'll notice that it only comes in capital (uppercase) letters. But unlike the font Engravers MT in Figure 7.3, some of the uppercase letters in this font are smaller than the others.

Fig. 7.5
Not all fonts have both uppercase and lowercase letters; some make do with just uppercase.

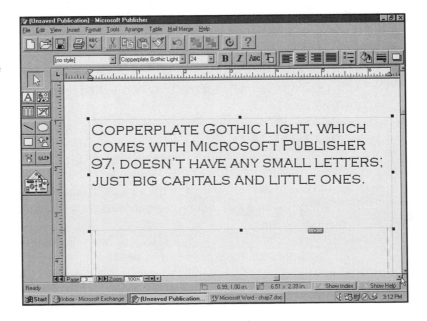

A font like this allows you to use all uppercase letters for effect, while still maintaining the distinction between what would normally be uppercase and lowercase letters in, for example, a proper name.

You don't have to use a special font like Copperplate Gothic Light to achieve this look. Publisher lets you apply this "small capitals" style to any font.

 Highlight the text you want to appear in small-capitals style and click the Small Capitals button. Uppercase letters in the text you highlighted don't change, but lowercase letters become smaller uppercase letters. Numerals and other symbols don't change.

THIS IS AN EXAMPLE OF SMALL CAPITALS. NUMERALS LIKE 1, 2, 3 LOOK THE SAME.

Today's special on the Character menu

There are several other ways to format your text that aren't available at the click of a button, but aren't far away, either.

To access them, highlight the text you want to format, and then choose Format, Character (or right-click and choose Character from the shortcut menu). The Character dialog box appears (see Figure 7.6).

Fig. 7.6
You have detailed control over the look of individual characters or groups of characters in your text.

There are several options to choose from, including some you can't access anywhere else. The Sample box shows you the effects of the options you choose so you can see what they look like before applying them to your publication.

A few exotic options

To the right of the General options is another set of options called Effects. Small Capitals is here, along with several other effects: All Capitals, Underline All, Underline Words, and Double Underline. In the bottom-left corner of the dialog box are the Super/Subscript options. Figure 7.7 shows what these formatting options look like when applied to text.

Fig. 7.7
You can apply all of these formatting options and more to your text.

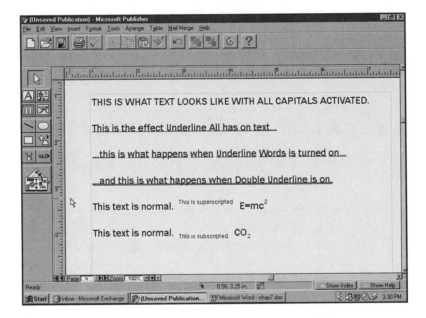

Here's a description of your formatting options:

- **All Capitals** turns all lowercase letters into capital letters. Numerals and other symbols don't change.

- **Underline All** underlines the entire selection.

- **Underline Words only** underlines text; it doesn't underline the spaces between words.

- **Double Underline** puts two fine lines under the highlighted text instead of just one. Unfortunately, you can't select it with Underline Words; if you choose this one, you're stuck with underlined spaces as well.

- **Superscript** makes the highlighted text appear slightly above and quite a bit smaller than normal text. You might use this option to indicate footnotes in a term paper, or to reproduce a mathematical formula such as the famous example in Figure 7.7.

- **Subscript** makes the highlighted text appear slightly below and quite a bit smaller than normal text. Chemical formulas make frequent use of subscripts.

This dialog box also lets you change the color of a font. And yes, there are still more special formatting options available to you in Publisher, but we'll explore those in the next chapter.

Q&A *Is there any limit to how many different fonts and effects I can use in a single text frame?*

No. You can make every character a different font, if you want. It might slow down your computer and your printer quite a bit, depending on your system, but the main hazard is producing a publication that will be mistaken for a ransom note.

I ñeed to üse some ôther characters

Most fonts contain certain basic characters—the letters of the alphabet, numerals, punctuation marks—but many of them also contain special characters which you can't easily access through your keyboard. Where, for example, can you find the acute accent (é) common in French words?

Publisher gives you easy access to these special hidden characters through the Insert menu. Just place your cursor where you want to insert the special symbol and choose Insert, Symbol. You see the Insert Symbol dialog box, which displays all the characters available in your current font (see Figure 7.8). You can access all your other fonts through the Font list box.

Click the symbol you want, and then click OK. The symbol appears where you had your cursor.

Fig. 7.8
Here you can access
characters you might
not even have known
existed.

Modern Hieroglyphics

Among the fonts Publisher supplies are several picture fonts, such as Almanac, Parties, and Wingdings. Picture fonts consist entirely of special symbols, everything from bullets and arrows to the symbols used on playing cards to tiny images of telephones and airplanes.

Figure 7.9 shows a few examples from some of these picture fonts. You can make some of these images very large and use them as clip art; others

work best to highlight ordinary text. Instead of using ordinary black dots to set off each number in a list of phone numbers, for example, you can use a tiny image of a telephone.

Call up the Insert Symbol dialog box to see what's available in the various picture fonts and familiarize yourself with them. That way, when you need something a little special to spice up your publication, you'll know where to look.

Fig. 7.9
A picture might be
worth a thousand
words, but a single
font can contain
dozens of pictures.

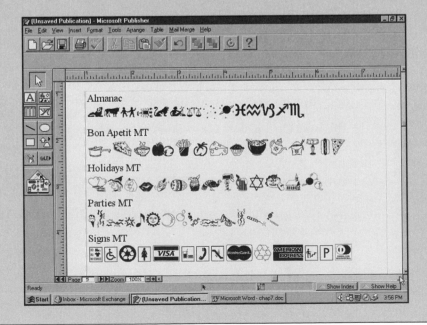

Lining up your paragraphs: margins, alignment, and tabs

There's more to the effective use of text than just choosing the right font. You also need to correctly space the text, align it properly, and generally make it readable and attractive.

Set your text frame margins

Remember what I said about a text frame being like a miniature word processor? Just like a word processor page, the text frame has its own margins—the space between the edge of the frame and the contents.

To set margins for a text frame:

1 Select the frame.

2 Choose F**o**rmat, Text Frame **P**roperties to open the Text Frame Properties dialog box shown in Figure 7.10.

Fig. 7.10
This is the place to customize a selected text frame.

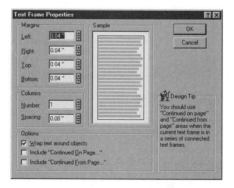

3 In the Margins area of the dialog box, specify the margins for all four sides.

TIP **Notice that the default margins set by Publisher are 0.04 inches.** That doesn't sound like much, but sometimes it can cause problems when space is tight. That's because if the text is too large to fit between the margins, it isn't displayed; instead it's stored in the overflow area. To get the largest possible text in the smallest possible text frame, reduce the default margins to zero.

Do you want columns?

Besides adjusting the margins of your text frame from the Text Frame Properties dialog box, you can also break it into two or more columns. Simply enter the number of columns you want in the Number box, and how much space you want between columns in the Spacing box. This is the easiest way to set your text in columns for a newsletter or similar publication.

Place your tabs

Setting tabs in a Publisher text frame is similar to setting tabs in most word processors. To begin with, notice that whenever you work in a text frame, the ruler highlights the area the text frame occupies (see Figure 7.11).

Fig. 7.11
The ruler highlights the width of the selected text frame.

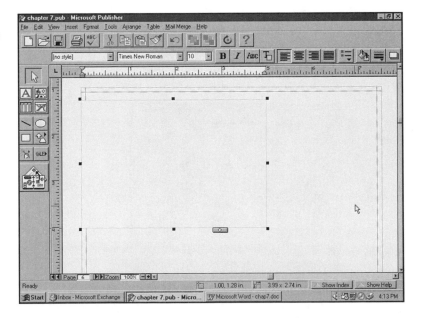

To set a left tab, click the ruler at the point you want the tab stop. When the cursor is on a line of text and you press the Tab key, everything to the right of the cursor jumps over to align with the tab you just set. You can enter as many tab settings as you need.

If you only select the text frame without highlighting any text, Publisher applies the tabs to the whole text frame. If you highlighted text, the tabs apply only to the paragraph in which the highlighted text appears.

To set a different type of tab, click the "L" that appears at the intersection of the vertical and horizontal rulers. A different symbol appears. Keep clicking to page through the four available types of tabs. In addition to the left tabs described above, you can use center tabs, right tabs, and decimal tabs.

Center tabs move the pointer to the tab setting and then alternate moving the text left and right so the text stays centered around the tab settings. This is handy for title or headlines over columns of text.

Right tabs move the pointer to the tab setting and then push text to the left as you type. This is helpful if, for example, you're typing a list of numerals, some with three digits and some with two, and want them to line up properly one above the other.

Decimal tabs move the pointer to the tab setting and push all text entry to the left until you type a decimal point. Then all text entry is placed to the right of the decimal point. This is the only way to align columns of numerals that have varying numbers of digits after the decimal point.

Once the type of tab you want appears, place the pointer on the ruler where you want the tab stop to appear, and click.

For more precise settings, or if you need to set a lot of tabs, select the text frame and choose Format, Tabs. The Tabs dialog box appears (see Figure 7.12).

Fig. 7.12

If you need more precision for your tabs, or you want to change the leading characters in front of a tab, use the Tabs dialog box.

In the Tabs dialog box, you can enter the precise location of a tab setting in the Tab Positions box, choose a type of tab setting and the kind of leader you want: None, Dot, Dash, or Line. You can also change the location of the default tabs, which are preset at every half-inch, or Delete All Tabs.

New text frames already have default left tabs set every half-inch. Use the Default Tabs control box in the lower right corner to change this default for future text frames.

Left, right, center, or justified?

How you align text between the margins can affect its legibility and its impact.

There are four choices for aligning text:

 Left—The left side of the text lines up and the right side is uneven.

 Center—Each line is centered and the left and right edges of the text are uneven.

 Right—The right side of the text lines up and the left side is uneven.

 Justified—Both the right and left sides of the text line up.

To set the alignment of a paragraph, click anywhere in the paragraph. Then click the appropriate alignment button from the text formatting toolbar. Figure 7.13 demonstrates all four types of alignment.

Fig. 7.13
Each type of alignment has its uses.

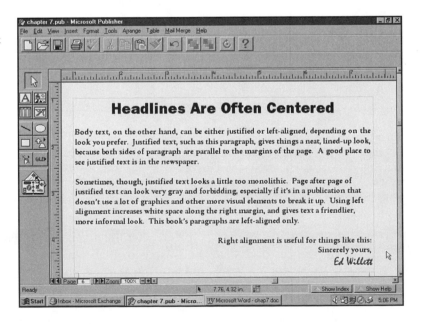

Hyphenation

To minimize wasted space in text frames, Publisher automatically hyphenates text (unless you disable hyphenation in the Options dialog box). Without hyphenation, long words get pushed to the next line, which can leave a big gap at the end of a left-aligned line or increase the space between words in a justified line. You can change the default option for specific text by selecting the text and choosing Tools, Hyphenate. The Hyphenate dialog box appears (see Figure 7.14).

Fig. 7.14
Sometimes, you want to change the way hyphenation works.

The Hyphenate dialog box works a little differently than most. The first choice always displays the reverse of the currently selected option, and it is already selected. If automatic hyphenation is operating, the choice is to Turn off automatic hyphenation. Just click OK to implement it. The next time you open this dialog box, the preselected choice is Automatically hyphenate this story.

Use 'em sparingly

Be careful when choosing to Center or Justify text. Centering doesn't work well with large blocks of text; it makes it difficult to read, because each line of the paragraph stops and ends at a different place. Reserve center alignment for titles and headlines.

Justified text can create additional problems. To make every line extend the same amount to the right, extra space has to be added between words. This can cause some very strange gaps.

Justified text is always turned off automatically for the last line of a paragraph—imagine trying to justify a line that has two or three words!

You can also opt to be shown every hyphen so you can approve it (or move it to another place in the word), by choosing <u>C</u>onfirm every automatic hyphen. When you turn automatic hyphenation off, this choice changes to <u>S</u>uggest hyphens for this story, in which case, Publisher shows you where it would put hyphens if you did ask it to automatically hyphenate the story, and asks if you want to insert one there.

 TIP **You can turn automatic hyphenation on and off by pressing** Ctrl+H. This makes it easy to decide whether your story looks better hyphenated or without hyphenation.

You can also change the hyphenation zone, the amount of space you're willing to accept at the end of a line before hyphenation occurs. The larger the zone, the fewer hyphens (but the more ragged the edge).

I need more space between lines and characters

Sometimes, your text just doesn't fit into the space you allotted for it. Maybe there's too much space left over at the bottom of a story, or the headline is just a little too wide.

Publisher deals with these common layout problems by allowing you to adjust the space between lines and between letters.

 Plain English, please!

Designers often talk about white space. That's the part of the publication that's blank, and it's an important element of design. White space allows the other elements of your publication to "breathe," making them stand out and catch the eye of your reader. Too much, however, can make your page look empty. As is true of most elements of page design, using white space correctly is a balancing act. **99**

Add some space between lines

To adjust the space between lines

1 Highlight the text whose spacing you want to adjust.

2 Choose F<u>o</u>rmat, <u>L</u>ine Spacing. The Line Spacing dialog box appears (see Figure 7.15).

Fig. 7.15

To avoid extra white space, or to create it, use these controls to decrease or increase the space between lines of text and paragraphs.

3 Adjust the controls as necessary. The Sample area shows you how your changes will affect your text.

- **Between <u>L</u>ines**—This adjusts the white space between lines of text. The default is one space, just a little bit taller than the tallest letters of the font, enough to make the lines of text easily readable.

   To change this spacing, click the up or down arrows of the Between Lines text box. Each click raises or lowers the value by a quarter of a space. You can enter precise values (0.9 space, for instance, or 1.1) by typing them directly in the text box.

- **<u>B</u>efore Paragraphs**—This adjusts the space inserted before each new paragraph. This is measured in points, not spaces; compare it to the size of your type to get an idea of the effect. For example, 24 points of space inserted before each new paragraph of 12-point text is the equivalent of two blank lines.

- **<u>A</u>fter Paragraphs**—Every time you press Enter to start a new paragraph, Publisher inserts the amount of space you specify in this text box. This control, too, measures in points.

4 After you make your changes, click OK. Figure 7.16 shows the effects of various line spacing.

Fig. 7.16

In the paragraph on the left, I increased the space between lines to 1.25; on the right, I decreased the space between lines to .75. The paragraph in the middle has the default line spacing.

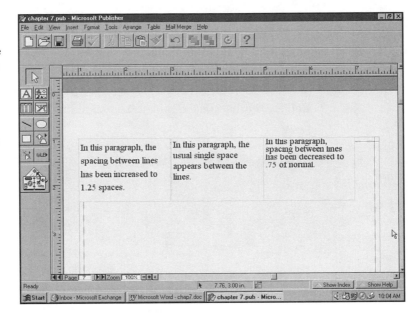

Spaces? Points? I'm confused...

The fact the space between lines is measured in spaces and the space between paragraphs is measured in points can be confusing. However, you can use either measurement system in any of the boxes.

Changing Between Lines to measure in points is particularly helpful. That's what printers normally use in measuring the space between lines, called **leading** (pronounced "ledd-ing"). If you send your publication to an outside printer, it helps you and the printer understand each other if you both use the same measurement system. For a printer, normal leading isn't "one space," it's 120 percent of the text's point size.

To change the Between Lines measurement to points instead of spaces, highlight the number in the box, and type in the number of points you want your text leaded, replacing the sp with pt (for example, you might type 11 pt over the original 1 sp). If you later want to change the leading again, you'll find the measurement is still in points. You can change the measurement back to spaces at any time by replacing the pt with sp.

You can also change the measurements of the Before Paragraphs or After Paragraphs text boxes from points to spaces. But when you return to the Line Spacing dialog box later, you'll find those text boxes still measure in points; they've converted your command to their preferred measurement system.

Q&A *I decreased the space between lines in my paragraph; now the tops of all the characters are cut off on the screen. What's going on?*

You can see this same effect in the right-hand paragraph in Figure 7.16. Publisher lets you decrease space between lines or letters to the point where letters print on top of each other. If the tops of letters are cut off, first print a test page. Sometimes, the text will print fine, nicely squashed together, despite what it looks like on-screen. If your letters print on top of each other, however, you have to increase the line spacing again.

Can I put more space between letters?

Printers also have a name for the space between consecutive letters. They call it **kerning**, which originally referred to the nonprinting metal that surrounded the raised letter on a single slug (character) of metal type. It's also called tracking.

Whatever you want to call it, you can adjust this spacing as easily as you adjusted the space between lines. To change the tracking of one or more paragraphs:

1 Highlight at least some of the text in all of the paragraphs you want to adjust.

2 Choose Format, Spacing Between Characters. The Spacing Between Characters dialog box appears (see Figure 7.17).

Fig. 7.17
Shrinking or expanding space between characters can help you fit more text into less space or, with some fonts, improve legibility.

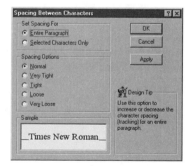

3 Choose Entire Paragraph (the default setting).

4 In the Spacing Options area, you can choose Normal, Very Tight, Tight, Loose, or Very Loose.

Tight means the letters move closer together than normal, while loose means they move further apart. The option you choose will be applied to all the paragraphs that contain highlighted text. (Even if you highlighted less than a whole paragraph, the entire paragraph will be affected.)

5 Look at the Sample area to see what your text will look like with the new spacing in place. Figure 7.18 shows examples.

Fig. 7.18

Altering the spacing between characters can help text fit into a tight space. On the left, the spacing between characters is Very Tight; on the right it's Very Loose, in the middle it's Normal.

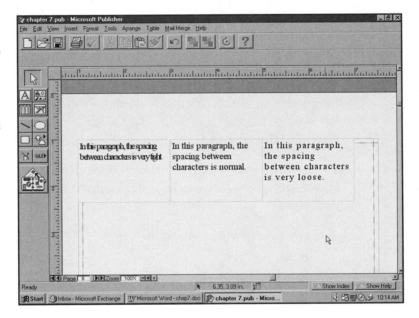

To change the spacing only between specific characters:

1 Highlight the characters you want to adjust, and choose Format, Spacing Between Characters. The Spacing Between Characters dialog box appears.

2 Choose Selected Characters Only. The dialog box changes the available options (see Figure 7.19).

Fig. 7.19
You can alter the spacing between as few as two individual characters—sometimes all it takes to make, say, overly long headline fit in its assigned space.

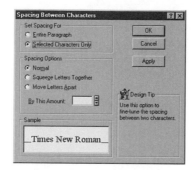

3 You can add or subtract a precise amount of space (measured in points) between the letters you highlight. First, select Squee<u>z</u>e Letters Together or Move Letters <u>A</u>part. Then choose the number of points you want added or subtracted from the spacing in the <u>B</u>y This Amount text box. You can return to normal spacing at any time by choosing Nor<u>m</u>al.

4 Look in the Sample area to see what your text will look like with the new spacing applied.

5 Click A<u>p</u>ply to change your text's spacing while keeping the dialog box open (you can double-check the results before making them official). Or click OK if you're sure you have the spacing right. The dialog box closes and your text adjusts to the new spacing.

Making Text Stand Out: Special Formatting

● **In this chapter:**

- **Writing purple (or any other color) prose**

- **Heading up my to-do list: make some lists!**

- **Getting fancy with first letters**

- **Doing it with style**

Color, fancy first letters, patterned backgrounds: text-formatting options in Publisher go far beyond just changing fonts, sizes, margins, and alignments. . . . . ❯

F or decades, "purple prose" has been a pejorative term among writers, implying an overabundance of flowery adjectives at the expense of readability. But with Publisher, even a lawnmower-repair manual can be written in purple prose—on a bright green background, if you like.

Writing purple (or any other color) prose

If you have a color printer, or if your publication will only appear on a computer screen, using colored text is another way to grab your reader's attention.

How do I change the text color?

In Chapter 7, you looked at the Character dialog box. One of the options in that dialog box allows you to choose a font color. However, you can access the same option directly from the workspace:

1 Highlight the text you want to color.

2 Click the Font Color button. The color palette opens, with several colored boxes (see Figure 8.1).

3 Click the box that contains the color you want for your text, and the color of your text changes.

Fig. 8.1
Choose from this offering of 35 colors for your text, but if that isn't enough...

If these aren't enough colors for you, click the More Colors button to open the Colors dialog box (see Figure 8.2). As the Design Tip in the dialog box says, the colors were placed in each column because they work well together. If you confine your choices to one column, you can avoid any horrible color *faux pas*.

Fig. 8.2

...choose from 84 coordinated colors (such as Periwinkle) in the Basic colors Color Model. If you still aren't happy...

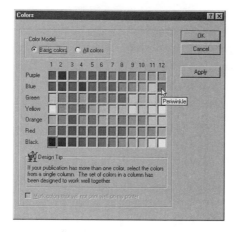

In the Colors dialog box, you can choose between Basic colors (the ones presented in the coordinated columns) or All colors. If you choose All colors, you open a different color palette (see Figure 8.3). Click the palette and crosshairs appear; move the crosshairs around the palette with your mouse until the color you like appears in the Color box below. You can adjust the brightness using the sliding control to the right of the palette, or you can enter numbers in the text boxes. (See Chapter 10 for a more detailed description of this dialog box.)

Fig. 8.3

...create your own color using the color palette and brightness control.

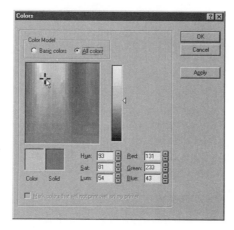

Q&A *I created a color I like in the Color box, but my text keeps appearing in the color that appeared in the Solid box, which is quite different. Why can't I get the color I designed?*

Publisher uses the color in the Color box if possible, but sometimes it isn't possible. If your system is operating in 256-color mode, you can only use the colors in the Solid box. If you're operating in Hi-Color or TrueColor modes, you can use the color in the Color box.

What other color controls can I use?

In the color palette that appears when you click the Font Color button, you can also choose the Patterns & Shading button. This opens the Fill Patterns and Shading dialog box, which has three options: Tints/Shades, Patterns, and Gradients. You can only apply Tints and Shades to text. (You can learn about the Patterns and Gradients options in the next section, which talks about background color.)

Tints/Shades presents you with a series of rectangles, showing the text color with a range of tints and shades applied (see Figure 8.4). When you choose a rectangle, the color appears in the Sample area. Click OK to make your text this color.

Fig. 8.4
Like the brightness control on your TV, Tints/Shades allows you to fine-tune the intensity of the color you choose.

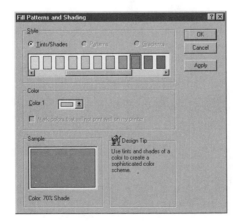

Color my world—or at least my background

Besides changing the color of your text, you can also change the color of the text frame's background. Just select the frame and click the Background Color button in the Text Formatting toolbar. Pick a color just as you did for your text.

TIP   **If you work with a black-and-white printer, the most common** text/background color combination to use, apart from black-on-white, is white-on-black (also called reverse text). To create that effect, make your text white and your background black.

Patterned backgrounds

To change the pattern of your background, click Patterns & Shading in the pop-up color selection dialog box. This time, when the Fill Patterns and Shading dialog box opens, the Patterns and Gradients options are available.

Choose Patterns and a variety of patterns you can apply to your background appears: crosshatching, brickwork, thatching, and more.

You also have to choose both a Base Color and a Color 2. The Base Color defaults to the current background color; Publisher uses it to draw the pattern. Color 2 defaults to white, so if you don't change the colors, the pattern you pick will be drawn in color on a white background.

Click the Color 2 drop-down arrow to see the color palette (see Figure 8.5).

Fig. 8.5
Tired of a plain color background? Choose a pattern to spice it up, and apply a second color.

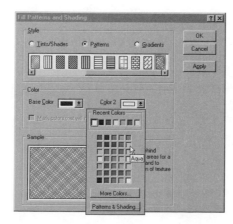

Making the gradient

Choose the Gradients option. You now have a selection of background options that look like an airbrush artist applied carefully graduated shades (see Figure 8.6). The Base Color continues to be the color with which the effect is applied; Color 2 is still the background color.

The best way to understand gradients is to try them; you can't truly appreciate them until you do. Check out the examples in Figure 8.7.

Fig. 8.6
Gradients are the most exotic background options Publisher has to offer. Used appropriately, they can make your text leap off the page.

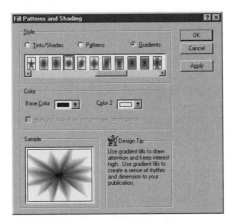

Fig. 8.7
Patterns and gradients have very different effects. Choose one that works well with your message.

CAUTION **Whenever you use colors, patterns, and gradients, remember that** the purpose of text is to be read. Mauve letters over an orange-and-green starburst might appeal to you, but will be almost impossible to read. Use colors, patterns, and gradients to draw the reader's eye, but be careful not to overwhelm your message.

Heading up my to-do list: make some lists!

The Lord High Executioner in Gilbert & Sullivan's *The Mikado* sings a song about his "little list," on which he has placed all the annoying people he'd like to eliminate. Whether you're a Lord High Executioner or just a very organized shopper, the time will come when you, too, will need to make a little list.

You can do it the hard way, using tabs and indents and alignment, or you can get Publisher to create a bulleted or numbered list for you.

 Plain English, please!

A bullet, in printing, has nothing to do with firearms. It's a graphic symbol—typically a fat black dot like a bullet-hole, hence its name—used to set off special lines of text. **"**

 To create a list, first draw a text frame or select an existing one. Then choose the Bullet or Number List button on the Text Formatting toolbar.

Publisher immediately presents you with six possible bullets and an option to see more. If you choose one of these bullets, you can start creating your list. Every time you press Enter, Publisher inserts a bullet at the beginning of the line and your text automatically indents. If your list item continues past the end of the line, the next line of text automatically indents to match the first line.

If this list isn't what you had in mind, you can modify it by clicking the Bullet or Number List button again and choosing More. The Indents and Lists dialog box appears (see Figure 8.8).

Fig. 8.8
Whether you have a little list or a big one, customize it to meet your precise requirements.

Number one, with a bullet

The Bullet Type area shows the same bullets you see when you first click the Indents & Lists button. Now, using the Size text box, you can make them larger or smaller.

If all of these bullets are shooting blanks as far as you're concerned, click New Bullet. This opens the New Bullet dialog box. Identical to the Insert Symbol dialog box (see Chapter 7), the New Bullet dialog box displays all the characters available for a font. It defaults to the Symbol font, but you can use the Show Symbols From list box to see all the characters in any font installed on your computer. Choose any character you want to use as a bullet; it appears in the Bullet Type area of the Indents and Lists dialog box.

TIP **Most fonts contain an ordinary bullet or two, but the best places** to look for a more exotic bullet are in the picture fonts we discussed in Chapter 7. From Greek letters to arrows to tiny telephones or slices of pizza, these special character sets can provide you with bullets that match your list's topic.

Next, enter the indentation you want in the Indent List By text box. This determines how far from the left edge of the text frame the text of each bulleted item appears (the bullets line up on the left edge).

Finally, in the Alignment list box, choose how you want the text to align. You have the usual alignment choices of Left, Center, Right, and Justified.

Number one, with a number

If you choose Numbered List in the Indent Settings area, the dialog box options change (see Figure 8.9).

Fig. 8.9
Use these options to set up a numbered list, useful for an agenda or a sequentially arranged publication.

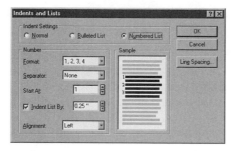

The indent and alignment options are the same as before, but the bullet boxes are gone. Instead you have three new options:

- The Format list box lets you choose to use numbers or letters for your list.

- The Separator list box lets you choose different elements to separate the number from the list: colon, parentheses, and so on.

- Start At lets you select which number or letter you want to begin the list. It doesn't have to be 1 or A.

TIP   **A bulleted list is more graphically interesting than a numbered list,** but a numbered list is better if, at some point, you want to refer your readers to a specific item within the list, such as "If you look at item number three on tonight's agenda…".

Indentation

In the Indents and Lists box, besides Bulleted List and Numbered List, you can also choose Normal. This option changes the dialog box so you can fine-tune paragraph indenting (see Figure 8.10).

Fig. 8.10
There are many more ways to indent a paragraph than just moving the first line over a few spaces.

In the Indents area, you can choose a Preset mode, which includes Flush Left (no indent), 1st Line Indent (standard paragraph indentation), Hanging Indent (first line flush left, subsequent lines indented—the way your bulleted and numbered lists indent), and Quotation (the whole paragraph indented from the left and the right sides).

You can also create your own indentation scheme. Use the Left, First Line, and Right options to set how far, in inches, the left side of the paragraph should indent from the left margin, how far the first line should indent, and how far the right side of the paragraph should indent from the right margin.

Figure 8.11 shows a few examples of indenting possibilities.

Fig. 8.11
The way you indent a paragraph affects its legibility and how it looks next to other text.

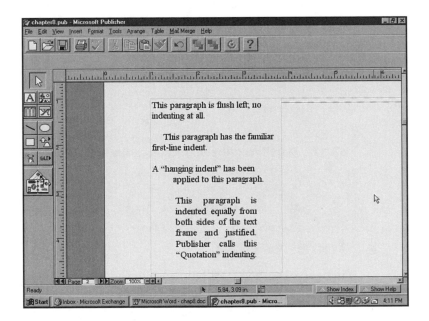

Getting fancy with first letters

There's another way to set off paragraphs: fancy first letters.

Drop caps, as they're sometimes called, add flair to a publication. They remove a publication from the realm of the gray and ordinary. Once upon a time, monks labored for days to create fancy first letters in the manuscripts they were illuminating. In Publisher, they're just a couple of mouse clicks away (the fancy first letters, not the monks).

1 Select the paragraph where you want to apply the letter. You don't have to highlight the whole paragraph; placing your cursor anywhere in it does the trick.

2 Choose F<u>o</u>rmat, Fa<u>n</u>cy First Letter. The Fancy First Letter dialog box opens (see Figure 8.12).

Fig. 8.12
No need to get thee to a scriptorium; you can have a fancy first letter in seconds.

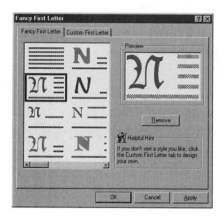

3 You have several possibilities. The gray lines represent lines of text, so you can see exactly how each of these suggestions will fit in your publication. Choose one to get a better look at it in the Sample area.

4 Click <u>A</u>pply, and you can check the results in your actual publication without closing the Fancy First Letter dialog box. Try others until you find the one you like.

5 If you decide you don't like any of them, click <u>R</u>emove, and your text reverts to normal and the dialog box closes. If you decide you do like one, click OK. Publisher applies the format to your text and the dialog box closes.

If you don't like any of Publisher's suggestions and want to create your own fancy first letter, click the Custom First Letter tab (see Figure 8.13).

Fig. 8.13

Use your own sense of style to create a fancy first letter that's perfect for your story.

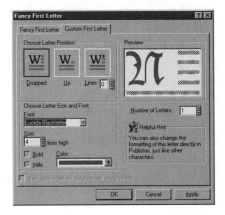

Designing your own fancy first letter

To create your own fancy first letter from the dialog box in Figure 8.13:

1 Choose the position. Choose <u>D</u>ropped to drop the first letter down into the body of the text; choose <u>L</u>ines to change the number of lines the letter drops. Choose <u>U</u>p to raise the letter above the top of the text.

2 Choose the font from the <u>F</u>ont list box. It can be any font; it doesn't have to be the same as the main body of the text.

3 Choose the size from the <u>S</u>ize box. The number in the Size box doesn't represent the first letter's size in points, but its height in lines of text. The maximum number of lines you can drop the letter into the text is always equal to this number: you can drop a 10-line-tall letter up to 10 lines into the body of the text, whereas you can only drop a three-line-tall letter three lines into the text.

4 If you want to make the first letter bold and/or italic, select the <u>B</u>old or <u>I</u>talic check boxes, or both.

5 Choose the letter's color in the <u>C</u>olor list box. This opens the pop-up color selection box you saw earlier in this chapter.

6 Select how many letters at the beginning of the paragraph you want in the Fancy First Letter format from the <u>N</u>umber of Letters text box. To set the whole first word in the fancy format, enter the number of letters in that word.

7 Click OK to return to the Fancy First Letter dialog box. Notice that your design is now one of the preset selections. This saves you from having to re-create it each time you want to apply it; from now on, while you work on this publication, it will be readily available.

8 Click <u>A</u>pply to preview the letter in your publication while keeping this dialog box open, or choose OK to add the letter to your publication and close the dialog box.

Fancy first letters really give a paragraph a classy look (see Figure 8.14).

Fig. 8.14
Even if your text isn't as inspiring as this William James quote, a fancy first letter can make it look meaningful.

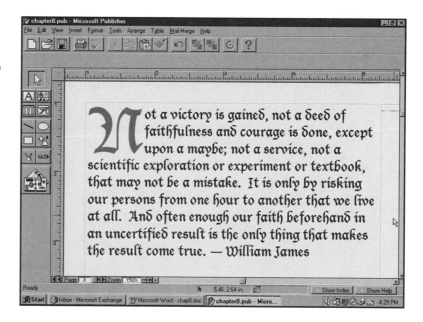

Do it with style

You finally have your text looking just the way you want it: the font, the size, the color, the spacing, and that fabulous Fancy First Letter are all to die for. It was a lot of work, but it's perfect.

Now you move to a new text frame. You want all the same formatting elements, but you don't want to go through all that work again. How can you avoid it? There are several ways, beginning with the Format Painter.

Format painting

Suppose you want the same indents and color schemes in two text frames. Just select the one that has the formatting you want, click the Format Painter—the pointer changes to a paintbrush—and click the second text frame. The indents and color scheme from the first text frame are instantly applied to the next.

CAUTION **The Format Painter is a help, but it's not perfect. Not all** formatting transfers. If there are two styles of text, for example, only one might make it to the new text frame. Fancy first letters don't transfer, either. Check the newly formatted text frame carefully to make sure it looks the way you want it to.

Pick Up and Apply Formatting

The Format Painter is good for transferring formatting from a single object to a single object; but if you need to transfer formatting from one text frame to many other text frames, all at once or one after the other, Publisher offers an alternative that involves much less mouse clicking:

1 Select the text frame whose formatting you want to transfer.

2 Choose Format, Pick Up Formatting, or right-click and choose Pick Up Formatting.

3 Select the objects you want to format by clicking them one after the other while holding down the Shift key.

4 Right-click the selected objects and select Apply Formatting, or choose Format, Apply Formatting.

5 The format from the first object transfers to all the selected objects.

Styles

Creating a style is another useful way to use the same text and paragraph settings over and over without having to re-create them each time. And unlike the Format Painter or Pick Up and Apply Formatting, it allows you to save a format on disk and apply it to other publications—even publications in other applications.

Here's how to create a style:

1 Choose Format, Text Style. The Text Styles dialog box appears (see Figure 8.15).

Fig. 8.15
Creating a style saves you the trouble of having to re-create complicated formatting instructions every time you start a new text frame.

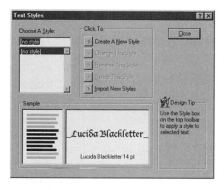

2 Click Create a New Style. The Create New Style dialog box appears (see Figure 8.16).

Fig. 8.16
Most of the text formatting options we've looked at appear in this one dialog box, which makes creating a style easy.

3 Name your style in the Enter New Style Name text box. The current settings will be identical to those of the text frame you are working in, so if its format is the one you want to use in other locations, click OK and your done.

4 If you want to make changes to the style before saving it, or create a new style sheet from scratch, click any of the buttons to open the formatting dialog boxes we've worked with in the last two chapters.

5 When the style looks the way you like, click OK. This takes you back to the Text Styles dialog box.

6 Click Close. You can now apply your style to other text frames in your publication.

Editing, renaming, or deleting styles

To edit, rename, or delete an existing style, choose Format, Text Style. Then highlight the style you want to edit, rename, or delete in the Choose A Style list box, and click the appropriate buttons.

- Choosing Change This Style opens the Create New Style dialog box; simply make your changes and click OK.

- Choosing Rename This Style shows you the current name of the style sheet and prompts you for a new name.

- Choosing Delete This Style deletes a style. Publisher asks you to confirm your decision and then removes the style from the list.

Imported or domestic?

Imported styles, when you shop for clothes, are usually more expensive. But Publisher allows you to import styles for free: not from Paris, but from other Publisher publications, from text documents, from HTML documents, and even from other programs, including Microsoft Word and Excel; WordPerfect; and Lotus 1-2-3.

To see a list of programs from which Publisher can import styles:

1 Choose Format, Text Style, Import New Style.

2 Click the Files of type list box in the resulting Import Styles dialog box.

3 Choose the type of file you want to look for (such as a Microsoft Works 3.0 file) and click once to select it. The dialog box now displays only files of that type as you browse through the folders and files on your disk drives.

4 When you find the file whose style you want to import, select it and click OK.

5 You return to the Text Styles dialog box, where all the styles contained in the file you selected now appear listed in the Choose a <u>S</u>tyle list box. Click Close to add the new style to those available in the publication you're currently working on.

Applying styles

To apply a style, select a text frame and choose a style from the Style list box. Styles apply to the whole text frame; even if you highlight only a word or two in a frame before applying a style, all the text in the frame will be affected.

TIP **If you know exactly how you want to format the types of text in** your publication, design styles before you draw your first text frame. The Create A New Style dialog box brings together in one place almost all of the formatting elements you've seen in this chapter. Rather than choosing menus here and clicking buttons there, you can do the same work in this one dialog box. Then just draw your text frames, apply the appropriate style to each one, input your text, and you're on your way to a finished publication in far less time, with far less effort.

Part III: Adding Graphics and Tables

Adding Graphics

● In this chapter:

● **Enough words! I want to add pictures!**

● **Browsing the Clip Gallery**

● **A nip here, a tuck there: making the picture fit the frame (and vice versa)**

● **Adding artwork from almost anywhere**

Add the right graphic, and your mundane text becomes marvelously memorable! . . . . **>**

Text is a great way to convey information, and has been ever since the Sumerians invented writing. But if text alone were enough for your purposes, you'd have been content with your word processor and wouldn't have bought Microsoft Publisher 97. The whole point of desktop publishing software is combining text and graphics into a seamless whole.

Illustrations break up blocks of gray text, draw the eye of the reader, highlight information in the text, and sometimes provide new information. Pick the right picture and you may not need text at all to get your message across.

Publisher 97 makes it easy for you to add pictures to your prose.

Where should my graphics go?

If you create a publication from scratch, the all-important decision of where to place your graphics is entirely up to you. If you work with a PageWizard, you will use preplaced graphic elements, but don't worry: it's easy to move a picture around if you decide you don't like its location.

The process is a lot like hanging a painting in your house; you put it where you think it'll look good. But after you move the furniture around, you might decide it doesn't look so great there after all, so you try it somewhere else. Fortunately, moving a graphic around inside Publisher doesn't leave nail holes behind.

Drawing a picture frame

Just as you had to draw a text frame to add text to your publication, so you must draw a picture frame to add a picture.

 To insert a picture frame, first click the Picture Frame button on the Publisher toolbar; then move your pointer to the page, positioning it where you want to insert the frame.

As with text frames, you can either click the mouse pointer once to have a picture frame appear instantly, or place the mouse pointer at a corner of the area where you want the picture frame to appear and drag diagonally away from it. When the frame is approximately the size you need, release the mouse button (see Figure 9.1).

Fig. 9.1

An empty picture frame looks just like a text frame, except for the absence of a Connect button at the bottom.

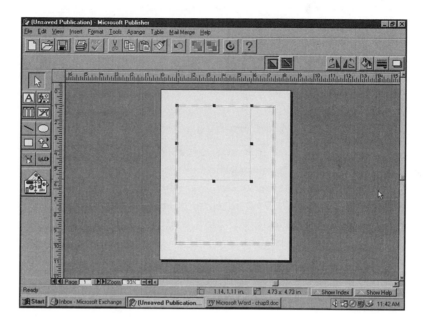

Like the text frame, the picture frame shows eight black handles when you select it; you must select the picture frame before you can put a picture in it. To select a picture frame, just click it once.

Now you've hung a frame, but a frame is no good without a picture. How do you get one to appear in that empty box? Like many designers before you, you need to make a trip to the Gallery.

Q&A *I placed my picture frame inside a text frame, but when I click it, all I select is the text frame. What gives?*

Sometimes, when you work with several text and picture frames together, a picture frame can end up "underneath" a text frame. If you click a frame that's been buried that way, even though it's still visible, you can't select it. To get at it, select the text frame covering it and push it "underneath" the picture frame by clicking the Send to Back button. If you have several frames overlapping, keep doing that until you can select your picture frame. See Chapter 16, "Fine-Tuning Your Layout," for more detail.

Fill that frame with something from the Clip Gallery!

After you select a picture frame, choose <u>I</u>nsert, Clip <u>A</u>rt, or right-click the frame and choose Insert Clip Art from the shortcut menu. You suddenly find a veritable smorgasbord of images at your fingertips, clip art provided with Publisher.

 ### *Plain English, please!*

Clip art is art that you didn't draw specifically for a publication, but instead found somewhere else. Before computer layout, you literally clipped such art, with scissors, from the pages of another publication or from a special book full of clip art (many newspapers and magazines still subscribe to such books, which arrive monthly). Then you had to paste the clip art into the new publication. Although using clip art on the computer requires no scissors, the name has stuck. **99**

What's in the Gallery?

As you can see in Figure 9.2, at the center of the Gallery is a box containing several small images. Across the top are tabs leading to the various sorts of things you can put in the gallery: Clip Art, Pictures, even Sounds and Videos.

Fig 9.2
Publisher makes it easy for you to find the artwork you need with this virtual art gallery, which also works with other Microsoft applications.

Clip Art consists of small drawings; Pictures is a collection of photographs. No sounds or videos are included with Publisher 97; for more information on adding sound and video clips to Publisher documents, see Chapter 15, "OLE: Objects Created in Other Applications."

At the left of the Clip Gallery is a list of subject categories.

Browsing the Clip Gallery is just like visiting a real art gallery; you can either walk through it from beginning to end or head straight to the room set aside for the particular kind of art you're most interested in. Click one of the categories, and you see only the images related to that category. Sometimes, the images can be a little small for easy viewing; Clip Gallery even provides a "magnifying glass." Check the Magnify box and Publisher enlarges the picture you select for your closer examination.

You can also search the Clip Gallery by clicking Find. Like a friendly guide at a real art gallery, Find can help you locate a particular picture based on a descriptive word, a portion of its name, or its graphics format. When the Find dialog box appears (see Figure 9.3), simply fill in the information you have in the blanks provided and choose Find Now.

Fig. 9.3
The Clip Gallery Find dialog box helps you pick out useful images from the hundreds available in the Gallery.

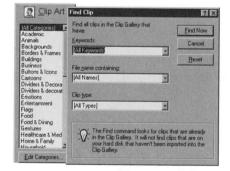

CAUTION The Clip Gallery Find command will only find files that have been added to the Gallery; if you have clip art you'd like to use that hasn't been added to the Gallery, Clip Gallery Find won't turn it up.

Importing Gallery clips

When you find the item you want, you can either double-click it or choose Insert.

Fit the picture to the frame, or the frame to the picture?

Once you choose Insert, the Clip Gallery closes and the Import Picture dialog box immediately appears, offering you two choices: Change The Frame To Fit The Picture or Change The Picture To Fit The Frame (see Figure 9.4). If you choose to change the frame, your frame adjusts to fit the picture; if you choose to change the picture, your picture stretches in one dimension or another. This can have unfortunate effects, as you can see in Figure 9.5.

Fig. 9.4
The Import Picture dialog box appears every time you import artwork into a picture frame.

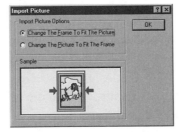

Fig. 9.5
Changing the picture to fit the frame is very effective with decorative, abstract patterns. But take care not to distort more realistic artwork such as this piano in unacceptable ways.

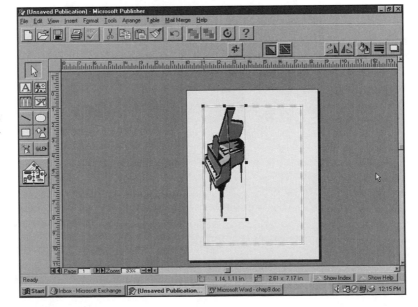

Making changes to the Gallery

Microsoft Clip Gallery is actually a separate program that works not only with Microsoft Publisher but with other Microsoft programs. If you have programs such as Word and PowerPoint installed, you've probably seen the Clip Gallery and already have lots of clip art in it.

In addition to the clips provided by Microsoft, you can add pieces of your own clip art and picture collection to the Gallery.

To insert your own clip art into Clip Gallery, open the Gallery and click Import Clips. This opens the usual Windows 95 dialog box for browsing your hard drive. Just locate the file you want to add to the Gallery and click Open.

Publisher adds the file to the Gallery, and the Clip Properties dialog box opens, providing you information about the size and file type of the clip. It also allows you to associate descriptive keywords with it and choose what category to place it in—rather like choosing which room of a gallery to hang a new painting in (see Figure 9.6). Carefully organizing your collection becomes more and more important as you add clip art to the Gallery—at least, it does if you're planning to find it again.

Fig. 9.6
The Clip Properties dialog box makes organizing your clip art a breeze, and provides more detailed information about each picture.

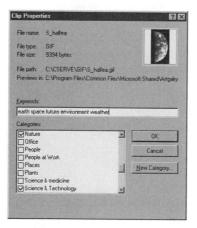

You can access the Clip Properties dialog box for any item in the Gallery by selecting the item and then clicking Clip Properties, or by right-clicking the item and choosing Clip Properties from the shortcut menu.

That shortcut menu also gives you two other tools for cleaning up the Gallery. You can delete an item from the Gallery by right-clicking it and choosing Delete Clip. You can also right-click and choose Update Previews, which prompts the Gallery to search your hard drive and remove previews for clips that have been deleted, update previews of files that have changed, specify the new location of clips that have been moved, and remove duplicate previews.

More clip art: Clip Gallery Online

If you have access to the World Wide Web, you also have access to extra Clip Gallery items.

 In the Clip Gallery dialog box, click the Internet button. This launches your Web browser and takes you automatically to Clip Gallery Live, a special World Wide Web page maintained by Microsoft at **http://198.105.232.29/**.

Once you accept the Terms of Agreement displayed on the introductory screen, you can browse or search a new collection of clips, organized the same way as those in Clip Gallery. For example, I browsed the Food and Dining category under Clip Art to bring up the six clips shown in Figure 9.7.

Fig. 9.7
The easy-to-use Clip Gallery Live offers an ever-changing selection of clip art, in addition to that provided with Publisher 97.

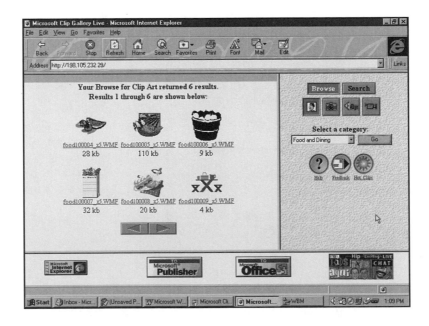

Click any clip you like, and it automatically downloads into your Clip Gallery in the appropriate category.

Microsoft is always adding new artwork to Clip Gallery Live, so it's a great place to find fresh images for your publication.

You can add artwork from almost anywhere

Of course, just as sometimes you hate everything the curator chooses to hang on the walls of an art gallery, you might find nothing in Clip Gallery or Clip Gallery Live you can use. Perhaps, you absolutely have to have a picture of a cow and, inexplicably, the Clip Gallery doesn't have one. But maybe you have a disk full of clip art that contains an absolutely fabulous cow, or you know of another publication on your disk that contains the perfect cow, or you took a great photo of a cow on your last vacation. Maybe you're even talented enough to draw a cow. Publisher makes it possible to add any of these possible cows to your publication.

Inserting a picture file that's not in Clip Gallery

You can add any picture (provided it's in a format Publisher recognizes) from a hard, floppy, or CD-ROM drive to your publication.

1 Draw or select a picture frame.

2 Choose Insert, Picture File, or right-click the frame and choose Insert Picture File from the shortcut menu.

3 The Insert Picture File dialog box asks you to select a file (see Figure 9.8). Publisher lists, by default, all the formats for storing computer graphics it recognizes. You can also search for files in a particular format by choosing from the Files of Type list.

Fig. 9.8
Use the Insert Picture File dialog box to insert picture files from outside Clip Gallery.

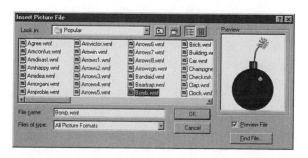

4 Locate the file you want (select <u>P</u>review File if you want to see what an image looks like before you import it) and double-click it, or choose OK.

5 The Import Picture dialog box appear; decide whether to change the frame or the picture as you did previously and click OK. Your imported file appears in the picture frame.

❝ *Plain English, please!*

When you import a picture, Publisher looks for files that have any one of a variety of strange identifiers, including PCX, WMF, and BMP. The letters specify the way in which graphic information is stored in that file: WMF, for instance, stands for Windows Metafile. But you don't have to know any of that: if Publisher shows it in the Insert Picture File dialog box, then you can use it in your publication. ❞

The types of picture files Publisher 97 can import are PC Paintbrush, JPEG, Windows Bitmaps, CorelDraw Picture, Computer Graphics Metafile, Micrografx Designer/Draw, Encapsulated PostScript, Kodak Photo CD, Tagged Image File Format 5.0, Windows Metafiles, WordPerfect Graphics, CompuServe GIF, Macintosh PICT, Enhance Metafiles, Portable Network Graphics, AutoCAD Format 2-D, and Targa.

Copying artwork from another publication

You might remember seeing an image in another publication that would be perfect for your publication. Publisher lets you go get it.

1 Open the publication that contains the graphic you want, using whatever application it requires.

2 Using the tools provided with that application, select the graphic and copy it to the Clipboard.

3 Return to Publisher. Go to the page of your publication where you want to place the copied image, click once on the page where you want the copied image to appear; then click the Paste button.

The copied object appears in a new picture frame, which you can then adjust as necessary (see Chapter 10, "Adjusting Graphics," for more information).

Adding a scanned image

Scanners allow you to turn photographs and other images into files your computer can display and manipulate. Using a scanned image is exactly the same as using any other image, if it's already stored on your drive. However, you might want to scan an image directly into a Publisher publication. Publisher lets you do that—provided, of course, you have a scanner. If you don't, the scanner options are not available.

1 Draw or select a picture frame.

2 Choose Insert, Scanner Image, or right-click the frame and choose Insert Scanner Image from the shortcut menu.

3 If you have more than one scanner, you have to choose which one to use; then click Acquire Scanned Image.

4 Start the scanning process, using the software provided with your scanner and whatever settings you want to apply to the final picture.

5 When you finish scanning, exit the scanning software. The Import Picture dialog box appears. Make your choice, and the scanned image appears in your publication (see Figure 9.9).

Fig. 9.9

Publisher's capability to use scanned images opens up many design possibilities for you. Here I've scanned in a photo of myself. You can also include handwriting, freehand drawings, and more.

TIP **Most scanners allow you to scan things in a variety of resolutions.** The higher the resolution, the more data storage space the resulting picture file will take up. To cut down on file sizes, limit the resolution you scan a picture at to the resolution of the printer you'll be printing it on. If you use a 300 dpi laser printer, there's no point in scanning in a picture at 1,200 dpi. It'll look great on the screen, but it's still only going to print at 300 dpi!

CAUTION **Images don't appear out of thin air; somebody creates them. The** creator of an image owns the copyright to that image; that means nobody else can copy it or make use of it without permission. The clip art provided with Publisher and other computer programs is provided for the free use of purchasers of those programs, but there are many other images you can easily pick up, off the Internet, for example, or by scanning them in from a magazine, that you are legally not entitled to use. Failing to respect copyright has landed more than one desktop publisher or Web page designer in trouble. Be careful to only use images you have a legitimate right to use.

Drawing your own artwork

It's not an option for everyone, but some people can draw their own artwork on the computer and actually come up with something usable. If you have the talent, Publisher makes it easy for you to create your own illustrations.

1 Draw or select a picture frame.

2 Choose Insert, Object, or right-click the frame and choose Insert Object.

3 You see the Insert Object dialog box, which includes a list of the types of programs that allow you to create objects to imbed in Publisher publications. (See Chapter 15, "OLE: Objects Created in Other Applications," for details.) Choose the graphics program you want to use, such as Microsoft Draw or Paintbrush.

4 The graphics program appears, either as it usually does or on top of Publisher, with a work window occupying the picture frame, as in Figure 9.10. Draw your artwork, then save it or close the program. Publisher automatically places the artwork you created in the selected picture frame.

Fig. 9.10
You can create graphics using other programs and place them directly in your publication. Here, I used Microsoft Paintbrush to create an image in a preselected picture frame.

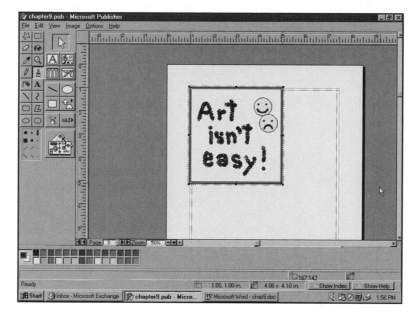

TIP **You can draw crude images using the line, rectangle, circle, and** shape tools provided with Publisher, but it's much easier to use a dedicated graphics program. The greater flexibility they give you will reflect in the quality of the graphics you produce—not that you can tell that in the example I created!

10

Adjusting Graphics

● In this chapter:

● **Getting the right picture in the right place**

● **This picture needs to be bigger!**

● **Rotation: when right-side up just isn't good enough**

● **Are there any cool colors, tints, and shades?**

Get maximum impact from your graphics by changing pictures from "almost right" to "absolutely right" with Publisher's graphics tools. . . . . >

How many times have you bought a new piece of artwork and hung it in what you thought was the perfect place in your home or office, only to discover that it clashes with the couch or makes the room look lopsided? How many more times have you hung it before you're perfectly satisfied?

Finding the perfect place for artwork is sometimes as much a process of trial and error as good planning. It can be the same with putting graphics in a Publisher publication. An item might look fine in your rough sketch, but when you actually insert it, it overpowers the text it's supposed to complement and ruins the balance of the page—or else it seems to fade out of existence because it isn't strong enough.

Be flexible and experiment. Whether you need to replace your picture entirely or just move it an inch or two, it's easy to do.

By the way, if you're reading this book sequentially, several sections of this chapter will look a little familiar. That's because some of the things you do with frames—such as moving, resizing, and coloring—are the same no matter whether the frames hold text, pictures, a table, WordArt, or some other object.

It's the wrong picture!

To replace one picture with another, double-click the picture frame whose contents you want to change. This opens Clip Gallery. Choose the picture you want to replace the current picture with, and click Insert. The new picture automatically replaces the old.

You can also replace one picture with another by selecting the picture frame and choosing Insert, Picture File. Browse your computer to find the picture file you want and double-click it or click OK.

It's in the wrong place!

To move a picture to another location on the same page:

1 Select the picture frame and move the mouse pointer over it. The arrow changes to a set of crossed arrows and an image of a moving van (see Figure 10.1).

2 Hold down the left mouse button and "drive" (meaning drag) the moving van to the new location for the graphic. During the move, a light-gray rectangle the same size as the picture frame represents the graphic.

3 When the frame is where you want it, release the mouse button to "hang" the picture in its new location.

Fig. 10.1
Just as you might rent a moving van to transport artwork from one place to another, use Publisher's moving van to relocate graphics.

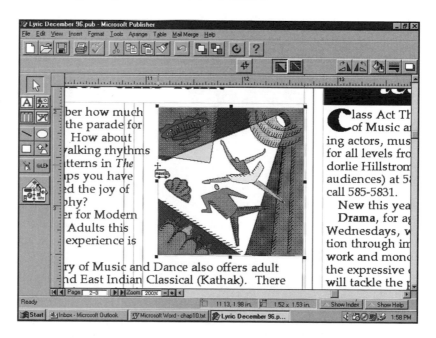

Can I put it on a different page?

You might decide an image would work better on an entirely different page—but since you can't see that page, you can't just load up the moving van and drive your artwork to it. Here's one way to get it there:

1 Select the picture frame you want to relocate.

2 Using the moving van, drag it right off the page, onto the scratch area—the gray area surrounding your pages.

3 Move to the page where you want to place the picture. It will remain visible even while the pages change (see Figure 10.2).

4 Drag the picture off the scratch area onto the page and place it wherever you like.

Fig. 10.2
The scratch area is a virtual desktop where you can store clip art and other items while you flip from one page to another.

TIP **An alternative method for moving objects, graphics, and text from** page to page is to cut and paste. This is faster than dragging, especially if you use the keyboard shortcuts. (It can also be confusing if you move a lot of pictures around from page to page, so it's probably best to use the scratch area if you want to relocate more than one or two pictures.) Just select the picture you want to move and click the Cut button. The picture disappears. Move to the page you want to place it on and click the Paste button. The image reappears in the same place on the new page as it was on the original page. Now drag it wherever you want.

Q&A *I cut a picture from one page and, without thinking, copied something else from another page without ever pasting the first picture. Can I get it back?*

Unfortunately, no. If you use Cut, it's important to immediately go to the page you want the picture on and paste it in place, or you run the risk of losing it. Another option is to use the Copy button instead of the Cut button; that way the original is still in your publication where you originally put it, no matter what happens to the copy. If you use Copy, though, you eventually have to go back to the original page and delete the picture, making the process a bit more complicated than just using Cut.

I pasted the picture I cut from another page onto a new page that already had text and other elements on it. Before I dragged it into place, I selected something else. Now my picture is hard to separate from all the other elements on the page. How do I select it again?

To select your picture again, click it. This selects the top element of all the overlapping elements. Click the Send to Back button; then click your picture again. If it still isn't selected, click Send to Back again. Keep doing this until the picture you want is the one selected. Drag it into place, and then check the page carefully to make sure you didn't accidentally change its appearance. For more information on working with overlapping elements, see Chapter 16, "Fine-Tuning Your Layout."

It's the wrong size!

Sometimes, after placing a picture in your publication, you're happy with the location, but not with the picture's size. It may be too small for details to be clearly visible, or too big to fit comfortably in the space you've chosen for it.

Handles: get a grip

As noted earlier, all frames in Publisher have selection handles you can use to adjust their size. Resizing a picture frame is just like resizing any other kind of frame:

1 Select the picture frame you want to resize.

2 Aim your mouse pointer at one of the selection handles. The pointer changes to a box labeled RESIZE, with arrows extending horizontally, vertically, or diagonally from it, depending on which handle you chose.

3 Drag the handle in the direction of one of the arrows, and the frame (again visible as a light-gray rectangle) alters the size accordingly. As soon as you release the mouse button, the picture refills the frame (see Figure 10.3).

Fig. 10.3
If you're not careful when you resize your picture, it will end up looking like this.

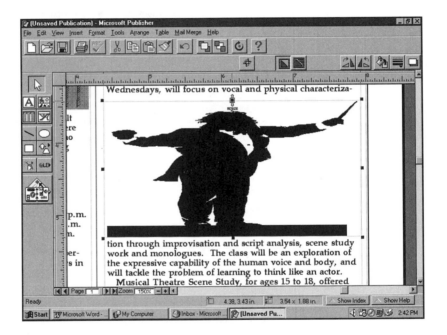

Using the scale option

Take another look at Figure 10.3. The picture's not only a different size, it's a different shape. And it has become distorted—the conductor is squashed!

Sometimes, that kind of distortion helps you achieve a special effect you're striving for, but not with a realistic picture like this one. How can you resize a picture without running the risk of distorting it?

You can always do it by eye, adjusting the frame until the picture looks right, and sometimes that's good enough—but sometimes it isn't. When it isn't, you need to use the Scale Picture command instead.

With the picture selected, choose Format, Scale Object (or Scale Picture; the name changes depending on where the image came from), or right-click the picture and choose Scale Object from the shortcut menu. This opens the Scale Object dialog box (see Figure 10.4), in which you can set the Scale Height and Scale Width as percentages of the original size. You can also reset the picture to its Original Size. Click OK and the picture instantly changes.

Fig. 10.4
If you set Scale Height and Scale Width at exactly the same percentage in the Scale Object dialog box, your picture resizes without distortion.

> **TIP**
>
> **When you resize a picture, one dimension, either height or width,** usually takes precedence over the other. Maybe the picture can only be two inches tall, and width doesn't matter, or maybe it has to fit into one column, and can be any height at all. Hold down Shift while using the handles to make the picture the exact size it needs to be in the most important dimension; this ensures that the proportion of height to width remains the same.

It's framed wrong!

Sometimes, the problem with a picture isn't the size, it's the content; there's too much of it. For example, say you scan in a photo of yourself taken last summer. You think it's a great picture of your face, but you really don't want the hot dog in your hand appearing in your business report.

The Crop Picture tool lets you eliminate unwanted elements from your picture frame.

1 Select the picture frame.

2 Click the Crop Picture button.

3 Move the pointer to a frame handle. The arrow changes to two pairs of crossed arrows with the word CROP.

4 Drag the handle toward the middle of the picture (see Figure 10.5).
A light gray line shows you exactly where you cropped to.

5 Release the mouse button. Part of the picture disappears, as though you
just covered it with paper. Don't worry; it's still there, and you can get it
back just by moving the handle back to its original position.

6 Adjust the sides of the picture frame until it displays exactly what you
want.

Fig. 10.5
Use the Crop Picture
button to remove
unwanted elements
from a picture.

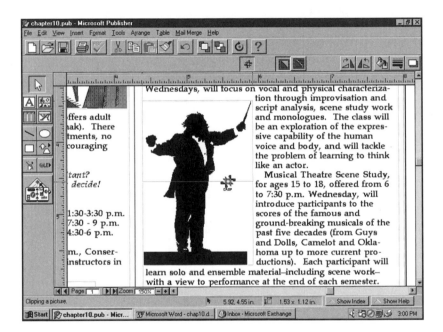

 TIP   **Imported pictures often include empty space around the image.**
Use the Crop Picture button as soon as you import a picture to remove that
space, so the edges of the frame exactly match the edges of the image. This
makes it easier to resize the image: you won't have to allow for any space
surrounding the image when you try to make it fit perfectly into your
publication.

Better yet, tightly crop the image in a graphics program before you import
it. This can save space and speed up Publisher's performance.

Q&A ***What happens if I crop a picture, cut and paste it, and then change my mind about the cropping? Can I uncrop the pasted version?***

Yes. Cropping does not destroy any part of the picture; it just hides it. When you cut or copy a cropped image, Publisher also copies the invisible part of the picture. You can uncover that invisible part again by using the Crop Picture button.

It's angled wrong!

Publisher 97 lets you rotate any object to any angle: a powerful feature that helps you achieve just the right look for your publication, by squeezing graphics into awkward spaces.

The most common form of rotation is turning an object 90 degrees. The Rotate Right and Rotate Left buttons in the Picture Formatting Toolbar let you do this easily. Simply select the picture you want to rotate and click either button.

Breaking out of right angles

To rotate a picture in anything other than multiples of 90 degrees, click the Rotate button on the Standard toolbar to open the Rotate Objects dialog box (see Figure 10.6). Use the clockwise or counterclockwise arrows to rotate the image a little at a time, or enter the specific number of degrees you want the image rotated in the Angle control box. You can cancel rotation at any time by clicking No Rotation.

Fig. 10.6
The Rotate Objects dialog box lets you rotate an image (or text) frame to the left or right by a specific number of degrees.

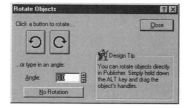

The keyboard-mouse option

An even easier way to rotate an object is to press and hold the Alt key, while pointing the mouse at the corner handle of any frame. The arrow changes to two arrows chasing each other in a circle, above the word ROTATE.

Click and hold the left mouse button and move around the picture. A line drawing of the frame rotates as you move the mouse (see Figure 10.7). You can also flip the frame quickly by dragging your mouse directly across the middle of the picture. When you have the picture aligned the way you want it, release the mouse button.

Fig. 10.7
The ability to rotate frames frees you from the tyranny of right angles, and offers many fresh opportunities for eye-catching designs.

TIP **When you rotate an image using the Alt+mouse method, your** pointer is connected to the center of the object by a line. You can stretch this line out as far as you like. Use it to align your rotating object with the corners of the paper, other objects, or diagonal lines. It also helps you remember which way is up! That's easy to forget because only an outline of the frame rotates at first.

It's the wrong color!

If you have the capability to print in color, you have another powerful weapon in your desktop-publishing arsenal to use in the ongoing battle for the reader's attention. And if you can change that color at will, you can precisely target your tactical efforts.

Publisher 97 allows you to do just that, choosing from a broad palette of basic colors or creating your own colors.

Basic colors

To recolor a picture, select the picture frame. Then choose F_ormat, _Recolor Object (or right-click the picture and choose Recolor Object from the short-cut menu).

The Recolor Object dialog box appears (see Figure 10.8). It contains a Preview box that shows the selected picture and has a palette of basic colors on the left.

Fig. 10.8
The Recolor Objcet dialog box lets you see what your picture will look like in a new color.

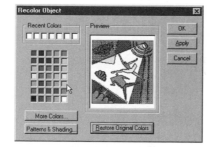

As you move the mouse over the boxes, the name assigned to each color appears. In addition to ordinary colors like Orange and Blue, you'll find Pumpkin, Peach, Saffron, and Cobalt.

Click any color and the Preview box shows what the picture looks like in that color. Click _Apply and the picture in the publication takes on the hue you selected, but the Recolor Object dialog box remains open so you can experiment with other colors. Click OK to accept the color change and return to your publication.

The next time you open the Recolor Object dialog box, you'll see the last color you selected in the leftmost box of the Recent Colors area. This can help you match colors from picture to picture.

If even Teal and Sienna aren't enough variety for you, click the More Colors button to open the Colors dialog box (see Figure 10.9).

More colors

Here you have even more colors to choose from. As Microsoft's Design Tip points out, the colors in each numbered column are designed to work well together. Choose all your colors from the same column to give your publication a more unified look.

Fig. 10.9
Double your colors; double your fun. With more colors, you have more design options.

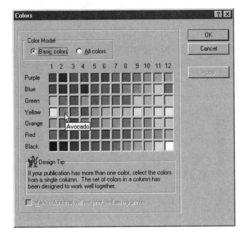

Look at the names of these colors. In addition to Coral and Maroon and the rest, there are boxes cryptically labeled RGB (204,51,102) and the like. Select All colors at the top of the dialog box instead of Basic colors, and you'll see why.

Take a look at Figure 10.10. Instead of discrete boxes of colors, there's a palette where the colors flow from one to the other—like someone spilled several cans of paint across the screen. Crosshairs respond to the movements of your mouse; by moving the crosshairs around the palette, you can come up with all the hues that Publisher doesn't include in its basic color menus.

Fig. 10.10
If the 84 choices Publisher gives for basic colors aren't enough, you can create your own using the All colors palette.

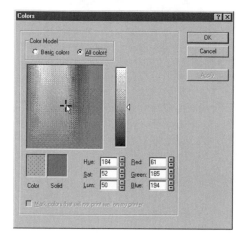

In the Color and Solid boxes, you see the color you created (Color), and the solid color most like it (Solid). Publisher applies your custom color if possible, but sometimes, depending on the object you recolor and the display capabilities of your computer, it can only use the solid color.

To the right of the color palette is a tall, skinny rectangle containing the color you chose in shades from very dark to very light. This is like the brightness control on your TV: Slide the mouse pointer up the rectangle, and your color gets lighter; slide it down and the color darkens.

The six text boxes at the lower right contain numbers that change as you maneuver the crosshairs and slide the mouse pointer. If you want, you can precisely set all the parameters of the color using these boxes. After you choose the color you want, click OK to return to the Recolor Object dialog box.

Tints and shading

There's one more button to try in the Recolor Object dialog box: Patterns & Shading. Clicking it opens the Fill Patterns and Shading dialog box in Figure 10.11.

Fig. 10.11
Here you can apply tints and shades to your chosen color—another way to control your color's brightness.

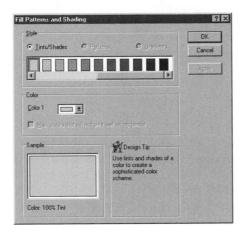

HUE, SAT, LUM, and RGB

Hue, Sat, and Lum might sound like some of Donald Duck's lesser-known nephews, but they're not. They're the three elements that make up the colors you see on the screen.

Hue is the pure color, with numbers assigned from 0 (red) to 120 (green) to 240 (blue) back to almost-red at 359. **Sat** is short for saturation and represents the intensity of the color, from 0 (gray) to 100 percent (the pure color). Finally, **Lum**, or luminescence, is the color's brightness. It's what you control in the skinny rectangle next to the color palette in the All colors Color Model (or with the brightness control on your TV set).

For even finer tuning of color, you can adjust the **RGB** settings. All the colors on your computer are composed of mixtures of red, green, and blue. Increasing the setting of each color alters the mix of all three. If you play with the Red, Green, and Blue boxes in the All colors Color Model, you notice that, as you increase or decrease the value of one of the colors, the value of Hue also changes, but more slowly.

Most users never need to touch these boxes, but if you want to precisely match a color someone else has used, these boxes allow you to do so.

This dialog box features three areas: Style, Color, and Sample.

During recoloring, you can only choose one Style option: <u>T</u>ints/Shades. The options are from 0 percent Tint (white) at the far left of the selection box to 100 percent Tint (pure color) at the center, and then down to 0 percent Shade (black) at the far right.

The Color area shows the color you choose. Clicking the <u>C</u>olor 1 selection box opens the Recent Colors dialog box, which in turn offers the More Colors button, which leads back to the other color palettes we've discussed.

Finally, at the bottom, a sample of your color with the current tints and shades appear. Click OK in the Fill Patterns and Shading dialog box and again in the Recolor Object dialog box. Publisher applies the tint or shade to your picture.

Oops! I liked the original better

No matter how many times you change the color of your picture, if you finally decide you should have stayed with the original colors, there's a way to undo all the damage you've done. Just click the <u>R</u>estore Original Colors button in the Recolor Object dialog box, and you're back where you began!

11

Let's Table That

● **In this chapter:**

- **First, how do I make a table?**

- **Now, how do I put information in my table?**

- **How do I make changes to my table?**

- **Can I add graphics?**

Tables are an eye-catching way to present lots of information in a small space...and Publisher makes them easy to create . . . .

Sentences and paragraphs are a great way to impart information. But sometimes, you don't need all those words; all you need is to present data with a few identifying labels, as on the tear-out card in this book. That's when you need a table—a space-efficient and graphically interesting way to present information.

Building a table—without Carpentry 101

 To create a table, click the Table button on the Publisher toolbar. The pointer arrow changes to crosshairs. Either place the crosshairs roughly where you want the table to go and click once (if you have single-click object creation activated) or place the crosshairs where you want to anchor the upper-left corner of the table, and drag down and to the right until you fill the space you allotted for your table. Release the button, and the Create Table dialog box immediately appears (see Figure 11.1).

Fig. 11.1
Choose a preset table style and then polish it to your specifications.

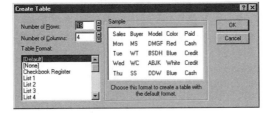

Rows and columns

In the upper-left corner of the Create Table dialog box, you see two controls for setting the number of rows and columns. The default numbers are based on how big a table you drew. Changing these numbers changes the size of your cells; the smaller the numbers, the bigger the cells.

 **Plain English, please!**

A **cell** is a room where a prisoner is kept, the basic unit of all living things— and the little rectangle formed by the intersection of a row and a column in a table. You enter data in a cell, something like a tiny text frame. **"**

Preset styles

If you want, you can shop for Publisher tables in the Create Table dialog box much as you might shop for a kitchen table in a furniture store window. Publisher offers a number of styles of tables; view one by clicking a format in the Table Format list. A small example appears in the Sample area. If you see one you like, click OK, and Publisher applies that format to the table frame you drew. If you just want a very basic table to build your own design on, choose (None) in the Table Format list. This creates a table with no borders, shading, or special character formatting.

Fine-tuning a format

If you see a format that has some elements you like and others you don't, you can choose to apply only portions of it to your table...but not when you first draw the table. Instead, choose (None) from the Table Format list when you first draw the table and click OK. Now open the Auto Format dialog box by choosing Table, Auto Format. This time, the dialog box includes an Options button. Choose the format you want to partially apply to your table from the Table Format list; then click Options. This adds a Formats to Apply area to the Auto Format dialog box. The Formats to Apply area contains four options.

- Select Include Text Formatting to retain text style selections such as Bold and Italic. If

you don't select this check box, all text will appear in normal style.

- Select Include Patterns & Shading to retain the shaded and colored cells you see in some of the preset styles. If you don't select this check box, all the cells will be white.

- Select Include Text Alignment to retain the text's positioning in each cell. In many of the preset styles, the text is centered in each cell; in others it is aligned to the right margin. If you don't select this check box, all text will be set flush left.

- Select Include Borders to retain any lines delineating cells, rows, or columns, or surrounding the whole frame. If you don't select this check box, no lines appear.

Plugging stuff in

The sample tables in the Create Table dialog box also include sample text. That text doesn't appear in your newly created table (see Figure 11.2). Just like a brand-new kitchen table, it's bare. Your kitchen table isn't of any use until you start putting place settings and maybe a nice vase of flowers on it, and your Publisher table isn't of any use without text—although maybe it could use a nice vase of flowers, too.

Fig. 11.2
Although the table frame looks different than those created for graphics and text, it has the same handles; and you can move or resize it the same way. It strongly resembles an Excel spreadsheet!

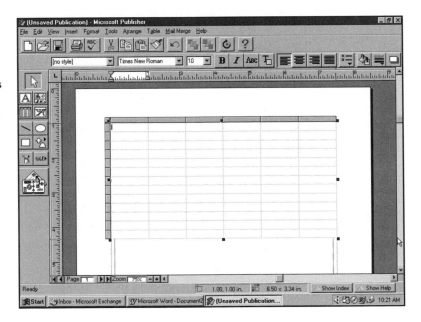

Just start typing

You can type text in each cell of the table just as though it's a miniature text frame.

Click a cell to move the cursor there. You can also press Tab to move from one cell to the next, or Shift+Tab to move from one cell to the previous one. You can also navigate from cell to cell using your keyboard cursor keys.

TIP **If you type in more text than the cell can hold, the cell** automatically grows larger. This can cause the table to grow longer, which can mess up the rest of your layout. To avoid this, lock the table size by choosing Table, Grow to Fit Text (which is active by default; choosing it again deactivates it). You can still type as much information as you want in any cell, but the extra text isn't visible and the table doesn't expand to hold it.

Use fill to escape drudgery

If you want to have the same text in several different cells of your table, you don't have to type it in over and over. For text that repeats in a variety of places throughout the table, use Cut and Paste. For text that repeats over and over again in the same row or column, use the Fill Down and Fill Right commands.

To use the Fill Down command, highlight the cell in which the repeating text begins, then drag your mouse down until you reach the last continuous cell in which you want the text to appear. (Make sure you don't accidentally highlight cells where you don't want the text to appear!) Choose Table, Fill Down, and every cell you highlighted fills with the text you typed in the topmost cell.

CAUTION **Be careful when using Fill Down or Fill Right: the repeating text** will overwrite any text you might already have in the highlighted cells.

You can highlight cells from the bottom up, too, but you can't Fill Up. Whether you start highlighting from top or bottom, it's the text in the topmost cell that is inserted in all the cells.

Repeating elements can likewise be easily inserted across a row by highlighting them and choosing Table, Fill Right. All the cells fill with the text that appears in the leftmost cell of the highlighted series.

Can I use data from another program?

If the data you want to insert as a Publisher table has already been entered in another program, you don't have to type it in. You can't import it like you do graphics or text, but you can easily copy it and paste it into place.

1 Open the program in which you originally entered the data.

2 If the data is already in a table, select the table and copy it to the Clipboard.

3 If the data isn't already in table format, insert a tab between each item of what will form a row, and press Enter at the end of the row. Each tab-separated item will appear in a different column in the row. After you apply tabs and returns to all the data, highlight it and copy it to the Clipboard.

4 Return to Publisher.

5 If you want to insert the data into a table you already created, select the table and place the cursor where you want the data to start appearing.

6 Choose Edit, Paste Special, and you see the Paste Special dialog box in Figure 11.3. You have several options, which can change depending on what form the data you want to insert currently takes.

In general, the options are:

- (Original Program) Object—If this option is available, and you choose it, the data won't be inserted as a table at all; it will be inserted as an embedded object that can't be edited using Publisher's tools, but can be edited in Publisher using the original program's tools. For more information on embedded objects, refer to Chapter 15, "OLE: Objects Created in Other Applications."

- Table Cells with Cell Formatting—Choose this if you want to insert the material from the other program into an existing table, and you're sure it's formatted properly. This option is only available if you've selected an existing table before choosing Edit, Paste Special.

- New Table—This inserts table-formatted information from another program into Publisher as a brand-new table, which Publisher draws automatically.

- New Text Frame—If you import text that hasn't been preformatted to fit in a table, this might be your best choice. Publisher inserts the text in a new text frame it draws automatically. After your text is in a text frame, you can format it and add tabs and returns; then you copy it to your table.

- Picture—Publisher converts the text you saved to the Clipboard into a picture and pastes it into your publication. You can't edit it, but you can use the picture formatting tools we talked about in Chapters 9, "Adding Graphics," and 10, "Adjusting Graphics," on it.

- Formatted Text—Choose this one, and all the selected text copies to a single cell of your table. Generally, this is not what you want.

- Publisher Object—This inserts whatever you copied directly into Publisher as an object of the appropriate type. If, as in this example, you copy text, this choice will paste it into a new text frame, just like the New text frame option. If you were copying a picture, it would paste it into a new picture frame, and so on. This choice is only available if you haven't selected an existing table.

Copying data from some programs such as Excel even allows you the option of linking your Publisher publication to the other program, which means that when the data changes in the other program, your table in Publisher is automatically updated. (Again, see Chapter 15 for more information.)

Fig. 11.3
Paste Special is just that: a special way to paste information into Publisher that offers you more options than just clicking the Paste button.

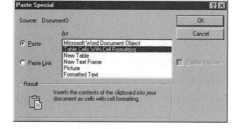

Working with Excel spreadsheets

If you work with Microsoft Excel and want to import cells from an Excel spreadsheet into an existing Publisher table, the procedure is even easier. Open Excel, copy the cells from the spreadsheet you want to import, return to Publisher, select the cell in your table where you want the data to begin appearing, and choose Edit, Paste (or press Ctrl+V).

Dressing up your table: a floral centerpiece, perhaps?

When you set your kitchen table for a special dinner party, you might change your mind about what plates to use, what flatware really suits the mood, and what candlesticks look best. The same thing can happen when you set your Publisher table. Maybe you used a preset design and it's not quite right, or maybe you designed your own and you want to give it that final layer of polish that distinguishes good design from mediocre.

Most of the formatting options available to you when you work with text frames are also available to you when you work with a table (see Chapters 7, "Formatting Characters and Paragraphs: The Basics," and 8, "Making Text Stand Out: Special Formatting"). The primary difference between using these tools in a text frame and using them in a table is the method of highlighting the text.

How do I select things in a table?

You can highlight one or several cells in a table by dragging the mouse across them while holding down the left mouse button. However, often when you work on a table, a single change in format will apply to all the cells in a row or column—you want to make them all bold, for instance—and there's a simpler way to highlight all the necessary cells.

To highlight an entire row or column, select the table; then click the selector (the fat gray box) on the left side or across the top that corresponds to the row or column you're interested in. You can highlight more than one row or column at a time by holding down the left mouse button and dragging the pointer across several selectors.

Now format the highlighted text just as you would the text in a text frame. Choose foreground and background colors, patterns and shades, fonts and sizes, line spacing, and spacing between characters (see Figure 11.4).

Resizing rows and columns

As noted previously, if Table, Grow to Fit Text is active, text that is too long for the space provided automatically starts a new line, swelling the depth of its own cell and the table as a whole.

Fig. 11.4
Careful formatting of the text in a table helps distinguish column headers and other labeling elements from data elements.

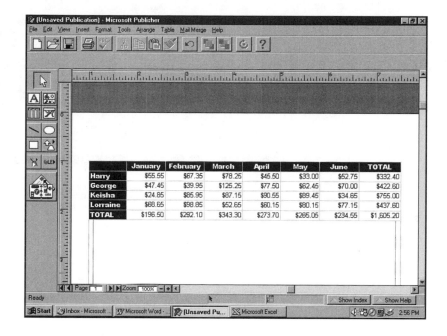

You might want to alter the size of the cell to avoid that, perhaps lengthening it so the text inside it still fits on one line. To do this:

1 Select the table.

2 Move the mouse pointer over the column or row selectors. When the arrow passes over the intersection between two rows or two columns, it changes to an image of two parallel lines attached to arrows going in opposite directions, labeled ADJUST.

3 Now hold down the left mouse button and drag the line in the direction you want to expand or shrink the row or column. It alters accordingly. The external frame of the table also changes. A dotted line appears to show you the new dimensions (see Figure 11.5).

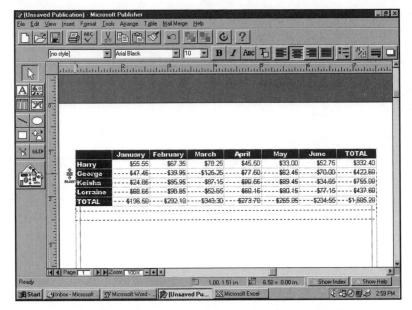

Fig. 11.5
As you resize a row or column, you can judge the impact on the dimensions of the table as a whole by watching the dotted lines that appear.

I need to add a row (or column) here

If someone arrives unexpectedly for dinner, you have to find room for another place setting at your kitchen table. In the same way, sometimes data arrives late to your Publisher table and you discover you need additional rows and columns. To add a row or column:

1 Highlight a row immediately above or below where you want to add rows, or a column immediately to the left or right of where you want to add columns.

2 Choose Table, Insert Rows or Columns, or right-click the table and choose Insert Rows or Columns from the shortcut menu. The Insert dialog box appears (see Figure 11.6).

Fig. 11.6
Insert as many additional rows or columns as you need in an existing table. Make sure you know where your cursor is first, though!

3 Choose Row(s) or Column(s); then choose the Number of Rows (or Columns) you want to insert.

4 Choose whether you want the row or column to appear Before Selected Cells or After Selected Cells.

5 Click OK. Publisher adds the new row or column, empty of data, to your table (see Figure 11.7).

Fig. 11.7
Don't worry if you misjudged the number of rows or columns you need; you can always add more.

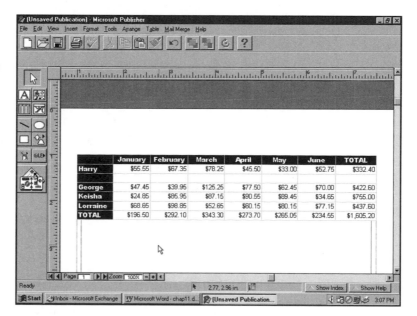

I want to get rid of a row or column

To delete a row or column, highlight it; then choose Table, Delete Rows or Delete Columns.

Copying, cutting, and pasting cells

To cut or copy the data in one or more cells, highlight the cells; then choose Edit, Cut Cells, or Edit, Copy Cells. You can then paste the data from those cells into new cells.

CAUTION **When you paste data from one cell into another, any data** currently in the cell you're pasting into will be overwritten.

TIP **To create a cell larger than normal, perhaps for a title bar running** across the top of the table, merge two or more cells together. Highlight the cells you want to merge and choose Table, Merge Cells; or right-click the table and choose Merge Cells from the shortcut menu.

Give those cells some elbow room

Like a text frame, each cell has its own internal margins—which, also like a text frame, default to .04 inch. To change these margins, place your cursor in a cell without selecting any of the text it contains, and then right-click the table and select Table Cell Properties; or choose Format, Table Cell Properties. The Table Cell Properties dialog box appears (see Figure 11.8). Adjust the margins using the four controls.

Fig. 11.8
If text almost-but-not-quite fits in a cell, you can sometimes squeeze it in by reducing the cell margins to zero.

TIP **Remember that all of the formatting tools available to you in a** text frame are available to you in a table, too. That means if you have trouble fitting text in a table, you can reduce the font size, tighten up the spacing between characters or lines, or change to a narrower font. The number of formatting tools available in Publisher means there's always more than one solution to a problem.

Lines and borders

In the next chapter, we'll look at adding borders to all kinds of frames. But with tables, there's a particular kind of border that's an important element inside the frame: borders around individual cells or groups of cells.

1 Highlight the cells you want to work with.

2 Choose Format, Border. The BorderArt dialog box appears (see Figure 11.9).

Fig. 11.9
How lines flow around
the cells in your table
is completely under
your control with the
BorderArt dialog box.

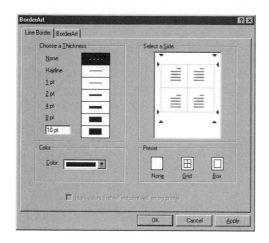

3 From the Preset options at the bottom of the dialog box, choose Non<u>e</u> (to remove any lines already present), <u>G</u>rid (to put lines between rows and columns), or <u>B</u>ox (to put a border around the outside of the selection only).

4 If you want lines only between rows, or only between columns, or only along one, two, or three sides of the entire selection, or even a combination of these, begin by choosing Non<u>e</u> from the Preset options. Now you can add just the lines you want.

5 In the Select A <u>S</u>ide area, you see a simple grid of four cells, surrounded with gray lines. To switch any of those gray lines from printing to nonprinting, simply click it. This marks it with two black triangles, one at either end.

6 To add more than one line, press Shift and click each line in turn, as shown in Figure 11.10.

7 Set the thickness to any point size you want with the Choose A <u>T</u>hickness options. You can also choose a line color from the <u>C</u>olor drop-down list.

8 Choose <u>A</u>pply to see what your added lines look like without closing the dialog box, or choose OK to accept the lines you installed and close the dialog box. Figure 11.11 shows a table with lines installed.

Fig. 11.10
Apply different thicknesses and colors to the lines in your table to achieve different eye-catching effects.

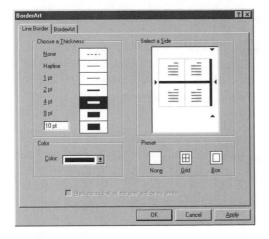

Fig. 11.11
Adding lines gives your table an organized, business-like look.

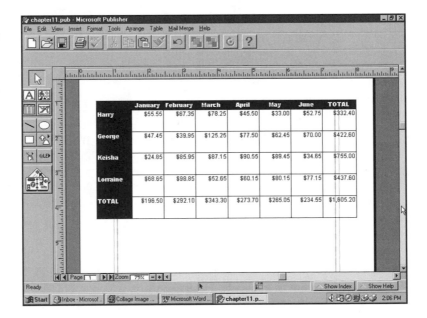

The other tab in the BorderArt dialog box, also called BorderArt, allows you to add borders that are fancier than just ordinary lines, including borders made from a series of pictures. You'd seldom use these kinds of borders inside a table, but you might want to add one to the outside of a table. We'll discuss BorderArt in detail in Chapter 12, "On the Border."

Adding a picture to a table

When you finalize your table, you can spruce it up by adding a picture to it. Simply draw the picture frame on top of the table and add a picture to it just as you would anywhere else (see Figure 11.12). And you thought I was joking about adding a vase of flowers!

CAUTION **Text in a table won't flow around a picture the way text in a text** frame does, so be careful not to obscure the text with the picture. The text, after all, is presumably more important!

Fig. 11.12
A touch of artwork can lift a table from the ordinary to the extraordinary, and make the reader look twice at its contents.

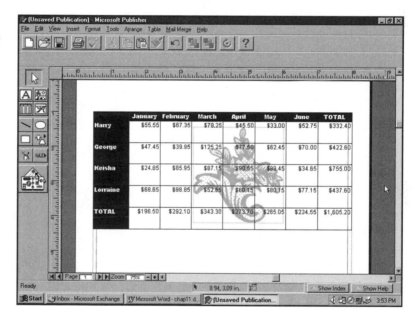

Part IV: Special Effects

12

On the Border

● **In this chapter:**

- **I like my art in a frame!**

- **What are my options?**

- **Not all borders have four sides**

- **How can I add even fancier borders?**

Borders enhance text, graphics, and tables—and Publisher offers you plenty of borders to choose from. Wrap your publication in lightning bolts or hearts . . . .➤

Most towns have at least one store devoted to framing things. It's not just artwork that's being framed, either; people also frame movie posters, needlework, even pressed flowers.

People frame things because those things are special to them. They want to highlight them in a room that may be crowded with other things to look at. They frame them so they can enjoy them better and visitors can admire them, too.

That's the same reason you put a border around objects in Publisher: to make them stand out from a crowded page and catch the interest of visitors—in this case, the readers of your publication.

And just like real life, you don't have to limit yourself to framing artwork. In Publisher, you can put distinctive, decorative borders around text and tables, too.

Add a simple border

The simplest border is a line, and Publisher makes it easy to put one around any object. Follow these steps:

1 Select the frame—text, graphic, or table, it doesn't matter—you want the border to surround.

 2 Click the Border button in the Formatting toolbar. Up pops a menu that offers several options.

3 Click whichever of the four lines matches the thickness you want. Publisher instantly applies that line to your object.

4 If you want to remove a border that's already there, choose None. Whether it's a simple line border or one of the fancy borders you'll see later in the chapter, it disappears.

5 If you don't like any of these choices, choose More. The BorderArt dialog box appears (see Figure 12.1). You can also open this dialog box by choosing Format, Border.

Yes, this is the same BorderArt dialog box we looked at in the last chapter, when we were talking about tables, with one slight difference: since I selected a picture frame—not a table—for this example, the options related to placing borders around cells within a table don't appear.

Fig. 12.1
You have complete control over the thickness, color, and positioning of a border around any text, graphic, or table frame in Publisher.

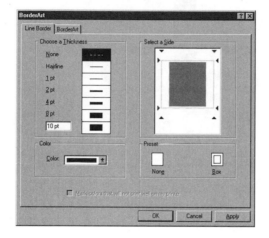

TIP **If the BorderArt dialog box—or any other dialog box you open—** blocks your view of the object you're working on, you can move the dialog box out of the way by grabbing its title bar and dragging it somewhere else on your screen.

Through thick or thin

The first choice you have to make is what thickness of line you want around your object. The preset options range from None to Hairline (0.5 points) to 10 points (remember, a point is 1/72 of an inch). If even 10 points isn't thick enough, you can type whatever thickness you want in the text box at the bottom of the Choose A Thickness list (see Figure 12.2). Your choice appears in the Select A Side box so you can get some idea of what it will look like around the object you're framing.

Fig. 12.2
Make a border of whatever thickness you want, and preview it in the sample box.

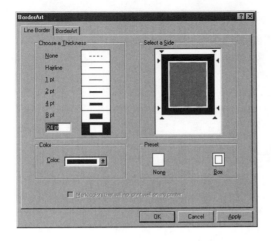

Light or dark, red or green?

You're not limited to just a solid, boring black line around your object. You can make a shaded line or a colored line, using this same dialog box.

Open the Color drop-down list to see the color palette we used with text and pictures in earlier chapters. (Chapter 10, "Adjusting Graphics," discusses selecting color in detail.) Pick a color from this basic selection or choose More Colors or Patterns & Shadings to see more possibilities (see Figure 12.3).

Fig. 12.3
If you want to set off your text frame, graphic, or table with a colorful line border, you can create it here.

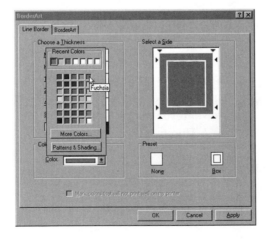

A border doesn't have to have four sides!

You know from everyday life that a border doesn't necessarily have to have four sides. After all, the border between Canada and the U.S. is really just a single line that mostly follows the 49th parallel.

Borders in Publisher don't have to have four sides, either. They can have three, two, or just one.

In the Select A Side box in the BorderArt dialog box, there's a triangle at each end of the four lines that make up the border.

Aim your mouse pointer at any of the marked lines inside the box and click the left mouse button. All the triangles disappear except the two marking the line you clicked (see Figure 12.4).

Fig. 12.4
Select which side of the border you want to change by clicking it. To select more than one, hold down the Shift key and click them one after the other.

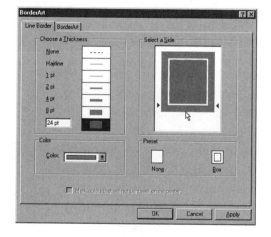

Now choose the thickness of line you want to appear on that side of your object from the list at the left. The other lines will stay the same.

You can select or deselect all four lines at once by choosing Box or None in the Preset area. None removes all lines, while Box replaces all lines with lines of the default thickness. To select two or three lines at once, hold down the Shift key while clicking the lines one after another.

In Figure 12.5, all lines were removed by choosing None; then the bottom line was selected and a custom 24-point line applied.

Fig. 12.5
Applying different sizes to different sides of a frame's border can better highlight the contents of the frame.

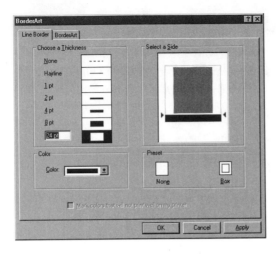

If you want to continue experimenting, click Apply; the changes you made to the border apply to the frame you selected, but the BorderArt dialog box remains open so you can make more changes. If you're satisfied with your choices, click OK to return to your publication (see Figure 12.6).

Fig. 12.6
This is what the border from Figure 12.5 looks like applied to a WordArt frame in a calendar.

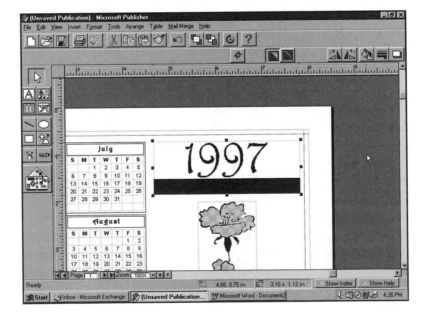

TIP   **Be creative with your borders. Make two sides thick and two sides thin,** or all four of a different weight. Use a different color on each side. A simple border outlining all four sides of your text, graphic, or table might be the best choice—but then again, it might not. Take advantage of Publisher's flexibility to experiment with fresh designs.

Getting fancy

In your home, a simple metal frame might work best for a quiet watercolor, while a richly hued Renaissance oil painting cries out for an ornate frame of gilded wood. In Publisher, sometimes a picture or fancy text needs a more interesting border than just a plain line.

The Publisher equivalent of gilded wood frames is BorderArt.

Choosing your border

You've already been using the BorderArt dialog box. To access BorderArt, click the BorderArt tab within that box (see Figure 12.7).

Fig. 12.7
Abstract designs, fancy lines, ice cream cones, and flowers: BorderArt offers all kinds of borders to spice up your text, graphics, or tables.

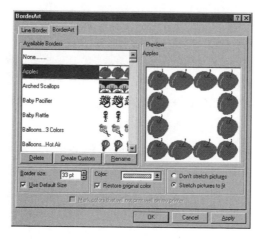

To browse the borders, scroll down through the A<u>v</u>ailable Borders list. Highlight a border to see it in the Preview box; you can check out how it looks in your publication by choosing <u>A</u>pply. If you do this, the BorderArt dialog box remains open for further experimentation in case you don't like the result.

Even if you like the border you choose, you might not like how thick or thin the program makes it by default. It might completely overwhelm your text, graphic, or table like the ornate frame of the Renaissance oil would overwhelm the pastel delicacy of a watercolor. Or it might disappear around the object like the metal frame of the watercolor would around the oil.

Adjust the thickness of your BorderArt using the <u>B</u>order Size option. Enter how thick you want the border to be in points. If you check the effect and decide you like the original, recommended size, you can return to it by selecting <u>U</u>se Default Size.

I chose Apples in Figure 12.7 to go with an advertisement I'm creating for a grocery store. In Figure 12.8, you can see what this border looks like.

Fig. 12.8
BorderArt that relates visually to the subject of the frame it's surrounding adds extra impact to the topic at hand, like an exclamation mark at the end of a sentence!

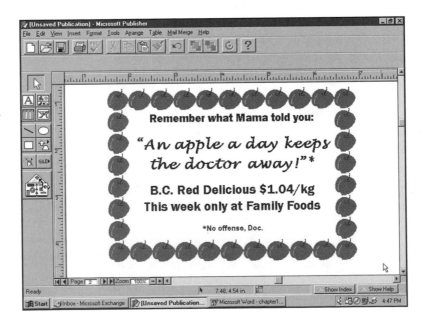

Q&A ***Can I modify BorderArt to print on only some sides of my object, the way I could modify an ordinary border?***

No. BorderArt always surrounds all four sides of the frame.

Won't a thick frame of BorderArt make the framed object take up more room?

No. The amount of space taken up remains the same; the object itself shrinks to fit inside the BorderArt. This can cause problems with text frames—text may slip into the overflow area—so check your publication carefully if you add BorderArt.

Create your own BorderArt

A new feature in Publisher 97 gives you the ability to create your own BorderArt out of any image you may have on your computer.

To create your own BorderArt from the BorderArt dialog box:

1 Click Create Custom.

2 The Create Custom Border dialog box opens (see Figure 12.9). If you want to create a border using one of the pictures in the Clip Gallery, make sure to select Use Clip Gallery to choose picture. If you want to create a border using a picture file that's not in Clip Gallery, remove the check in the box.

Fig. 12.9
With the Create Custom Border dialog box, you can use any picture file you have on your computer to design your own BorderArt.

3 Click Choose Picture. If you choose a picture from Clip Gallery, this will open Clip Gallery. If you don't choose a picture from Clip Gallery, this lets you browse your computer's drives.

4 Choose the picture you want, and double-click it.

5 Type in a name for your custom border when asked to do so, and click OK. Publisher adds your border to the list available whenever you call up BorderArt.

If you later want to remove your custom border, or any other border in the list of available borders, just highlight it on the list and click Delete. You can also change the name of any border by clicking Rename.

Finally, you can change the color of your selected BorderArt with the Color menu, just as you can change the color of a Line Border. Experiment as much as you like; you can put things back the way they were by checking the Restore original color box.

Adding a shadow

An effect similar to a border that's also available for use with any frame—as well as some of the more unusual shapes discussed in Chapter 13, "Getting Creative with Shapes"—is a shadow.

A shadow (shading that outlines the right and lower edges of a frame) makes the frame appear to be hanging slightly above the page and adds an intriguing three-dimensional look to your publication.

 To add a shadow, select the text frame, graphic, or table you want to apply the shadow to, and click the Add/Remove Shadow button on the Formatting toolbar.

In Figure 12.10, I applied a thin regular border and a shadow to a text frame.

Fig. 12.10
Shadows add a three-dimensional effect to your publication that can visually lift important information off the page.

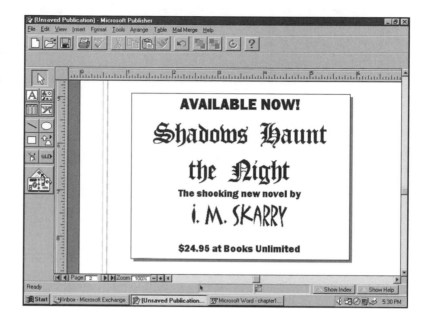

Q&A ***Can I add a shadow to a frame that already has BorderArt around it?***

Yes. Remember, BorderArt actually takes up space inside the frame you drew; the drop shadow will appear outside the original frame. No matter what kind of BorderArt you apply, the drop shadow will be rectangular: it won't outline each individual drawing that makes up the BorderArt.

Me and my shadow

The Shadow Publisher applies is always the same thickness and always the same color: gray.

Here's an easy way to create a shadow that's a different thickness and a different color:

1 Draw a box exactly the same size as the frame you want to add the shadow to.

2 Click the Color Object button on the Formatting toolbar, and fill the box with whatever color you want the drop shadow to be.

3 Position the box where you want the shadow to appear, usually just slightly offset from the object being shadowed.

4 Select the object you want shadowed and click Bring to Front. Presto! A shadow designed to your specifications appears. (Make sure the object you want to cast a shadow isn't clear, or the shadow will show through it!)

Using this method, you can also create a shadow filled with a pattern or a gradient, for an even more unusual effect.

13

Getting Creative with Shapes

● In this chapter:

- How can I draw a line, a rectangle, or an oval?

- How can I create fancier, more eye-catching shapes?

- Is there any way to draw shapes without so much mouse-work?

- How do I make my shapes look sharper?

You don't have to be da Vinci to create attractive designs with Publisher's built-in drawing tools . . . . ▶

Why do I need drawing tools? Sometimes clip art is overkill. You don't need a full-color image of the Earth from space; all you need is a circle. You don't need a picture of a beautifully wrapped Christmas gift; all you need is a box.

Similarly, sometimes BorderArt offers both too much and too little: graphics that are too fancy, in a shape that's too simple. Because it's applied to Publisher text, picture, or WordArt frames, BorderArt is limited to a rectangular shape (or a diamond shape if you rotate it).

If you need a simpler border around a more complex shape, you need Publisher's drawing tools.

The shortest distance between two points...

You can't get much more basic than drawing a straight line. And even people who flunked high school art because they couldn't draw a straight line can draw one with Publisher.

 Publisher's four drawing tools appear grouped together in the Publisher toolbar. To draw a line, click the Line button.

The pointer changes to crosshairs. Position the crosshairs on the page where you want your line to begin; click and move the crosshairs to where you want the line to end.

In Figure 13.1, you can see the line being drawn. It stretches and shrinks like a rubber band as you move the cursor around. When you release the button, Publisher plants the line in the default thickness (one point) and color (black).

Fig. 13.1
Indicate the shortest distance between two points with Publisher's line-drawing tool.

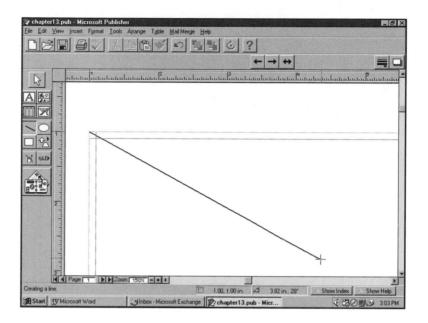

Adding arrowheads

You can add arrowheads to one or both ends of your line, before you begin or after it's in place. You can also alter the line's size and color.

To add arrow tips to one or both ends of your line, click one of the Add/Remove Arrow buttons in the Formatting toolbar. The Add/Remove Left Arrow button adds an arrow tip to the left end of your line (or the top, if it's vertical). The Add/Remove Right Arrow button adds an arrow tip to the right (or bottom) end. And the Add/Remove Both Arrows button adds arrow tips to both ends. Clicking any of these buttons again removes arrow tips you already added. If you click any of these buttons before you draw your line, the arrow tip appears when you draw it (see Figure 13.2).

Fig. 13.2
Arrow tips on one or both ends of your line are useful for creating flow charts or other publications where you need a sense of direction.

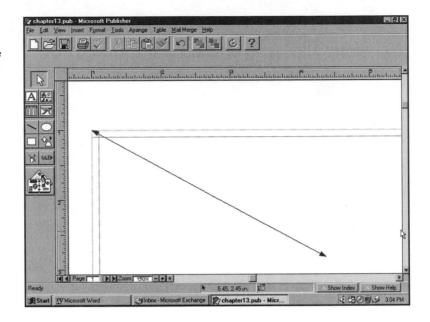

Thick or thin?

You can also preselect the thickness of your line before you begin drawing, by clicking the Line button in the Publisher toolbar, and then clicking the Border button in the Formatting toolbar.

This opens a drop-down list with four preset values to choose from. Pick the weight of line you want to use and click it. The drop-down list closes, and the next line you draw is the thickness you chose. Until you change the thickness again, every line you draw appears in this thickness.

How do I change a line after I draw it?

There are many more line-drawing options. After you position your line, select it and click the Border button again. You can apply one of the thicknesses you didn't use the first time, or you can click More to open the Line dialog box shown in Figure 13.3. You can also access this dialog box by right-clicking a line and choosing Line Properties from the shortcut menu.

Fig. 13.3

When is a line more than the shortest distance between two points? When it has been formatted from the Line dialog box.

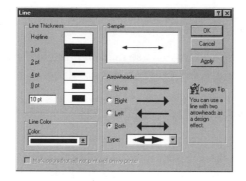

You can choose the thickness from those offered in the Line Thickness area or enter your own. You can also choose a color for your line by opening the Color drop-down list. Then select from a large selection of arrow tips by clicking the Type drop-down list.

A few clicks in this dialog box, and the arrow in Figure 13.2 becomes the far more interesting arrow in Figure 13.4. Choose Apply to see your changes without closing the Line dialog box, or choose OK if your arrow is now exactly what you want.

Fig. 13.4

Applying a new thickness, new arrow tips, and a new color to a line can change both its appearance and usefulness in your publication. This line is more forceful than the thin one in Figure 13.2.

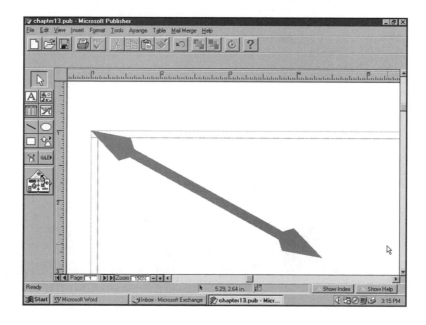

Drawing simple shapes

The most common shapes you'll use in designing Publisher publications are boxes and circles. Publisher makes it easy to draw both.

Boxing: drawing squares and rectangles

Drawing a square or rectangle in Publisher is exactly the same as drawing a frame, except there's no text or image to add afterward.

Click the Box button in the Publisher toolbar and the mouse arrow changes to crosshairs. Place the crosshairs where you want to anchor one corner of the box; then click-and-drag to the opposite corner of the box (see Figure 13.5).

 TIP **To ensure that your box is a perfect square, hold down the Shift key** while drawing. This keeps all four sides equal.

Fig. 13.5
Draw a box of any dimension with Publisher's Box tool.

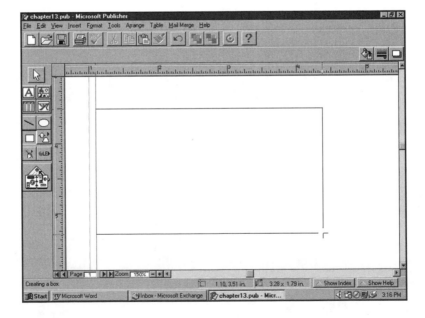

You can choose the thickness and color of the box's lines ahead of time, just as you did when drawing a line, or you can select the box after you draw it and change the line thickness and color.

 TIP **The formatting commands available to you when you draw a box** are the same as those available when you add a border to a text, picture, or table frame (see Chapter 12, "On the Border"). That means you can draw a box with only three sides, for instance, or replace its edge with BorderArt. If you need a fancy border around an object but can't, or don't want to, apply the border directly to the object, draw a box around the object and then apply BorderArt to the box.

Circles and ovals

 Click the Circle button to begin drawing ovals. Again, the pointer changes to crosshairs. This time, though, it's harder to position the shape. You can't position the crosshairs where you want the corner of the oval to be, because ovals don't have corners.

Instead, picture the oval you want to draw inside a box whose sides it just touches. Position the crosshairs where one corner of that imaginary box would be; then click-and-drag to the opposite (imaginary) corner.

After you start, you can see the oval you're drawing (see Figure 13.6). When the oval looks the way you want it to, release the mouse button.

 TIP **If you need a perfect circle, simply hold down the Shift key while** you draw. It's a much easier way to draw a circle than digging out that old high-school geometry set!

You can edit an oval's lines just as you can a box's, except BorderArt is not available, and you don't have the option of not printing part of it: you have to print the whole thing.

Fig. 13.6
Drawing an oval can
feel a little strange
because the crosshairs
indicating your mouse
position aren't actually
in contact with the
oval.

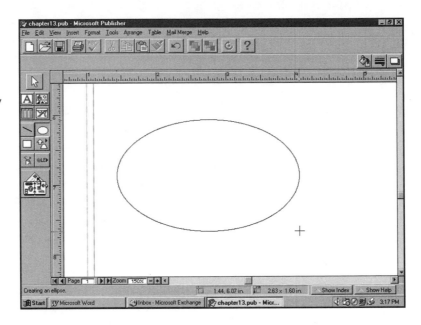

Starbursts and more

Sometimes, you want something a little more eye-catching, a little more
unusual, than just a circle or square. That's what the Publisher's Custom
Shapes tool provides.

 Click the Custom Shapes button on the Publisher toolbar and the small pop-
up window shown in Figure 13.7 appears.

Fig. 13.7
If boxes and ovals are
too plain for your
taste, you can probably
find something you like
here.

Choose any shape you like from here, and draw it just like you did the oval.
Again, the best way to position these nontraditional shapes is to picture them
inside a box that completely encloses the shape (see Figure 13.8).

Fig. 13.8
You can nicely match the oddest shape to the dimensions of another if you picture both inside imaginary boxes. Here, I've precisely overlaid a heart with a star.

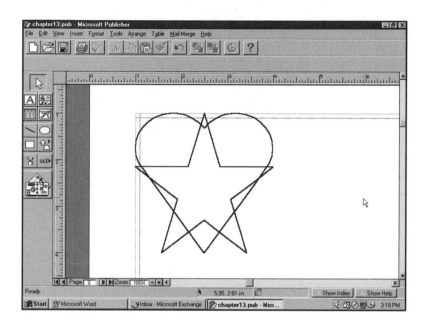

As usual, you can edit the line thickness and color of any of these shapes.

Fine-tuning shapes

If you click any of the shapes you just drew using Publisher's drawing tools, you see the familiar black handles appear around them. Resizing and moving shapes is the same as resizing and moving any of the frames you looked at in earlier chapters.

Resizing simple shapes

To resize a simple shape, select it and then place your mouse arrow over one of the handles. The pointer takes on a new shape and shows the word RESIZE. Click-and-drag the handle to where you want it to appear in the resized shape (see Figure 13.10). Release the mouse button, and the shape appears in its new size.

One-click drawing

There's an even easier way to draw shapes in Publisher than the method previously described.

As I mentioned in Chapter 4, "Do It Yourself," among the choices for customizing Publisher available under <u>T</u>ools, <u>O</u>ptions is Single-<u>c</u>lick object creation. Choose this command if it's not already selected.

Now, to draw an shape, just choose the tool you want, point your arrow at the place where you want the shape to appear, and click the left mouse button.

Like magic, your chosen shape appears in that spot. Of course, it might not be the right size and it probably won't be in quite the right place, which means you have to resize it and adjust its placement (see the next section of this chapter). You might not even save mouse-clicks or time with this option, but there's still a certain enjoyable feeling of wizard-like power inherent in pointing at a spot and zapping a shape into existence.

Every shape initially appears with exactly the same dimensions (based on what view you're in—50 percent, 100 percent, 200 percent, and so on). This method is useful for creating complex objects that consist of several simpler shapes layered on top of each other: for example, the star inside a pentagon inside a cross in Figure 13.9.

Fig. 13.9
One-click object creation makes it easier to create multipart objects like this one.

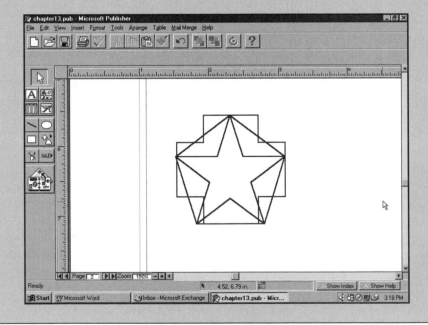

Fig. 13.10
Publisher provides a light gray outline of the shape as you resize it and doesn't erase the original shape until you release the mouse button, so you can see exactly what effect your efforts will have.

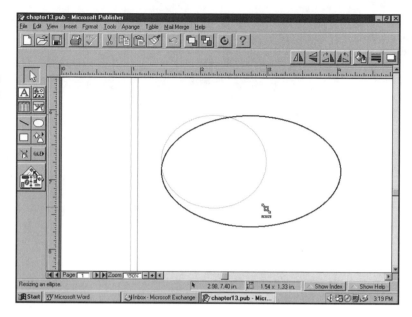

Fiddling with fancy shapes

If you draw some of the more ornate shapes such as cubes and then select them, you'll see an additional handle: a gray diamond. This indicates that there are other changes you can make to the shape besides adjusting its height and width. If you place your arrow over this gray handle, the pointer arrow changes to two parallel lines with arrows attached to them at right angles, labeled ADJUST. Click-and-drag the handle back and forth; light gray lines show you how that movement changes the shape.

Take a look at Figure 13.11. The cube at the left is the shape as originally drawn using one-click object creation. I moved the Adjust handle down to produce the shape in the middle; moving it up produced the shape at the right. Note that although the shape changes, its height and width remain unchanged.

Adjust handles only appear on some of the custom shapes, and their effect varies from shape to shape. If you see an adjust handle on a custom shape, experiment with it to see what effects you can achieve.

Fig. 13.11
The Adjust handle that appears on certain custom shapes means you effectively have a far greater number of shapes to play with.

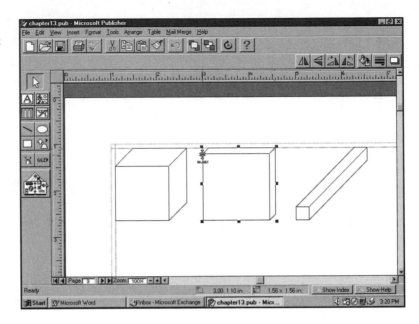

This shape would look better over there

You can reposition all of the shapes you draw with Publisher in the same way you can reposition any other Publisher object: simply select the shape and move the arrow over it until the arrow changes to the moving van symbol. Then just hold down the left mouse button and "drive" the shape wherever you want it to appear on the page.

TIP See Chapter 9, "Adding Graphics," for more details on relocating graphics.

Flipping shapes

Although some shapes, such as boxes and ovals, are symmetrical, some aren't. The 3-D boxes in Figure 13.11, for example, have a very definite orientation.

You might like a shape, but not the way it faces—maybe it leads the reader's gaze off the page. Publisher makes it easy to flip your shape. Simply select the graphic and click one of the Flipping buttons on the Formatting toolbar; or choose A̲rrange, R̲otate/Flip to open a drop-down list of options.

The Flip Horizontal and Flip Vertical buttons are self-explanatory. Figure 13.12 shows the rightmost box from Figure 13.10 the way it was originally drawn at the left—flipped horizontally in the center and flipped vertically at right.

Fig. 13.12
If you don't like the orientation of a shape, you can flip it with a single click.

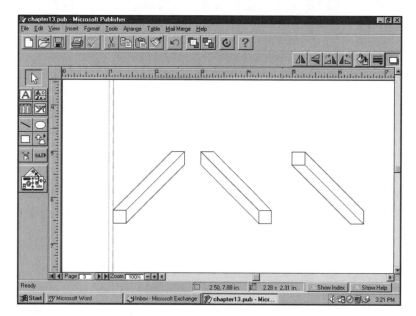

Rotating shapes

You can rotate shapes 90 degrees at a time by clicking one of the Rotate buttons. The Rotate Right button rotates shapes 90 degrees clockwise with each click; the Rotate Left button rotates them 90 degrees counterclockwise.

 You can also rotate a shape any number of degrees, from one to 365, by selecting it and choosing A̲rrange, R̲otate/Flip, C̲ustom Rotate. This brings up the Rotate Object dialog box, in which you can rotate the shape left or right by clicking a button or set a specific number of degrees you want to rotate the shape.

Another way to rotate shapes is to press and hold Alt while grabbing one of the shape's handles. The pointer arrow changes to ROTATE and lets you rotate the shape by hand.

For a more detailed discussion of rotating objects, see Chapter 10, "Adjusting Graphics."

You can add color to shapes, too

You've already seen how you can select the color of an shape's lines, but you have another color option with most of these shapes: you can choose a color to fill them with.

 To do that, select a shape, and then click the Object Color button in the Formatting toolbar.

You see a drop-down box of several basic colors to choose from. And you can see more colors by clicking More Colors or a selection of patterns, shading, and gradients by choosing Patterns and Shading.

For details on choosing a fill color, pattern, or gradient, see Chapter 8, "Making Text Stand Out: Special Formatting."

Shadowing

 Finally, you can add a shadow to your custom shape by clicking the Shadow button on the Formatting toolbar. The shadow forms by default along the right and bottom sides of the shape, but after you apply it, you can rotate and flip it with the shape (see Figure 13.13).

For a more detailed discussion of shadows, see Chapter 12.

Fig. 13.13

A shadow adds a 3-D effect to any shape, no matter how strange.

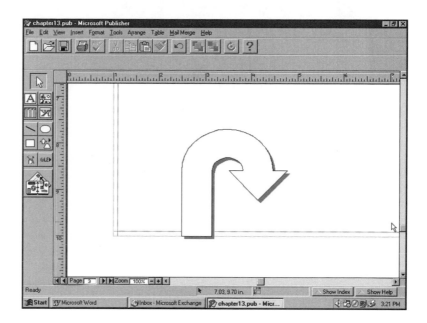

14

WordArt, for Characters with Character

● **In this chapter:**

- **What is WordArt?**

- **More stretches and pulls than an aerobic workour**

- **Can I add shadows to letters and make words odd shapes?**

- **How can I change colors, add a border, and use the rest of Publisher's graphics tools on WordArt?**

WordArt makes plain old text as malleable as graphics. Shape it and shadow it—make your publication shine! . . . . ➤

Most people think of text and graphics as two very different things. In fact, a lot of page designers don't much like text. They see it as dull and gray, cluttering up white space and distracting from the artwork, and they figure nobody reads it anyway. That's one reason the amount of text in magazines and newspapers has dwindled over the past few decades. It's a long way from the verbatim political speeches of 19th-century newspapers to *USA Today*.

But really, text is a form of graphics. Letters, after all, are nothing but little drawings, drawings that come in a wide variety of styles (fonts).

What if you could play with those drawings the way Publisher lets you play with other graphics—stretch them out, change their shapes and color, add shadows and other special effects? No one would find that dull!

WordArt lets you do all that, opening up a whole new world of design possibilities.

Creating WordArt

As with text, pictures, and tables, adding WordArt to Publisher begins with drawing a frame. Click the WordArt button on the Publisher toolbar, position the crosshairs where you want one corner of the frame to appear, and click-and-drag to draw the frame (see Figure 14.1).

Q&A *When I drew my WordArt frame, my regular toolbar disappeared! Did I do something wrong?*

No. WordArt, like Clip Gallery, is a separate program also used by some other Microsoft programs. When you draw a WordArt frame in Publisher, WordArt "takes over" the workspace, and its own menu bar and toolbar replace Publisher's menu, Standard toolbar, and Formatting toolbar.

Programs like this—that aren't part of Publisher but you can open in Publisher to create objects—are OLE programs. You can find out all about them in the next chapter.

Fig. 14.1

The first step to creating WordArt is to draw a frame like this one. Notice the new formatting toolbar that appeared. This is what you always see first when you draw a WordArt frame.

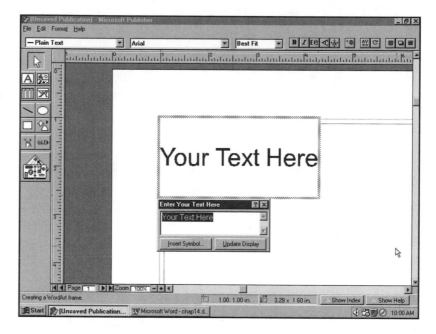

First, enter the text

Your new WordArt frame, you'll notice, is urging you to type in your own text. Type in your text, and it automatically replaces the highlighted Your Text Here in the dialog box. Then click Update Display to place your text in the WordArt frame.

If you need a character that's not on your keyboard, choose Insert Symbol. This updates the display with the text you already entered and opens the Insert Symbol dialog box (see Figure 14.2). Click the symbol you want to insert, and click OK to return to the Enter Your Text Here dialog box. The symbol you chose immediately appears in your WordArt frame.

The Enter Your Text Here dialog box remains open as long as you work in WordArt (unless you deliberately close it) so you can always update your text.

You're not limited to a single line of text in WordArt, either; you can press Enter after typing your first line to add a second line of text underneath it (see Figure 14.3). And more underneath that, if you want.

Fig. 14.2
You have access to all the characters a font contains through the Insert Symbol dialog box.

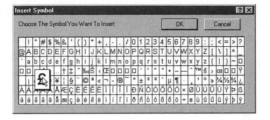

Fig. 14.3
You can add as many lines to headlines as you want in WordArt.

Then format it

Like an ordinary text frame, WordArt allows you to set all the standard parameters for text, such as font, size, style, alignment, and color, but adds a couple of interesting twists.

You find the formatting tools in the WordArt Formatting toolbar.

Fig. 14.4
The WordArt Formatting toolbar gives you both familiar and new tools to work with.

Button	Name	What you can do with it
— Plain Text	Shape	Form WordArt into interesting shapes like pentagons and circles.
Arial	Font	Choose a font.
Best Fit	Font Size	Make your text larger or smaller.
B	Bold	Make your text thicker and darker.
I	Italic	Make your text lean to the right.
Ee	Even Height	Make lowercase and uppercase letters the same height.
Flip	Flip	Stack the letters of your text on top of each other.
Stretch	Stretch	Expand text in all directions to the edges of the WordArt frame.

continues

continued

Button	Name	What you can do with it
	Alignment	Choose how you want your text aligned.
	Character Spacing	Adjust the spacing between letters and the use of kerning.
	Special Effects	Rotate and angle your text.
	Shading	Choose the colors and patterns you want to apply to your WordArt frame and text.
	Shadow	Choose a shadow effect to apply to your text.
	Line Thickness	Outline each letter of your text with a line of your choice of thickness and color.

Choose the font

Select the font and size the same way you do in a text frame. Click an option in either list box, and Publisher applies your choice to the text in the WordArt frame.

Notice, however, that the Size list box has a new option: Best Fit (see Figure 14.5).

Fig. 14.5
Best Fit is the default selection when you choose the size of your WordArt text.

You've already seen Best Fit in action. When you typed your text, it appeared in the WordArt frame much larger than it was in the Enter Your Text Here dialog box. If you added a second line, the characters automatically shrank to enable both lines to fit in the frame.

Best Fit makes your characters as large as they can be and still fit inside your text frame.

Give that text some style!

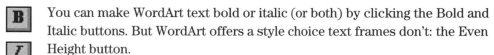

You can make WordArt text bold or italic (or both) by clicking the Bold and Italic buttons. But WordArt offers a style choice text frames don't: the Even Height button.

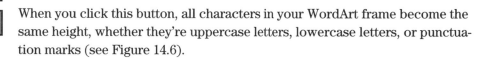

When you click this button, all characters in your WordArt frame become the same height, whether they're uppercase letters, lowercase letters, or punctuation marks (see Figure 14.6).

Fig. 14.6
That odd-looking character after the 500 is a comma blown up to capital-letter size.

Give it the marquee look

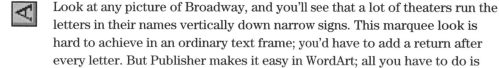

Look at any picture of Broadway, and you'll see that a lot of theaters run the letters in their names vertically down narrow signs. This marquee look is hard to achieve in an ordinary text frame; you'd have to add a return after every letter. But Publisher makes it easy in WordArt; all you have to do is click the Flip button (see Figure 14.7).

Fig. 14.7
This is an interesting effect, but you have to be careful how you use it. As you can see, punctuation really doesn't work at all!

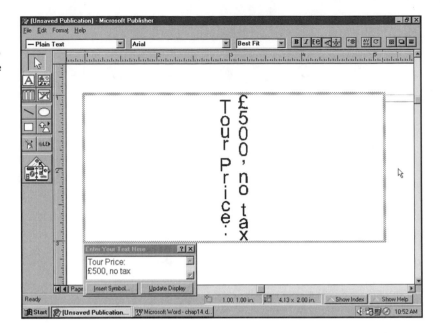

One size fits all

"One size fits all" is a phrase to be wary of when buying clothes, but it really does apply to WordArt frames. No matter how much or how little you put in your WordArt frame, you can make it fit snugly, filling the whole frame, by clicking the Stretch button or choosing Format, Stretch to Frame (see Figure 14.8).

Aligning WordArt text

You have the usual assortment of text alignments available to you for WordArt text. There are also a couple you haven't seen yet.

To align WordArt text, click the Alignment button. You see a list of six possibilities: Center, Left, Right, Stretch Justify, Letter Justify, and Word Justify. Click the one you want, and it applies to your WordArt text.

The first three options are the same as for a text frame:

- Center places the text in the center in the WordArt frame.

- Left places all the text in the WordArt frame flush against the left margin.

- Right places all the text in the WordArt frame flush against the right margin.

Fig. 14.8
Clicking the Stretch button expands the letters in all directions to fill your WordArt frame.

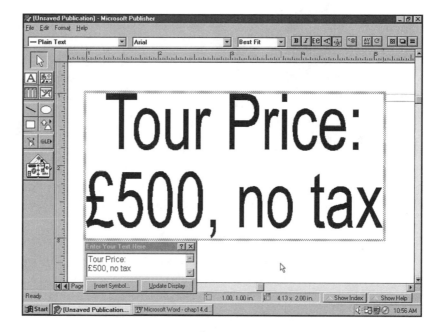

Justified text, you'll recall, is text that's flush against both the left and right margins. Unlike a text frame, a WordArt frame can use three versions of it:

- Stretch Justify justifies text by horizontally stretching the letters.

- Letter Justify justifies text by adding spaces between letters, regardless of their position in a word.

- Word Justify justifies text by adding spaces between words, without affecting the spacing between letters.

Look at the samples of all three kinds of justification in Figure 14.9.

Fig. 14.9
Each type of justified text WordArt offers has a unique look; choose the one that best suits your publication's design.

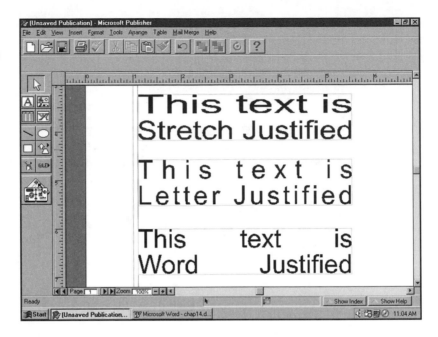

TIP

Although you can spread text in a WordArt frame over several lines, you cannot apply formatting to those lines separately: you can't, for example, center the text in the top line and align the text against the left margin in the second line. Whatever formatting choices you make apply to all text in the WordArt frame, indiscriminately.

If your design needs a series of lines of text in different formats and only WordArt gives you the tools you need to make them look the way you want, draw a series of WordArt frames, one for each line. It's a bit clumsy, but it works; and if you group them together, you can resize them all at once.

To group several WordArt frames, click them one after the other while holding down Shift. Publisher draws a gray frame around all of them, with a button at the bottom. Click that button, and the frames will be grouped together to create one large object you can resize and move around at will. For more detailed information on grouping objects, see Chapter 16, "Fine-Tuning Your Layout."

Rotating and sliding

You can rotate an entire WordArt frame just as you can rotate other frames in Publisher (I talk more about using Publisher's standard tools on WordArt later in the chapter), but you also have access to an entirely different rotation tool within the frame.

 Click the Special Effects button, or choose Format, Rotation And Effects. The Special Effects dialog box appears. Figures 14.10 through 14.12 show you the effects of using the Rotation and Slider options.

Use the Rotation control to set how many degrees you want to rotate the entire body of text. Click the down or up arrow buttons to change the number of degrees, or type in a specific value. Positive numbers rotate the text counter-clockwise, while negative number rotate it clockwise, so applying a value of 45 degrees makes the text slope up.

Use the Slider control to set the angle at which characters tilt. The default setting is 50 percent, which is straight up and down. Increasing this number tilts characters toward the left; decreasing it tilts them toward the right, until you reach the maximum allowable tilts of 100 percent (sharply tilted left) and 0 percent (sharply tilted right).

By setting both controls, you can create a variety of effects. For example, combining the 45-degree rotation of Figure 14.10 with the 100-percent slide of Figure 14.11 gives you the oddly off-kilter text in Figure 14.12.

Fig. 14.10
Text doesn't have
to be horizontal in
WordArt! Use the
Rotation control to
slant it up or down.

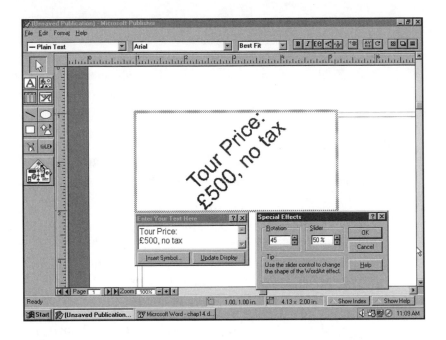

Fig. 14.11
The Slider control
can make your text
lean left or right faster
than a poll-perusing
election-year
politician.

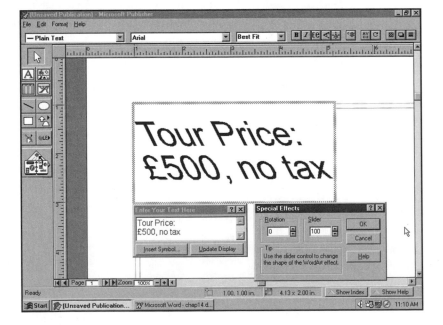

Fig. 14.12
Use the Rotation and
Slider controls together
to create entirely new
effects.

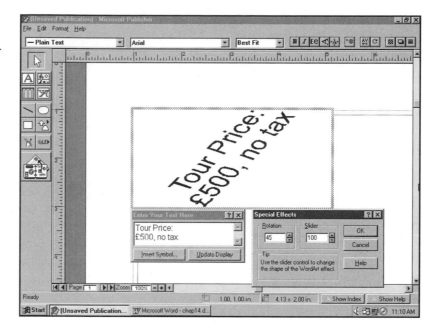

Character spacing

Making text fit in just the right amount of space is always a challenge. Of
course, in WordArt, you can click the Stretch button and fill the entire frame
by altering the shape of the letters, but sometimes that distorts text too
much.

1 Click the Character Spacing button. The Spacing Between Characters
dialog box appears (see Figure 14.13).

2 You have five options for changing the space between characters in
your WordArt text: Very Tight, Tight, Normal, Loose, or Very Loose.
Choose the tracking you want. (Tracking is the spacing between all the
letters in a block of text.) In Figure 14.13, the top example has Very
Tight tracking, the middle example has Normal tracking, and the
bottom example has Very Loose tracking.

3 When you select a tracking option, the Custom box shows you the
percentage of normal spacing the preset spacing selections represent.
If you don't like any of the preset spacing, enter a number in the
Custom box.

 **CAUTION** **If you have Best Fit or Stretch applied to your WordArt, adjusting** the character spacing will have different effects than if you choose a specific font size. With Best Fit selected, the font size changes as you change the character spacing, because tighter tracking allows a larger font to appear, while looser tracking means you must use a smaller font. You can see this effect in Figure 14.13, where all three examples have Best Fit selected. You can also see a similar effect when you choose Stretch.

Fig. 14.13
You can adjust the spacing between letters in your WordArt from zero percent of normal (all letters print over top of each other) to 500 percent of normal.

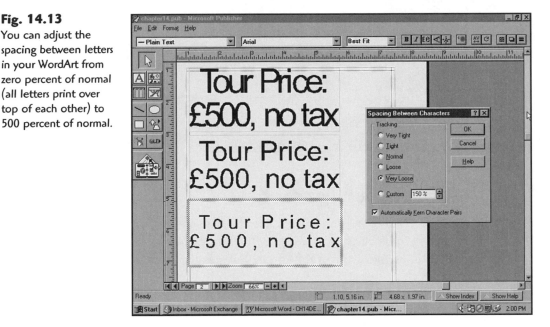

4 You must also decide if you want to Automatically <u>K</u>ern Character Pairs. Certain pairs of letters look better if they're moved closer together than other characters. A and V are one such pair, which is why they're on the Character Spacing button. If you select this check box, WordArt automatically kerns those awkward pairs; WordArt adjusts the spacing between them so they look their best. If you're trying for a particular effect with your WordArt that automatic kerning messes up, then don't select this check box.

5 After you make your choice, click OK; the dialog box closes and you're back in business editing your WordArt text.

Fine tuning the text: color, shadows, and borders

You've already looked at a long list of formatting options for your WordArt text, but there's a lot more to come, starting with color.

Add a dash of color

The Shading dialog box for WordArt offers options similar to those that come up when you click the Object Color button for other Publisher frames.

Click the Shading button. The Shading dialog box appears (see Figure 14.14).

Fig. 14.14
The Shading dialog box lets you specify colors and patterns for your WordArt characters: burgundy bricks with saffron cement, for example.

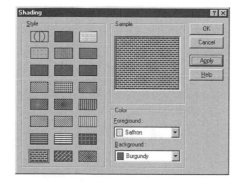

There are a lot of patterns to choose from, plus foreground and background color. These choices are similar to those offered with other frames. The biggest difference here is that the patterns are applied to your text.

The foreground color is the color with which the selected pattern is drawn on the background color.

Use outlines to make your text more legible

The bricks pattern in Figure 14.14 unfortunately makes the characters a little hard to read. Some of the other patterns in the Shading dialog box can make the characters even more illegible.

Adding an outline to each character alleviates that problem. Click the Line Thickness button, or choose For ma t, Bord e r to access a selection of lines. The Border dialog box appears (see Figure 14.15).

Fig. 14.15
You can choose the thickness and color of the line you want to outline your WordArt characters.

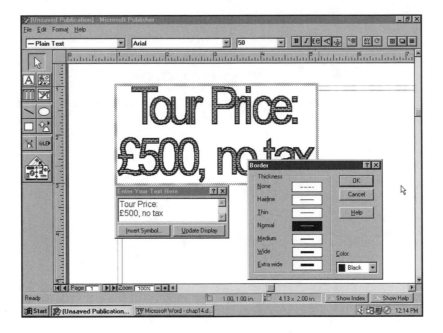

Choose how thick you want the outline, from N one to Hair l ine to E xtra Wide. As soon as you click an option, you'll see it applied to your WordArt text in the background; click OK when you like the way your text looks.

TIP **Although you might have some fonts in your collection in which** the characters appear as empty outlines, Publisher does not support an Outline format that you can apply to any font.

However, you can achieve that effect using WordArt. Just click the Shading button and choose solid white for the text color; then click the Line Thickness button and apply an outline.

The Shadow knows...

The Shadow button's function is different in WordArt than it is with other frames. Instead of putting a shadow around the frame, it lets you add shadows to the text. Click the Shadow button to open the Shadow dialog box (see Figure 14.16).

Fig. 14.16
The Choose a Shadow boxes give you an idea of how each shadow will look applied to your text, but the only way to tell for sure is to try each one.

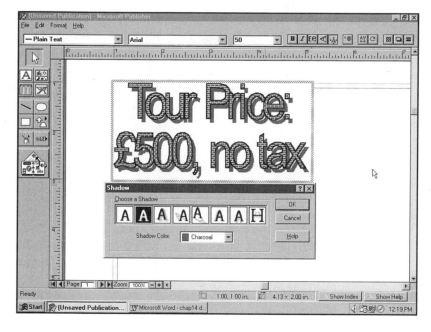

In addition to choosing from various shadow options, you can choose a color for the shadow.

Some shadows take up quite a bit of space and, as a result, your WordArt text will shrink to allow the shadow enough room in the frame. Fortunately, previewing the effects is easy; your WordArt text automatically changes as soon as you click any of the Shadow controls.

Even cooler cool effects: shape shifting

So far, although you changed the width and height of your WordArt text and even added a shadow, you haven't done anything all that different from what you can do in a text frame. Sure, you have a few more special effects to play with, but the text still marches across the page in a nice straight line—even if that line slants up or down. Is this all you can ask of text?

No. Straight lines are only one possibility in WordArt. There's one other formatting option available to you in WordArt that's also one of the most powerful: shapes.

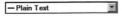

When you first draw your WordArt frame, the Shape list box shows a straight line and the words Plain Text. Click the arrow of the Shape list box to see a list of other available shapes (see Figure 14.17).

Fig. 14.17
The shapes give you an idea of what your text would look like; feel free to experiment.

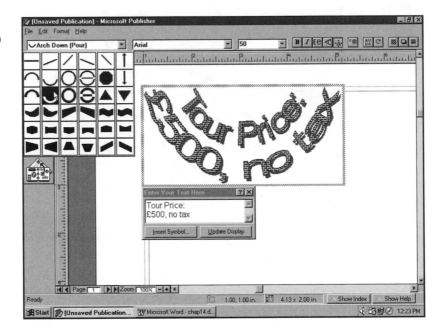

Decide what shape you want and click it. The list closes and Publisher applies the shape to your text.

Shapes give text added emphasis. You can create a cautionary sign, for example, with text in the shape of a stop sign, a banner headline with the shape of a banner floating on the breeze, or an important announcement that emerges from the mouth of a megaphone. The possibilities are limited only by your imagination.

CAUTION   **WordArt shapes are powerful tools for giving your publication a** unique look but, like all tools, you should handle them carefully. Because WordArt shapes distort characters, they can sometimes make text difficult to read. So, too, can colors, shadows, and other effects.

Remember that your publication's purpose is to effectively communicate with a reader. Unless you only want to communicate the fact that you have a fancy computer system, use WordArt's more elaborate effects sparingly, and always know exactly what you're striving to achieve with them. That will stop you from giving in to the temptation to use special effects just because they're available. (Now if someone could just convince Hollywood....)

Can I use regular graphics tools with WordArt?

After you perfect your WordArt text, you can return to the workspace to work on other elements of your Publisher publication. Just aim the mouse pointer at anything on the page outside the WordArt frame, and click once. The WordArt toolbar disappears and the normal Publisher toolbars appear.

This doesn't mean you've exhausted all the possibilities for improving your WordArt frame. If you now select the WordArt frame by clicking it once, the WordArt toolbar doesn't appear. Instead, the WordArt frame sprouts black handles, just like any other Publisher frame. All the formatting possibilities available to you in a regular graphics frame, from resizing to recoloring, are now available for your WordArt frame, including options such as borders, background patterns, and gradients. See Chapter 10, "Adjusting Graphics," for more details.

Editing your creation

Say you finally used every formatting tool you can on your WordArt frame, and you end up with something that looks like Figure 14.18.

Trouble is, you don't like it. Oh, you like the BorderArt and gradient—you don't like the WordArt itself. How do you get your WordArt editing and formatting tools back so you can change it?

The easiest way is to double-click the WordArt frame. The WordArt toolbar you used earlier in this chapter appears.

You can get the same tools by selecting the frame, and then choosing Edit, Microsoft WordArt Object, Edit, or right-clicking and choosing Microsoft WordArt Object, Edit from the shortcut menu. But if your final choice from either the Edit menu or the shortcut menu is Open instead of Edit, you get something different: the dialog box shown in Figure 14.19, which handily contains all your WordArt formatting options. Make your changes and click OK.

Fig. 14.18
I changed the text shape, resized the frame, and added BorderArt and a background gradient. See what I mean about it being easy to go overboard with Publisher's formatting possibilities?

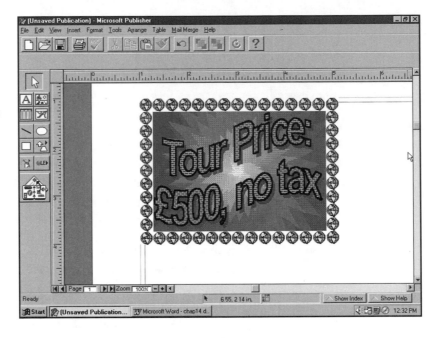

Fig. 14.19
This handy dialog box makes editing every aspect of WordArt easier than using the tools you originally drew the WordArt with.

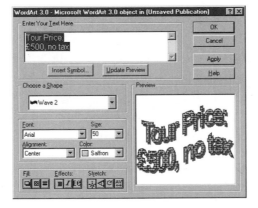

TIP **The dialog box in Figure 14.19 is actually easier to use than the** regular WordArt toolbar, so you might prefer to do all your WordArt creating from there. However, because it doesn't appear by default, you have to take a couple of extra steps to open it when you first draw your WordArt frame. First, click anywhere else in your workspace to deselect the newly drawn frame. Then select it again, right-click the frame, and choose Open. The dialog box in Figure 14.18 appears, ready for you to use it to create your new WordArt.

Q&A ***There's a third option under Edit, Microsoft WordArt Object. What does the Convert command do?***

Convert changes the fonts in objects created using an older version of WordArt 1.0 to the fonts that are closest to them in WordArt 3.0. This option is necessary because WordArt 1.0 and WordArt 3.0 don't use the same fonts.

15

OLE: Objects Created in Other Applications

● **In this chapter:**

- **What is OLE, and why should I care?**

- **Sound and video in a publication? Cool!**

- **Okay, explain the difference between embedding and linking**

- **Automatic and manual linking**

Sooner or later, you will probably want to add something to Publisher that it just can't provide. No problem! Create it in another program, and then just pop it into your publication . . . . ➤

What good is OLE anyway? Olé, of course, is what bullfighters yell as they face the bull. Roughly translated, it means something like, "What the heck am I doing here with this monster?"

OLE, on the other hand, is something Publisher users yell when they face a hole in their publication that none of Publisher's built-in tools can effectively fill. Translated, it means, "Object Linking and Embedding!"

That might sound like a mouthful of technical mumbo jumbo, but…surprise! You already had some experience using OLE objects. Remember those Clip Gallery objects? WordArt? How about the Excel spreadsheet you inserted in Chapter 11, "Let's Table That," or the Microsoft Draw object you inserted in Chapter 9 "Adding Graphics?" They're all OLE objects: objects you created in a program other than Publisher but added to your Publisher publication.

OLE lets you create specialized objects in programs designed just for creating those objects, embed those objects in Publisher, and access the tools you need to edit them by simply clicking the mouse a couple of times. Even more amazing is this: if you link the object in Publisher to its originating program, any changes you make to it in the original program (say, you work on your annual report and the spreadsheet tallying up the year's sales figures concurrently) are automatically reflected in Publisher.

 Plain English, please!

An embedded object is one you create and edit with another program, but is wholly contained in your publication. An embedded piece of artwork from a graphics program, for example, exists only in your publication, and the amount of disk space it requires for storage is added to the amount your publication already requires.

A linked object is one that appears in your publication but is actually stored somewhere else. A linked piece of artwork exists as a separate program: although you can see it in your publication and print it as part of your publication, all that is really stored in the Publisher file is the linked artwork's name and address. Like a well-trained dog, Publisher "fetches" the artwork from the program that created it (the source program) whenever it needs to display it or print it out. **"**

Inserting an OLE object

To add an OLE object, click the Insert Object button in the Publisher toolbar. This opens a drop-down list of the OLE-capable programs you most recently used in Publisher. If you choose More, the Insert Object dialog box appears, which has a complete list of all the programs on your computer that support OLE (see Figure 15.1).

Fig. 15.1
When you insert an OLE object, Publisher gives you a list of all the programs currently found on your computer that you can use to create OLE objects.

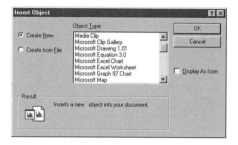

From this dialog box, choose:

- What type of object you want to add to your publication.

- Whether you want to create a new object or insert one from an existing file.

- Whether you want to display the inserted object in its entirety or simply as an icon. (For any publication that's meant to be printed, you obviously want the whole object to appear. But if you're, say, sharing the publication electronically with others on a network, you might choose to leave objects as icons; the viewer simply clicks the icon to see the OLE object.)

How do I create a new OLE object in Publisher?

If you choose Create New in the Insert Object dialog box and then click OK, a frame of default size (which varies depending on which program you use) appears within your publication, and the tools the originating program provides for creating a new object also appear—sometimes in addition to the Publisher tools, sometimes supplanting them.

In Figure 15.2, I've inserted a Microsoft Graph 97 chart into my publication. Notice how the Graph 97 toolbar replaced Publisher's standard and Formatting toolbars and altered the menu. Many OLE programs do the same thing.

Fig. 15.2
Need to add a graph? With OLE you can use the powerful graphing tools from other programs within Publisher.

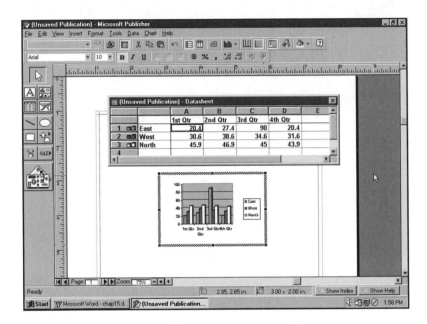

Once you use an OLE program, it's added to the list of recently used programs that appears when you first click the Insert Object button. Choosing a program from this list changes your mouse pointer to crosshairs and lets you draw a frame for your new object of whatever size you want. Or if you're in a hurry (and if you have the Single-click object creation option selected under Tools, Options), you can just aim in the general direction of where you want the object to appear and click once.

After you create an OLE object, return to Publisher either by clicking in the Publisher workspace outside the OLE program's box, or by closing the OLE program as usual. Make sure you save the object you created if the OLE program asks you to!

After you embed the object in Publisher, you can move or resize it as you can any other object. Other formatting options such as borders and BorderArt might also apply.

Or create it in the other program; then drop it into Publisher

Another option for creating an OLE object is to open the program you want to create the object in, work on it there, and then copy and paste the object into Publisher.

To do so, after you copy the object in the other program and open Publisher, choose Edit, Paste Special. The Paste Special dialog box opens (see Figure 15.3). The As list box displays various options, depending on the source of the object you paste. You can also choose to paste the object into your publication as an icon or to paste the object into your publication as a linked object—but only if Publisher supports that option for the program you copy from. Make your selection and then click OK.

Fig. 15.3
Choose how you want an object you copied from another program to be inserted into Publisher from the Paste Special dialog box.

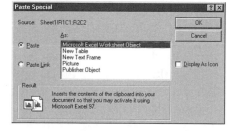

The OLE object appears in your workspace, and you can drag it where you want.

Sound and video? In a Publisher publication?

Among the possible OLE objects you can create in Publisher are some you probably never thought about embedding in a desktop-publishing publication: sound and video files.

You create these objects using other programs, just as you might create an Excel chart, but the only thing that appears in your publication is an icon. Figure 15.4 shows the icon for a MIDI file (Bach's Brandenburg Concerto) I embedded just below the previously inserted graph.

Fig. 15.4

You can even add sound and video to Publisher publications, although all you see when you print the publication is an icon.

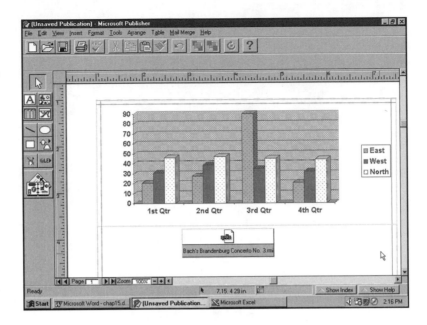

To play a sound or video object, select the object; then right-click. Choose the name of the object from the shortcut menu, and select Play. The appropriate program opens and you'll hear or see the contents.

Q&A ***All right, I give up. Why would I want to embed sound or video objects in a publication?***

Don't think of Publisher as a program that's only good for creating publications for print. You can now use Publisher 97 to create HTML documents for publication on the World Wide Web or on an intranet. You might also want to share your publication electronically over your office network or with friends. When you intend a publication only for viewing on other computers, there's no reason to limit yourself to static, soundless images and text: you can make your Publisher publication a full-fledged multimedia presentation!

For example, you can use this capability in a training publication, where embedded sound files provide audible help to students and embedded video files demonstrate the procedures they must learn.

Embedding or linking?

You can embed any of the objects you see when you click the OLE button, however, you can't link all of them.

The difference is that if you make changes to an embedded object in Publisher, those changes appear only in your publication. That's fine if the object only occurs in your publication. But if you use an object—say, a spreadsheet—created in another program that might change several times before you finish your publication, wouldn't it be great if any changes were automatically reflected in your publication, so it's always up-to-date? Well, that's what linking accomplishes.

In fact, you can use that same spreadsheet in many different publications being created by many different people, and all of them would be up-to-date —if the spreadsheet is installed as a linked object. That's because the object really only exists in one place, the computer on which it originated. All of the other publications use copies of it, which refer back to the original and update themselves as changes are made.

Even on your own computer, linking objects saves time, because you only have to make changes in one location, and the other copies take care of themselves.

You can only create a linked object using certain programs that are complete in and of themselves, such as Microsoft Word or PowerPoint. Some programs such as Clip Gallery are only "helper" programs that must be called up from within another program. Programs like that can only create embedded objects in Publisher.

To insert a linked OLE object within Publisher:

1 Click the Insert Object button or choose Insert, Object. The Insert Object dialog box opens again. This time, choose Create from File instead of Create from New.

2 Type the name of the file you want to use as a linked object, or use the Browse button. When you find the file you want, select the Link check box.

Fig. 15.5
Choosing Create from
File lets you insert an
existing file and create
a link to it, if its
originating program
supports linking,
that is.

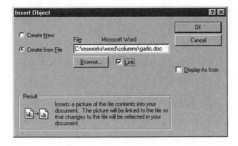

3 If you don't want the file to appear in your publication but only a representative icon (such as the MIDI file icon in Figure 15.4), select Display As Icon.

4 After you make your choices, click OK. The file you selected appears in your publication as a linked file.

To make sure your recent changes are included in your linked object, choose Edit, Links. This opens the Links dialog box in Figure 15.6, listing all the linked objects you have in your publication. You have several choices:

- Update Now takes a look at the selected object and its source file, and changes the linked object to match any changes to the source file.

- Open Source opens the program in which you created the linked object so you can make further changes.

- Change Source lets you change the file to which the object is linked. For example, you can use this option to update a spreadsheet in an existing brochure from a 1996 file to a new 1997 file.

You can also change the update options in the Links dialog box. If you select Automatic Update, the object in your publication automatically changes whenever changes are made in the source program. If you select Manual Update, any changes made in the source program only show up in your publication when you choose Update Now.

Fig. 15.6
Here you can see, update, and edit all the linked objects in your publication.

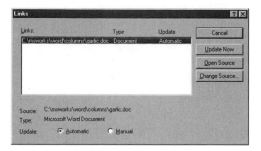

Editing OLE objects

To edit OLE objects, simply double-click them. That automatically opens the source program. Make the changes as you normally would, and close the program. Make sure you save the changes if the program prompts you to do so.

Part V: Putting It Together

16

Fine-Tuning Your Layout

● **In this chapter:**

- **I have frames on top of frames. How do I keep them straight?**

- **Making text flow around objects**

- **I want everything lined up perfectly!**

- **Grouping objects together**

- **Can Publisher help me check my layout?**

No frame is an island! Frames affect the frames they overlap. Get them to play nicely together to make your publication look its best; then get Publisher to help you give your layout one final check-up . . . . ▶

Creating a Publisher publication would be a cinch if it consisted of a single text frame—but, of course, it doesn't. Desktop publishing is all about combining a variety of visual elements in an effective way. It's like creating a publication by drawing each individual element on a separate sheet of transparent plastic, and then stacking the sheets on top of each other. If you don't stack them in exactly the right way, some things might get covered up that you want to see, while other things you'd prefer to cover up might be visible. You have to shuffle all the sheets until everything looks the way you want it to.

Publisher makes that shuffling process easy by giving you a set of tools to move any element to wherever in the stack of overlapping elements you want it.

Frames on top of frames

The basic tools for shuffling elements are the Bring to Front and Send to Back buttons in the Standard toolbar.

 To see the effect of these buttons, create two overlapping objects, like those in Figure 16.1. I put a picture frame (containing an image of garlic) over a text frame full of text (also about garlic. Hey, I like garlic!). The picture frame has a gray background; the text is reversed, white on black.

 As you can see, the garlic covers part of the text frame. The text has wrapped around the garlic's frame in an awkward, hard-to-read manner (text-wrapping is discussed later in this chapter). To change that, select the picture frame; then click the Send to Back button or choose Arrange, Send to Back. Now the text frame is obscuring the picture (see Figure 16.2).

Fig. 16.1

Here a graphic frame containing a happy bulb of garlic has been placed on top of a text frame.

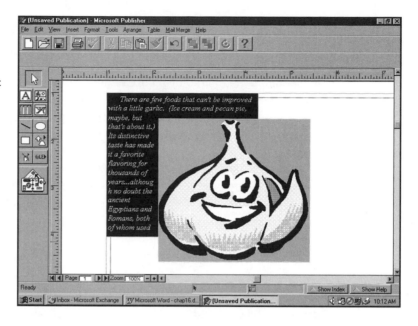

Fig. 16.2

The object you want fully visible should be on top of the stack. In this case, I selected the garlic's frame and placed it under the text by clicking the Send to Back button.

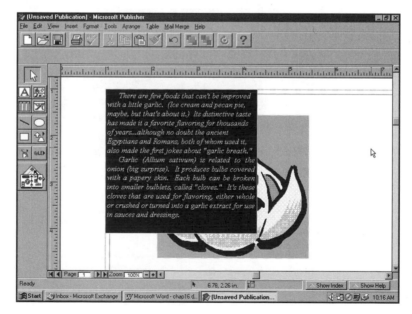

Send farther, bring nearer; when you arrange more than two frames

Send to Back and Bring to Front are either/or buttons: either the object you select is clear at the bottom of the stack, or it's on top. If you have more than two overlapping frames, you might want to position a particular frame somewhere in the middle, instead.

In this case, I'd like to create a three-sided BorderArt border around the text frame, while leaving the garlic barely visible in the background. To do this, in Figure 16.3, I added a third frame, a clear rectangle with BorderArt applied. Right now it's on top, so it's obscuring parts of both the other frames.

Fig. 16.3
Now there are three objects overlapping each other and interfering with your view. The empty border is on top, the text is in the middle, and the picture is on the bottom.

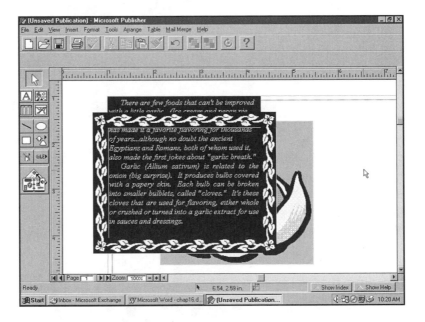

I select the empty border, then choose Arrange, Send Farther. This moves the rectangle one layer closer to the back, leaving it sandwiched between the text frame and the garlic (see Figure 16.4), producing the effect I had in mind.

Fig. 16.4
This is the effect I had in mind, but I had to move things around to get to it.

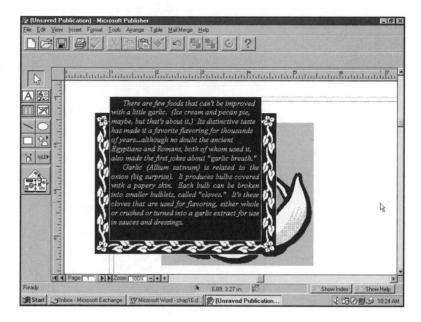

Choose A̲rrange, Bring C̲loser to reverse the effect; or you can select the garlic and choose A̲rrange, Bring C̲loser to place it between the text frame and the empty border.

When it's tough to get to the frame you want to move

It's very easy to say "select this" and "select that," but when you stack several frames over each other, it can be difficult to grab the one you want. That's because when you point at a stack of frames and click the mouse button, Publisher selects the frame on top.

There are two ways to get to the frame you want. One is to make judicious use of the arranging tools discussed in the previous section, sending the top frame to the back, then the new top frame after that, and so on until the frame you want comes to the front. If the frames are all exactly the same size, that's the only option open you have.

If the frame you want is distinctly smaller, or a very different shape than the other frames in the stack, you can select it by "lassoing." Point your mouse arrow somewhere on the publication where there are no frames, and click the left mouse button. If you now move the mouse, you see that your arrow draws a rectangle.

That rectangle is your "lasso." If you draw it around an object, Publisher selects that object. If you can manage to draw it around only the frame you want to select out of a stack, Publisher selects only that frame (see Figure 16.5). You can then edit it and arrange it as you see fit.

Fig. 16.5
Here I carefully lassoed the half-buried picture frame containing the garlic. Because the picture frame is the only object in the stack that is completely surrounded by the lasso, it's the only one that will be selected when I release the mouse button.

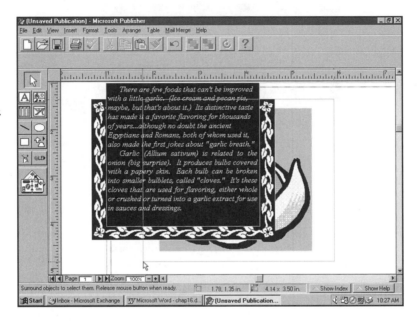

Using the lasso, you can also select more than one frame at a time: useful if you want to form them into a group. (See the section "Organizing objects into groups," later in this chapter.)

Keeping things straight

There's a general rule of thumb that's true for all desktop publishing jobs. Quickly designing a publication doesn't take long at all. Drawing in the text and graphic and table frames is a snap. Importing text or clip art? Nothing to it.

But giving everything that final polish, making sure frames aligned with the margins, that lines meet boxes smoothly, that the text in adjacent columns lines up—*that* takes time.

It would take even more time if Publisher didn't provide you with some useful tools for the purpose.

Lining up objects

Publisher can automatically line up objects with each other or with the margins of your page. You can choose to line up the left edges of some or all frames with the left edge of the object that extends furthest in that direction—or do the same thing to the right. Or you can align their centers with each other.

You can also align objects from top to bottom: you can align the top edges of all the selected frames with the top edge of the highest frame, align the bottom edges with the bottom edge of the lowest frame, or, again, align their centers.

Or rather than align objects with each other, you can align them with your margins. To see the difference, compare Figures 16.6 and 16.7.

Fig. 16.6
Here I aligned three different elements along the left edge of the leftmost object.

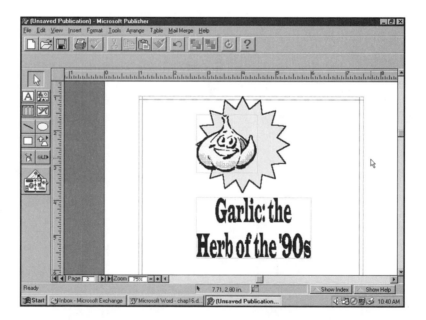

To use Publisher's automatic alignment tools:

1 Select the objects you want to align by clicking them one after the other while pressing and holding Shift. You can also lasso them with the mouse (see Figure 16.8).

Fig. 16.7
I aligned these objects along the left margin of the page.

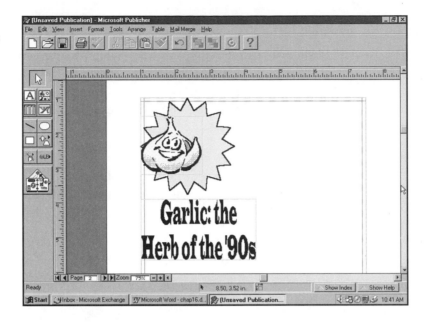

Fig. 16.8
One way to select several objects you want to align is to lasso them with the mouse.

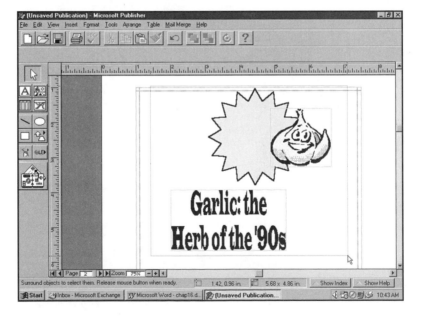

2 Choose Arrange, Line Up Objects. The Line Up Objects dialog box appears (see Figure 16.9).

Fig. 16.9
Publisher automatically lines up several objects at once in a variety of ways, saving you a lot of nitpickety labor.

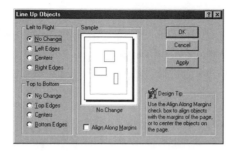

3 If you want to align objects along the margins instead of with each other, select the Align Along Margins check box.

4 Choose the types of Left to Right and Top to Bottom alignment you want. The Sample area gives you an idea of how those choices will affect your chosen objects.

I choose Left to Right, Centers, which is probably the choice you'll make most often. As you can see in Figure 16.10, it can make sense out of even the most uneven collection of objects.

Fig. 16.10
Centers lines up objects along the centers of their frames—a particularly useful capability.

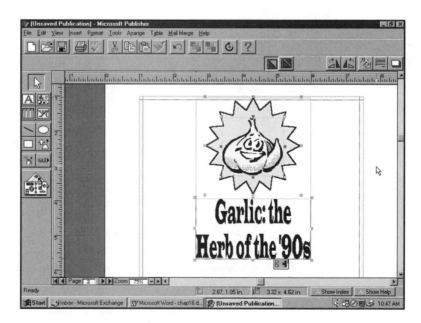

5 Click Apply to view the results in your publication without closing the Line Up Objects dialog box. (You can undo any alignment changes by choosing No Change in either the Left to Right or Top to Bottom sections.) After you're sure you have the effect you want, click OK.

Nudging objects

The mouse is a wonderful gadget, but it's sometimes hard to make extremely precise movements with it.

There's no need for that in Publisher; it provides a way for you to nudge an object a little closer or a little further away from another object without fighting with the mouse.

Select the object you want to nudge, and choose Arrange, Nudge Objects. The Nudge Objects dialog box appears (see Figure 16.11). Click any of the directional arrows in the Nudge Control area to nudge the object just a bit in that direction.

Fig. 16.11
Clicking any of the arrows moves the selected starburst .13 inch (the default distance) in the indicated direction.

You can adjust how far each nudge moves an object by selecting the Nudge By check box and entering a distance in the text box (it can be up to two inches). You can enter the distance in centimeters, inches, picas, or points by typing **cm**, **in**, **pi**, or **pt** after the numerals.

TIP **You can also nudge objects by holding down the Alt key and** pressing one of the arrow keys. Each time you press an arrow key, the object moves whatever distance you last entered in the Nudge Objects dialog box.

Feeling lost in your own publication? You need a good guide!

In northern Saskatchewan, sport fishing is a major industry. People come from all over the world to try their hand at catching the wily northern pike.

And the first thing the smart people do is hire a guide—otherwise, they'd waste time fishing in places where there are no fish, or worse, just disappear into the bush.

Publisher has guides, too. They keep you from fishing aimlessly for the goal of perfectly aligned objects and help ensure you don't get lost in your quest for a professional publication.

In fact, Publisher has two kinds of guides: layout guides and ruler guides.

Layout guides, discussed in Chapter 4, "Doing It Yourself," are the lines that show you where the margins of your page and the borders of any rows and columns are. They're generally set when you begin a publication and remain unchanged while you work on it. **Ruler guides** are lines you add to your publication to help you place objects in precise locations.

To draw a ruler guide, point at either the vertical or horizontal ruler, hold down Shift, and click and hold the left mouse button. Your mouse pointer changes to the ADJUST pointer. If you point at the horizontal ruler and drag the mouse down, a horizontal line that stretches clear across your publication will follow; point at the vertical ruler, and you can create a vertical line (see Figure 16.12). These lines don't print; they only appear on the screen.

Fig. 16.12

You can add as many ruler guides as you want to help you precisely position objects in your publication.

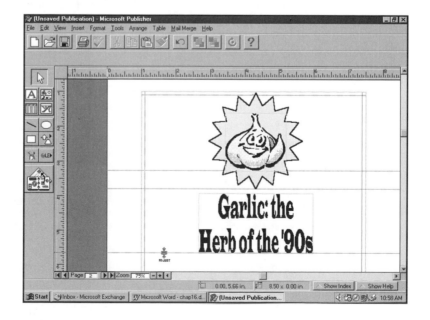

Snap to it!

The guides in Publisher look like ordinary lines, but they have a secret power. With the Snap To command, you can make them sticky, and you don't have to smear glue on your monitor to do it. This gives you another way to align objects; if the left edges of all the objects are stuck tight to the same ruler guide, you know they're aligned. In fact, if you have the Snap To options activated when you first design your publication, you might not need to use Publisher's automatic alignment tools at all, because any frames you draw that are in contact with the guides will already appear aligned.

The guides aren't the only things you can make sticky with Snap To commands. You can also make the invisible lines indicated by ruler marks sticky, or objects themselves. You can use all of these options to keep objects aligned while you draw them.

There are three Snap To options on the <u>T</u>ools menu:

- Snap to Ruler <u>M</u>arks—If you drew lines down and across the page from the marks on the horizontal and vertical rulers, you'd create a grid. With this option selected, Publisher acts as if that grid has been drawn, using sticky lines. It won't let you position an object anywhere where its left border and top edge aren't perfectly aligned with a ruler mark. This can help you align objects at precise distances from margins or other objects.

- Snap to <u>G</u>uides—This makes objects snap to ruler guides or layout guides when they get close. This is particularly useful when you're viewing a full page; the small size of the image can make it difficult to tell whether you have things properly aligned. With Snap to <u>G</u>uides active, you can simply shove objects up against a guide to ensure their alignment. And even if you make the guides invisible so you can see what the printed page will look like (by choosing <u>V</u>iew, Hide <u>B</u>oundaries and Guides), objects continue to snap to them.

- Snap to Obje<u>c</u>ts—With this, you can make objects magnetic, too, so the edge of one object snaps to the edge of another if you bring them close together. This can help you eliminate unsightly gaps.

I recommend turning on the Snap To options only when you really need them; otherwise, you'll soon become annoyed by frames' tendency to stick to everything in sight, especially if you want to deliberately fudge an alignment to make a little more room for a picture or another bit of text, or just because you think it looks better. The Snap To options are like the grammar checker on a word processor: helpful up to a point, but downright annoying when you know what you're doing and have some special effect in mind that doesn't fit in the software's view of how things should be.

Objects of a feather group together

When you first design a publication, you spend most of your time working with individual frames. You have to create each one, fill it with text and graphics, and properly format it.

But suppose you create a complex advertisement for a newsletter that contains pictures and WordArt and you suddenly realize you have to make space on that page for one more story you forgot. Your only option is to shrink the size of the ad; but shrinking all the frames that went into making it is going to take forever.

Publisher has the solution: it offers you a way to group related objects together and manipulate them all at once. In this case, you can resize all of them at the same time and by the same amount.

Organizing objects into groups

To form a group, select all the objects you want it to include by holding down Shift and clicking each object in turn, or by lassoing them all with the mouse. A blue box surrounds all the selected objects. At the bottom of this box is the Group button: it always appears when you select more than one object.

Click the Group button, and the objects you select group together. Essentially, they become one large object whose dimensions are determined by how far the various member objects extend in all directions. In Figure 16.13, I grouped the items I worked with earlier.

Fig. 16.13
With a click of a button, you can lump together objects of different types in a single group.

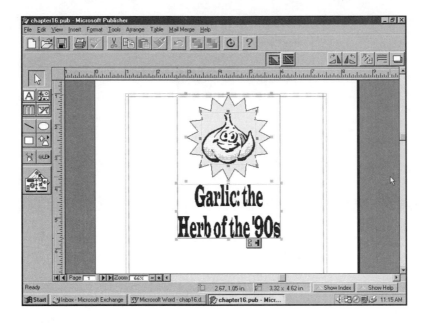

To dissolve the group, click the Group button again.

Group therapy

Once you group objects, you can work with that group as though it were a single object. You can move or rotate it and copy, cut, delete, or paste it.

You can also click the Shadow and Border buttons, but any shadows or borders you apply don't surround the group; they surround the individual objects in the group. If you want every object in the group to have a border, that's useful, but if you want a border around the group itself, you have to draw the border separately. (Of course, after you draw it, you can add it to the group.)

Q&A *I resized a group containing many different types of objects, but I ended up with a mess. Some objects seem to have adjusted to the new size while others didn't. What's going on?*

The key to working with a group is remembering that, although it acts like a single object, all of the objects inside it retain their original characteristics when you resize it. While the graphics and WordArt elements easily adapt to the new size, the text in text frames and tables keeps its original point size, which might be too large or too small for the resized frames.

After resizing a group containing text or table frames, make sure you check each individually and adjust the text size as required.

Going with the (text) flow

When a blizzard is blowing, the wind—carrying millions of snowflakes—rushes along pretty smoothly until it runs into a house or car or some other stationary object. The result is turbulence. The snow, no longer carried smoothly along, falls to the ground and creates a drift.

Similarly, your text might flow along just fine through your publication until it encounters another object. The result, if you're not careful, can be turbulence in your design.

Publisher gives you several ways to deal with this situation.

That's a wrap

Whenever you draw a picture frame or select an existing one, two text flow buttons become active in the picture Formatting toolbar.

 The Wrap Text to Frame button is selected by default. It makes text that comes in contact with the picture flow around the outside of the frame (see Figure 16.14).

Fig. 16.14
No matter how oddly shaped the graphic, text politely stays outside its frame if you select the Wrap Text to Frame button.

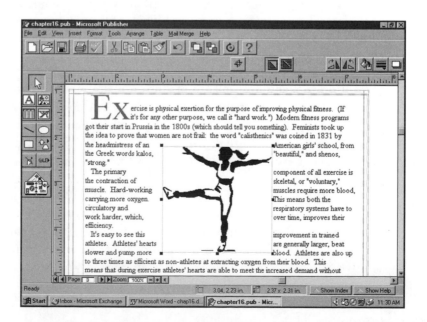

Click the Wrap Text to Picture button, and the text starts snuggling up against the picture, ignoring the margins of the text frame (see Figure 16.15).

Fig. 16.15

The peppy exerciser from the previous figure looks a little claustrophobic now that I selected the Wrap Text to Picture button.

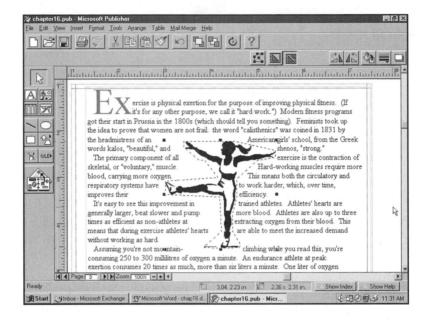

When you're in Wrap Text to Picture mode, the Edit Irregular Wrap button becomes active.

The Edit Irregular Wrap button allows you to carefully mold text around a picture, ensuring it remains readily legible while better integrating the graphic into the text.

Click the Edit Irregular Wrap button. The usual eight selection handles give way to many more, all around the perimeter of the picture. Place your arrow on one; the arrow changes to an ADJUST symbol. Click-and-drag the handle wherever you want. The text wrap outline changes its shape accordingly (see Figure 16.16). (Note that if you pull one of these handles inside the picture itself, it also acts as a kind of cropping device, hiding part of the picture.)

 TIP **The flow of text around a picture isn't always pretty; you can end up with ugly breaks in words, words all by themselves, and other problems. Don't automatically accept the way the computer chooses to wrap text; use the Edit Irregular Wrap button freely. Nothing undermines the professional look of your publication more than badly wrapped text.**

Fig. 16.16
Edit the text wrap outline to fine-tune the flow of text around a graphic.

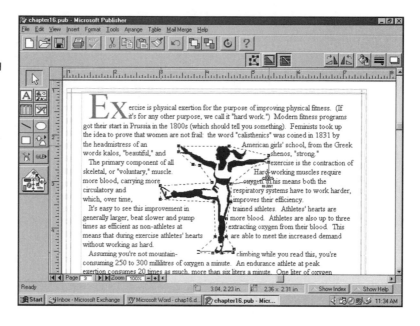

Massaging the margins

You can also adjust how close text wraps to a picture or its frame by selecting the frame, clicking the right mouse button, and choosing Object Frame Properties. The Object Frame Properties dialog box appears (see Figure 16.17).

Fig. 16.17
In the Object Frame Properties dialog box, you can precisely adjust how close text can come to your picture.

You have the choice of wrapping text around the Entire Frame or around the Picture Only. If you select the former, the Margins area has four text boxes in which you can adjust how close text can come to each side of the frame. As usual, you can enter measurements in centimeters (cm), inches (in), picas (pi), and points (pt).

If you choose the Picture Only option, only one control, Outside, will appear in the Margins area. The margin you enter applies around the entire picture. Return to your workspace to see the effect; then use the Edit Irregular Wrap button to fine-tune it.

Get out the microscope: the Design Checker

So, now you've sorted out all the overlapping elements, and you think your layout looks pretty good. Every text, picture, table, and WordArt frame is just where it belongs. This publication is an award-winner if you ever saw it. In fact, you're finished!

Well, maybe. For several years, I was editor of a weekly newspaper. Every story from every reporter flowed through my computer terminal, and from my terminal straight into the typesetting machine. I perused every word, every sentence, every paragraph with an eagle eye, determined that this would be the week when not a single typographical error would find its way into print…

…and every week, I was disappointed. Every week, I missed something. Sometimes, the errors were so glaring I cringed when I picked up the paper and wondered how on earth I could have failed to see a mistake that obvious.

It's not easy producing a perfect publication on your own. What you really need is a second pair of eyes to look things over.

Publisher gives you that second pair of eyes. It already knows the kinds of problems users commonly run into; it will examine your document, find potential problems, and let you know where they are. Then you can decide what, if anything, you need to change. Design Checker is like having an assistant whose sole job is to proofread your work.

To activate this tireless assistant, choose Tools, Design Checker. This opens a dialog box, which asks if you want to check all pages or a range of pages. You can also choose to have Publisher look at background pages.

After you make those selections, click Options to open the Options dialog box as shown in Figure 16.18.

Fig. 16.18
Tell Publisher what layout problems you want it to look for. It's ready to help.

From here, you can choose to have Publisher look at all or some of several common problems:

- Empty frames—These are frames that contain no information, and therefore can usually be deleted. Empty frames can cause other frames to change position, so you really don't want them cluttering up your publication.

- Covered objects—Publisher will warn you of any objects that overlap other objects. If you overlap objects on purpose, you might want to remove the check from this option.

- Text in overflow area—Choose this option to make sure you didn't cut off stories prematurely by trying to cram too much text into too small a text frame. If you have, some of the text will be hidden in the text overflow area. You need to enlarge the frame or reduce the text size (or edit the text) to make sure no text is missed when you print. (See Chapter 5, "Before You Add Text, You Have to Add Text Frames," for more information about text frames and the overflow area.)

- Objects in non-printing region—Most printers won't print objects that are too close to the edge of the page. With this option selected, Publisher will warn you of any objects in that situation.

- Disproportional pictures—This asks Publisher to let you know if you change the proportions of any of the pictures you inserted, which could mean they'll appear distorted.

- Too many special effects—In Publisher jargon, "special effects" are pictures, WordArt, and BorderArt. If you check this option, Publisher warns you of any pages that have more than five special effects, on the theory that this might result in a cluttered look.

- Spacing between sentences—When I learned to type, I learned to put two spaces at the ends of sentences. In desktop publishing, you should really only have one. This option will warn you of any extra spaces after the ends of sentences. (Putting in two spaces is a hard habit to break, believe me!)

- Too many fonts—Using too many fonts can make a publication look overly busy and unorganized. With this option checked, Publisher warns you if you used more than three fonts.

- Too many colors—Using too many colors can also make your publication look cluttered. Publisher will also warn you if you used more than three colors.

After you choose the layout problems you want Publisher to look for, click OK. If Design Checker finds a problem, the Design Checker dialog box in Figure 16.19 appears.

Fig. 16.19

Design Checker describes the problem it found in your layout, offers suggestions for fixing the problem, and links you to pertinent areas of the Help files.

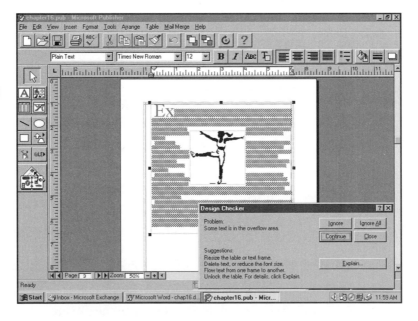

Notice that, behind the Design Checker dialog box, a story in the publication has been selected. That's the text frame where the problem was found. You can go to the publication immediately and correct the problem without closing the Layout Checker; just move the dialog box out of the way while you work. All of Publisher's tools remain active even with the Design Checker dialog box open. This makes it easy to correct each problem as you identify it; then move on to the next.

Sometimes, of course, the "problem" Design Checker turns up isn't a problem at all; it's something you did deliberately to create a specific effect. If you look at the identified problem and like the way it looks, then leave it. *You* are the final arbiter of how your document should be put together.

You can also choose to have Design Checker Ignore the problem or Ignore All problems of that type, Close the Design Checker dialog box, or ask Layout Checker to Explain (which opens a section of the Help files). Click Continue when you're ready for Layout Checker to continue checking your publication.

CAUTION **Two common problems that Design Checker won't check for are** widows and orphans (single words or sentences that get stranded at the top and bottom of pages due to page breaks). To remove a widow or orphan, add a few words before it to put at least two lines at the top of the page, or take out a few words to drop it to the bottom of the page.

The X-Files: Unexpected side effects

Finally, when you give your layout the *final* final going-over, be prepared for the unexpected. A tiny adjustment to a text frame can change the words that flow around a graphic three columns over—and completely mess up your carefully cultivated word-wrap. Making a picture just a little bit larger can bump the end of the story below it into the never-neverland of text overflow. Altering the point size of a subhead can leave you with blank space at the bottom of the page.

Figures 16.20 and 16.21 illustrate another common example. Here, changing the incorrect spelling of the word "intend" through Check Spelling has resulted in an extra line of text being added to the end of the story; a change that means half of the phone number now prints over the border of the page. You could easily overlook this change during proofreading and Design Checker might not even have caught it.

Fig. 16.20
Of course, you have to change an obviously misspelled word like "intnd"...

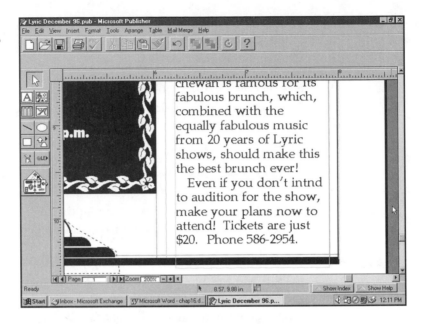

Fig. 16.21
...but even a tiny change like adding a single letter can have an unexpectedly large effect on some other area of your publication.

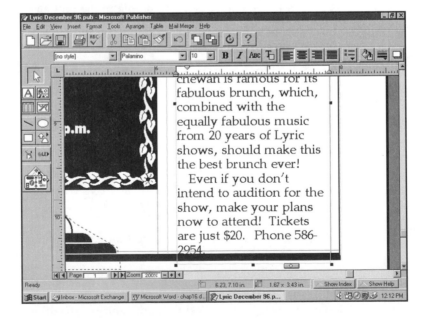

Whenever you make an adjustment, however minor, check to make sure it hasn't created an unexpected side effect somewhere else.

Unlike Fox Mulder of *The X-Files* TV series, you can't blame aliens whenever something goes wrong. You're in charge of your publication.

17

Mail Merge

- ● In this chapter:

- ● **Creating an address list for mail merging**

- ● **Customizing your address list**

- ● **Using mail merge with publications other than labels**

- ● **Filtering your addresses**

Publisher 97 makes it easy to personalize publications with its powerful new mail merge capability! . . . . ▶

Have you ever struggled to create mailing labels in your favorite word processor, all the time thinking, "Wow, this would be a snap in Microsoft Publisher!"?

Well, maybe not…but I have. Trouble was, Publisher didn't make it easy, because it didn't have a mail-merge feature. With the release of Publisher 97, however, that oversight has been rectified, and now you can create mailing labels, or personalize other publications, with ease.

You can create a database of information in Publisher that you want to merge with your publication. Or you can use information from a database you created in another program.

Creating a list in Publisher

To create a database file in Publisher, choose <u>M</u>ail Merge, <u>C</u>reate Publisher Address List. (Publisher calls the database file an "address list" because addresses are what are most commonly included in such a file; but as you'll see, it can actually be a list of anything at all.) This opens the New Address List dialog box in Figure 17.1.

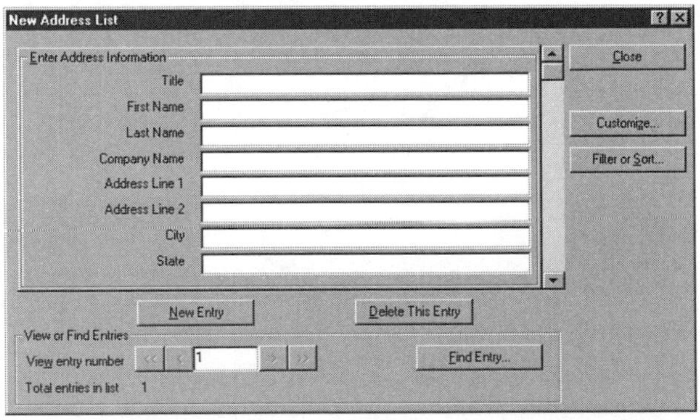

Fig. 17.1
The New Address List dialog box lets you specify the information you want to merge with your publication.

Publisher has already set up some of the most common fields used in address lists in the <u>E</u>nter Address Information area (a few fields don't immediately appear; scroll down within the arrow to see the hidden ones). To create an address list using these default fields, type your information in the blanks provided. You can move from field to field using your mouse, cursor keys, or Tab key.

 Plain English, please!

A **field**, in a computer database, is a category of information, such as address, first name, or country. **"**

When you fill in all the information for the first entry, click <u>N</u>ew Entry. This clears the fields, ready for you to type in the information for the second entry. Continue this process until you've typed in information for all the entries in your address list.

Once you finish the address list, click <u>C</u>lose. A Save As dialog box appears, so you can save your list wherever you like on your computer. Notice that address lists you save in Publisher are given the extension .mdb. Be careful not to change this or Publisher won't recognize the file as an address list when you want to open it again.

Editing your address list

Once you add more than one entry, you can move from entry to entry using the View Entry Number controls, and make any changes you think are necessary. You can either enter the specific number of the entry you want to view, or click the buttons marked with arrows. The single-arrow buttons take you forward or backward through the list one entry at a time; the double-arrow buttons take you directly to either the beginning or end of the list.

In a long address list, it's very easy to forget where something appears. If that happens, click Find Entry (see Figure 17.2).

Under Find this text, enter the text you want to find. You can choose to search all fields, or just a specific field. Click <u>F</u>ind Next, and Publisher takes you to the first occurrence of the text you want to see. Click <u>F</u>ind Next again to go to the second occurrence, and so on, until you reach the end of the address list.

Fig. 17.2
Find Entry lets you track down entries in your address list that you may have misplaced.

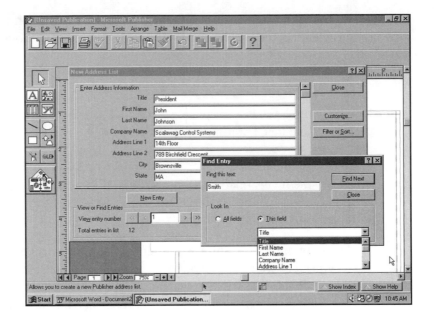

Customizing your address list

The fields that Publisher creates by default are very common and useful ones, but more than likely, they're not exactly what you need. That's all right, because Publisher lets you customize them to your heart's content.

To customize your address list, click Customize in the New Address List dialog box. You get the Customize Address List dialog box as shown in Figure 17.3.

Fig. 17.3
Match the fields in your address list to your specific needs in the Customize Address List dialog box.

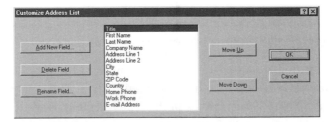

Here you see a list of all the existing fields in your address list. You can use the Move Up and Move Down buttons to move up and down in this list; or just use your mouse or cursor keys.

To the left of this list, you see three choices: Add New Field, Delete Field, and Rename Field.

- If you click Add New Field, Publisher asks you to type in a name for your new field and whether it should go before or after the field selected in the list box.

- Delete Field deletes the selected field. (First, Publisher asks if you're sure you want to go through with it.)

- Rename Field asks you to type in a new name for the selected field.

After you create the fields you want, click OK. The New Address List dialog box immediately reflects any changes you made (see Figure 17.4).

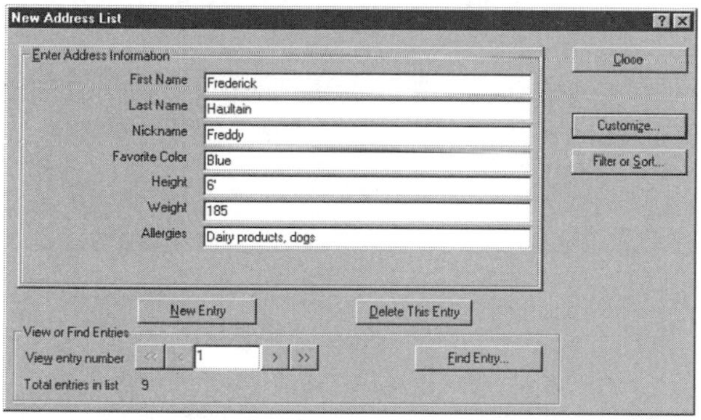

Fig. 17.4
Here's a modified New Address List dialog box, with several new fields added and others deleted.

When is an address list not an address list?

Calling the data file you create in Publisher to merge with your publication an "address list" is more than a little misleading, because the information you want to merge with your publication may not involve addresses at all.

"Mr. John Jones, you may already have won $1 Million!" Did you ever get a "personal" letter from Ed McMahon like this? It was created by merging information from a list of names. Publisher's mail merge feature allows you to do the same thing.

You can use it to personalize publications in other ways, too. For example, fundraising brochures for a symphony orchestra might be personalized to include each recipient's taste in music, gathered by a questionnaire at a recent contest. "Mr. Kapusianyk, you love Bach's Brandenburg Concerto," might read one letter, while the next would read, "Mr. McMillan, you love Beethoven's symphonies."

The possibilities are endless, because your "address list" can contain any information you want it to.

You can edit any Publisher address list at any time by choosing Mail Merge, Edit Publisher Address List, and calling up the list you want to work on.

Preparing to merge

Before you merge your address list with your publication, you need to have a place in your publication to put the new data.

To set up your publication for merging, place a new text frame where you want the information to appear, or place your cursor in an existing text frame at the spot where you want the information to appear (see Figure 17.5).

Fig. 17.5
You can add merged data to any existing text frame, whether it's blank or already contains text. In this case I want to add addresses to a brochure in the empty text frame at center.

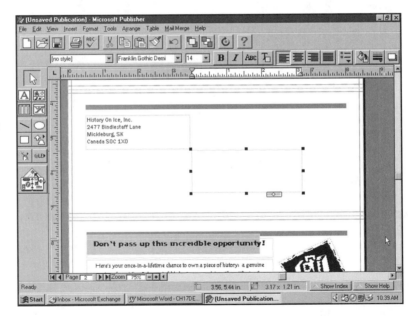

Now choose Mail Merge, Open Data Source. This gives you two options: Merge information from a file I already have, or Create an address list in Publisher.

Create an address list in Publisher is exactly the same as the Create a Publisher Address List command we discussed earlier. To actually use that address list in your publication after it's created, choose Merge information from a file I already have. This lets you browse your computer for the database file you want to use. Once you find it, double-click it or click Open.

Using information from another program

Often the information you want to merge with your publication already exists in another format. Maybe you're in charge of sending out the newsletter for your local amateur theater company, and you already have all your members' names and mailing addresses saved as a Microsoft Access database file.

Publisher doesn't make you type all that information in again as a Publisher database file. Instead, it lets you import it straight from the other program.

The various types of database files Publisher can read are listed in the pull-down box in the Open Data Source dialog box (see Figure 17.6). Choose the type of database file you want to look for, locate the file, and double-click it or click Open.

Fig. 17.6
As you can see, Publisher can make use of database files stored in a variety of formats.

Be a field marshall

Once you select a Publisher address list or other database file to use, you can tell Publisher in what order you want to insert the various fields, using the Insert Fields dialog box in Figure 17.7.

Fig. 17.7
When the time comes to merge information from a database file into your publication, Publisher lets you pick and choose which fields you want to insert, and in what order.

Highlight the field you want to insert from the list, and then click Insert. A field code—a marker labeled with the name of the field—appears in the selected text frame at the spot where you place your cursor (see Figure 17.8).

You can insert as many or as few fields as you want, in any order. You can also change text frames without closing the Insert Fields dialog box, so you can place field codes everywhere you need them with ease.

Once you insert all the codes you want to, click Close to return to your workspace.

Fig. 17.8
This is what my brochure looks like after I insert the field codes.

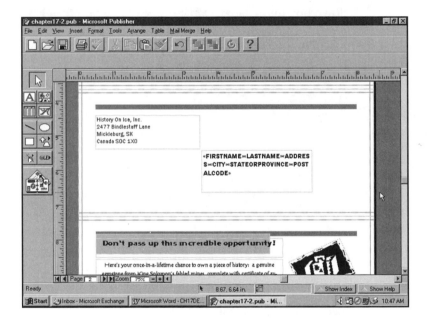

TIP Once you link your publication to a particular database file, you can insert field codes in any text frame at any time by choosing Mail Merge, Insert Field.

Q&A *Can I merge information from more than one data source in the same publication?*

No. If you choose Mail Merge, Open Data Source and your publication is already linked to a data source, Publisher asks you if you want to link to the new data source and warns that some of your fields may not get information from it. The rule is: only one data source per customer.

Format your fields

Notice that in Figure 17.8, the field codes are all crammed together without any space between them—not at all the way I want the address to look. You can format your field codes just as you would any other text, changing font, size, and so on, as long as you don't change the code itself.

In Figure 17.9, I've reformatted the field codes to look the way I want the address to look in the final publication, adding returns, spaces, and punctuation.

Fig. 17.9
Imagine what the finished product will look like as you format the field codes.

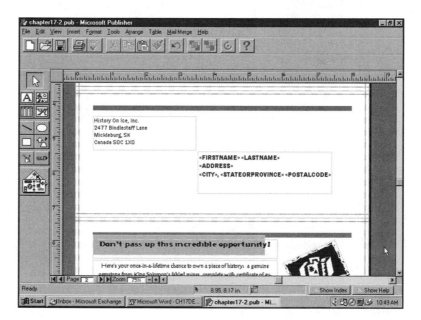

Merging

Now, at last, you can actually merge the data from your database file with your publication. To do so, choose <u>M</u>ail Merge, <u>M</u>erge.

In your publication, Publisher replaces the field codes with data from the database file, and the small Preview Data dialog box in Figure 17.10 appears.

Fig. 17.10
Examine each data entry individually with this control to make sure that the mail merge goes off without a hitch.

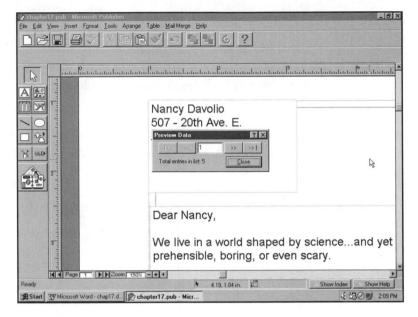

Use the controls to check out each entry. You can enter the precise number of the entries you want to examine, click the inner buttons to advance one entry at a time (either backward or forward), or click the outer buttons to take you to the beginning or end of the entries. As you move through the entries, they appear in your publication. (Move the dialog box out of the way if it's obstructing your view.) If you see a mistake, you can correct it in your publication; the Preview Data dialog box will remain in place while you do so.

 CAUTION **Even if the database file you want to merge is very long, take the** time to check each entry individually. A small typing error in the original data entry can result in an embarrassing mistake in the final publication, or render an address useless.

Filtering: when you don't want it all

Sometimes, you don't want to use all the information in your data source. Maybe your theater-company membership list includes both local members and distant members, and you only want to mail this particular newsletter to those who live in town.

Once you merge a data source with your publication, you can filter out the information you don't want.

To do so, choose Mail Merge, Filter or Sort (we'll talk about sorting in a minute).

The Filtering and Sorting dialog box in Figure 17.11 lets you fine-tune the data you use in your mail merge.

Fig. 17.11
You can be very specific as to which entries from your data source you want to merge with your publication.

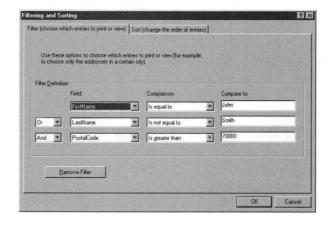

At left, you can enter up to three Fields to examine. In the rather silly example in Figure 17.11, I've chosen to look at FirstName, LastName, and PostalCode.

Once you enter at least two fields to look at, you can also decide whether you want to filter your data on the basis of something being true of the first field And something else being true of the second field, or of something being true of the first field Or something else being true of the second field. In the example, I used Or with the second field and And with the third field.

Next, you have to choose how you want to compare the fields to your filtering criteria. Under Comparison, you have a choice of: Is equal to, Is not equal to, Is greater than, and Is not greater than. You can apply the first two equally to numerical data and text; the last two apply only to numerical data.

Finally, you have to enter what you want to compare the fields to. Add it all up, and the only entries that will make it through the filter I created are those for people whose first name is John, or whose last name is anything but Smith, and whose ZIP Code is greater than 7000. John Smith, ZIP code 71284, would be selected; so would Ebenezer Cuddingsworth, ZIP code 70001; but Jane Smith, even though her ZIP code is the same as John's, would not be; nor would John Phillips, ZIP code 60999.

That's probably a more detailed filter than anyone would ever need, but it's nice to know the capability is there, isn't it? And if you decide your filter just isn't working, all you have to do to get rid of it is click Remove Filter.

If you keep the filter and click OK, you'll only be able to view those entries that make it through the filter.

Let Publisher sort it out

Sometimes, you want to insert your merged data in a particular order, typically, alphabetically or numerically. That's the function of the other tab in the Filtering and Sorting dialog box (see Figure 17.12).

Fig. 17.12
Publisher sorts your data numerically or alphabetically for you.

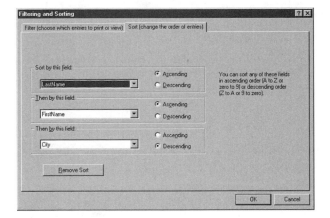

Decide the most important field you want to use to sort your data (in this case, LastName, a typical choice), and choose it from the drop-down list in the Sort by this field area. Then decide if you want to sort things in ascending (A to Z and 0 to 9) or descending (Z to A and 9 to 0) order.

If the field you want to sort by is likely to contain repeating data—more than one person with the same last name, for instance—then you can enter a second field to sort by in Then by this field, and even a third, under Then by this field. After that you're out of luck, but very few things can't be successfully sorted with three fields to work with.

When you click OK and return to previewing your entries, you'll find that your data now appears in the order you specified.

Of course, you can also cancel your sorting instructions by clicking Remove Sort.

Print Merge

The final step in merging data doesn't take place until you print your publication. We'll look at printing in detail in the next chapter, but the Print Merge dialog box that appears when you choose File, Print Merge (see Figure 17.13) offers four options that aren't in the regular Print dialog box.

Fig. 17.13
Print Merge is the final step in merging a database file with your publication.

- Rather than ask you which pages you want to print, Print Merge asks you which entries you want to print. You can choose All entries, or a range of Entries.

- If you're printing mailing labels, you can choose to skip over one or more rows by specifying the First row to print. This is helpful if you want to start printing labels on a page that's partially used.

- To print just one test page, to make sure your merged data looks the way you want it, click the Test button.

- Finally, if you want to avoid having blank lines wherever an empty field occurs, check the Don't print lines that contain only empty fields box.

 TIP **One of Publisher's PageWizards (see Chapter 3, "Create a Publication Pronto with PageWizards")** creates mailing labels in many of the most popular Avery sizes. Using this PageWizard is the fastest, easiest way to create labels.

18

Printing: The Final Step

● **In this chapter:**

- **How do I get my equipment ready to print?**

- **This isn't an everyday letter: printing odd jobs**

- **Uh-oh, something went wrong. Where can I find help?**

- **My five-year-old dot-matrix doesn't cut it; I need to take my publication to an outside printer**

Whether you print your publication on your own printer or send it to an outside printer, Publisher helps you take desktop publishing's Final Step. . . . . ●▶

There's a proverb that says, "A journey of a thousand miles begins with a single step." Your publication's journey into the outside world also begins with a single step: either printing (in the case of a traditional publication) or publishing to the Internet (in the case of a World Wide Web document).

In this chapter, we'll look at printing; in the next chapter we'll look at using Publisher to create a World Wide Web site and publishing to the Web.

Deconstructing the printing process

The final step of printing a publication in Publisher can actually be broken into several smaller steps. These vary depending on who's doing the printing, what kind of equipment is being used, and what type of publication you've created.

If you print your publication on your own printer, then the process begins with Print Setup.

Which printer? What paper? Which direction? Print Setup lets you choose

Practically every Windows 95 program that supports printing has Print Setup in some form or another. In Publisher, you access it by choosing File, Print Setup. The Print Setup dialog box appears (see Figure 18.1).

Fig. 18.1
Print Setup lets you choose your printer and your paper source, size, and orientation.

First, open the Name drop-down list to see a list of all the printers available on your system. Click a printer to select it, and more information about it automatically appears in the Status, Type, Where, and Comment fields below the Name list box.

Status tell you whether the printer is ready to use (such as, whether it's turned on and if it's the default printer). Type tells you what type of printer you selected (in Figure 18.1 it's the same as the name, but I could have named the printer something else entirely). Where tells you to which port the printer is connected. And Comments might provide additional information entered when you installed the printer in Windows 95.

Click Properties to see the Printer Properties control box. The controls available to you here depend on what kind of printer you chose. Typical controls include paper size and source, print resolution and density, how you want your printer to handle graphics, and so on.

After you select your printer, check out the Paper area. The Size list box lets you select what size of paper you want to print on; what's available depends on the printer you selected. The same is true of the Source list box; it lists sources of paper available on your printer. Sometimes, your publication won't fit comfortably on a size of paper your printer can use. See the "All jobs are not created equal" section later in this chapter for more information.

Finally, in the Orientation area of the dialog box, you can choose between Portrait and Landscape. If you have trouble remembering that Portrait orientation prints across the narrow direction of the paper, and Landscape orientation prints across the wide direction of the paper, don't worry. The Orientation area includes a preview reminder that makes it clear.

When you've made all your selections, click OK to return to the workspace.

 TIP **Unlike some programs, Publisher doesn't offer Print Preview,** which shows you exactly how the publication will look when you print it. On the other hand, any time you look at a Publisher publication on-screen, you're pretty well seeing what it will look like on paper.

To get an even better idea, turn off all the nonprinting elements that might be visible. Choose View, Hide Boundaries and Guides, and (if necessary) choose View, Hide Special Characters.

There's your Page Preview.

Even more printing options

You've selected your printer and paper and you know your publication is perfect, so you must be ready to print, right? Well, maybe. But there are a still a few more options to consider.

Choose <u>F</u>ile, <u>P</u>rint. The Print dialog box stands between you and seeing your publication on paper (see Figure 18.2).

Fig. 18.2
Do you want to print just some of the publication? How many copies should Publisher print? The Print dialog box is where you make these decisions—and others—about the print job.

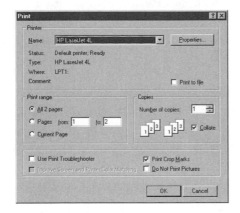

The Print dialog box has four areas: Printer, Print range, Copies, and an unnamed section at the bottom.

- The Printer area gives you another opportunity to change to a different printer. It also contains a check box called Print to file. Check this box to print the publication to a hard drive or floppy disk, to await printing to paper at a more opportune moment.

- In the Print range area, decide whether you want to print all the pages in the publication or just some of them. The default is <u>A</u>ll Pages (how-ever many pages you have). If you just want to print some pages—just pages two and three of a five-page publication, for example—click the Pa<u>g</u>es radio button and enter **2** in the <u>f</u>rom box and **3** in the <u>T</u>o box. To change your mind and print all pages after all, click the <u>A</u>ll Pages button again.

  You can also choose to print only the C<u>u</u>rrent Page, the page you're currently viewing in your workspace.

- In the Copies area, enter how many copies you want to print in the Number of copies box, and whether you want Publisher to Collate them.

 Plain English, please!

> To collate pages is to put them in their proper order. If you select the Collate check box and print multiple copies of a multipage publication, Publisher prints the pages of each publication sequentially: all the pages of the first copy, then all the pages of the second copy, and so on. If you don't select the Collate check box, Publisher prints each page of the publication individually the number of times specified: 15 copies of the first page, then 15 copies of the second, then 15 of the third, and so on.

- Finally, in the bottom area, you can choose to Use Print Trouble-shooter, Improve Screen and Printer Color Matching (if your printer supports it), or Print Crop Marks. These topics are discussed later in the chapter.

  You can also select the Do Not Print Pictures check box. If you do, Publisher replaces all the graphics in the printed publication with placeholders (light gray boxes crisscrossed by diagonal lines). This is useful for checking layouts because it speeds the printing process.

I'm late! I'm late! Printing on the run

 To quickly print your publication, don't bother with the Print dialog box. Just click the Print button in the Standard toolbar. Publisher sends the current page to the printer, using the last settings you entered in the Print dialog box.

All jobs are not created equal

Not all publications are designed to fit on letter-sized paper, legal-sized paper, or even 11"×17" paper. If you design a business card, a tent-fold card for a restaurant tabletop, or name cards for a birthday party, your creations will be much smaller than any of those types of paper.

On the other hand, other designs—a poster for a musical production, for instance, or a banner for a welcome-home party that has to stretch the length of a wall—will be much larger than most standard sizes of paper.

Fortunately, Publisher can handle even the oddest of odd jobs like these, large or small.

Printing publications smaller than your paper

When you design a publication that's smaller than a standard-sized sheet of paper, Publisher doesn't show you how it will fit on that paper. Instead, it shows the publication as it will look when cut to its final size, like the business card in Figure 18.3.

Fig. 18.3

Publisher displays small publications like this business card as they will look when finished, not as they will look when printed on a larger piece of paper.

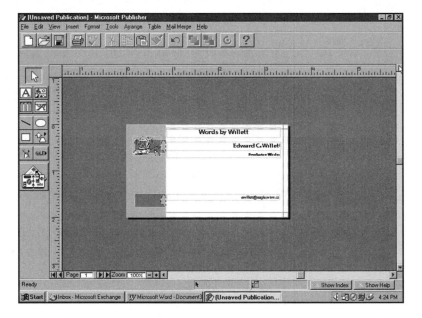

When you choose File, Print to print this kind of publication, however, notice that the Print dialog box has a Page Options button. Click it to open the Page Options dialog box (see Figure 18.4).

The Sample area shows how Publisher arranges the multiple copies on the page, but you can change it if you want by clicking Custom Options, which brings up the dialog box in Figure 18.5.

Fig. 18.4
In the Page Options dialog box, you can choose whether to print only one copy of your small publication per page or multiple copies.

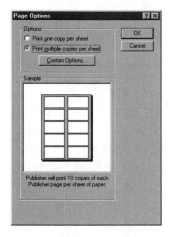

Fig. 18.5
Here's where you can fine-tune the way Publisher arranges small publications on the page for printing.

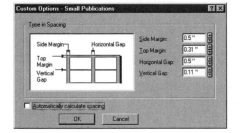

The top area is called Type in Spacing, and that's exactly what you do: Type the amount of space in inches you want in the Side Margin and Top Margin, as well as the Horizontal Gap and Vertical Gap between each pair of cards (use the drop-down arrows to switch to centimeters, picas, or points). The preview shows you what you're accomplishing.

To restore the default spacing, click Automatically calculate spacing.

Click OK to return to the previous dialog box, whose Sample area now shows the effects of the changes made in the Custom Options dialog box. Click OK again to return to the Print dialog box, and click OK one more time to finally start printing.

It's too big! Printing publications larger than the paper in your printer

To print publications such as banners and posters that are larger than any size of paper you can use in your printer, you need to use another unique dialog box. If your publication is too large for the size of paper you've chosen, a button called Tile Printing Options becomes available when you choose File, Print.

 Plain English, please!

You can print publications larger than the paper in your printer on several sheets of paper, each of which has just part of the publication on it. You assemble these sheets to create the whole publication, just like tiles fit together to created a pattern on a floor: hence, this method of printing large publications is called tiling.

Clicking the Tile Printing Options button opens the Poster and Banner Printing Options dialog box, which shows you how your publication will be divided among several sheets of paper (see Figure 18.6). The large white rectangle in the Sample area is your publication; the transparent rectangles drawn on top of it represent the separate pieces of paper on which it will be printed.

Fig. 18.6

Just as individual tiles can create a beautiful mosaic floor, so can you assemble a complete publication from pieces of paper that each contain only part of it.

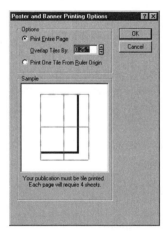

If you print the publication with these settings, it will take four pages, as shown in the Sample, to cover the whole design. You can change how much each tile will overlap the others by using the Overlap Tiles By control box. Click the arrows to adjust the overlap, or type in a specific number [again, in centimeters (cm), inches (in), picas (pi), or points (pt)].

TIP **Changing the overlap can make it easier to assemble the publication.** A larger overlap gives you more leeway as to where you put the seam: you can trim around entire letters and graphics, for example, rather than having to try to perfectly match their halves.

Adjusting the overlap can also ensure that the outside edges of the publication perfectly match the outside edge of the tiles. This can help you line up the printed tiles and make assembly that much easier.

The Overlap Tiles By box is only active if you choose the Print Entire Page button. Choose Print One Tile From Ruler Origin and the Sample changes to show only one regular-sized sheet of paper overlaying your oversized publication (see Figure 18.7).

Fig. 18.7
If you only need to print part of a large publication, perhaps to check how a particular picture will look or to avoid a nasty seam through a bit of WordArt, use Print One Tile from Ruler Origin.

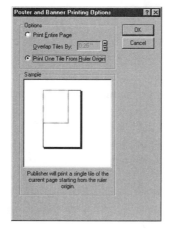

Publisher lines up that single tile with the zero markings on the vertical and horizontal rulers. Normally, those marks align with the upper-left corner of your publication, so that's where the single tile appears by default. However, you can change the position of the tile by changing the location of zero on one or both of the rulers.

To do that, point at either ruler or at the intersection of the two. Your mouse arrow changes to a two-headed arrow. Press and hold the Shift key, and drag the mouse to the point you want the zero markings to align to (see Figure 18.8).

Fig. 18.8
Relocating the zero marks on the rulers, as I'm doing here, and printing a single tile at a time can help you avoid awkward seams when assembling your publication, and give you an easy way to check just a portion of your publication during the design process.

If you return to the Tile Printing Options dialog box and select Print One Tile From Ruler Origin, you see the single tile has now moved in the Sample area (see Figure. 18.9).

Fig. 18.9
Now that we've moved the zero marks of the ruler, the single tile that will print has also moved.

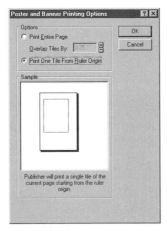

Click OK to return to the Print dialog box, and OK again to print your publication.

What if I want to print in color?

Publisher offers lots of great tools for using color with text, graphics, WordArt, and tables. But when you print to your color printer, you might be disappointed; sometimes, the color you print doesn't match the color on the screen.

Publisher can help avoid that disappointment: it offers you a couple of ways to ensure that the color on the monitor and the color on the printer are as close as possible.

CAUTION **To access the tools in this section, your color printer must support** Image Color Matching, so check your printer documentation before continuing with the rest of this section. If you don't have a color printer, this section isn't going to do you much good either!

To access Publisher's color-matching tools, choose <u>T</u>ools, <u>O</u>ptions. In the Options dialog box, choose <u>I</u>mprove screen and printer color matching (see Figure 18.10).

Fig. 18.10
The first step to successful color printing is to choose this check box in the Options dialog box.

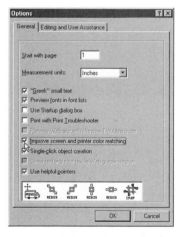

After you activate this option, other tools become available to you. For example, select an object and click the Object Color button, and then More Colors. As you can see in Figure 18.11, the <u>M</u>ark colors that will not print well on my printer check box is now available. If you choose this, Publisher puts X's through all the colors in the color palette that will not work well on your printer.

Fig. 18.11
Publisher provides you with friendly advice on using the colors that will work the best.

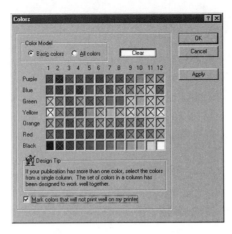

The second option that Publisher provides that can help you match monitor colors to printer colors is in the Print dialog box that comes up whenever you choose File, Print. Select the Improve Screen and Printer Color Matching check box, which does exactly what it says.

Individual color printers might offer other choices, including a selection of methods for matching screen and printer colors. From the Print dialog box, choose Properties and explore the various options your color printer provides.

Publisher's Print Troubleshooter is here to help

If you've worked with a variety of software packages, you already know that printing can be a tricky business. Sometimes, when you finally get through all the options pertinent to your publication and you're ready to print, you click OK for the final time, sit back...and something goes wrong.

Maybe nothing prints at all. Maybe your fonts look funny. Maybe graphics don't show up or don't look like they should.

Some problems require you to check your printer and computer and Windows 95 documentation, but Publisher does its best to give you a helping hand with print problems via the Print Troubleshooter (see Figure 18.12). You can set up Publisher so that Print Troubleshooter opens every time you print, or you can choose to activate it only when you have a problem. Either way, it can provide valuable hints that can lead to a successful resolution of your printing problem.

Fig. 18.12

If this looks familiar, it should; Print Trouble-shooter is simply a part of the built-in Help feature.

To keep Print Troubleshooter active all the time, choose Tools, Options, then check the Print with Print Troubleshooter check box. Now Print Trouble-shooter will open every time you print.

If you prefer to only activate Print Troubleshooter after something goes wrong, click the Use Print Troubleshooter check box in the Print dialog box and try printing again. Or you can simply choose Help, Print Troubleshooter when you need a printing tip.

When Print Troubleshooter appears, click Troubleshoot a Printing Problem to see the list in Figure 18.13. More specific problems branch off from here; with any luck, one of them will not only match the problem you're having, it will also offer the correct solution.

Fig. 18.13
The first step to finding an answer to a printing problem using Print Troubleshooter is to decide which of these general problems most closely matches the one you're having.

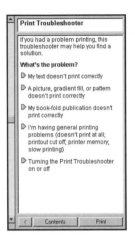

> **Print Troubleshooter**
>
> If you had a problem printing, this troubleshooter may help you find a solution.
>
> **What's the problem?**
>
> ▷ My text doesn't print correctly
>
> ▷ A picture, gradient fill, or pattern doesn't print correctly
>
> ▷ My book-fold publication doesn't print correctly
>
> ▷ I'm having general printing problems (doesn't print at all; printout cut off; printer memory, slow printing)
>
> ▷ Turning the Print Troubleshooter on or off
>
> < Contents   Print

This has to be perfect: sending publications to outside printers

Your inkjet or 300 dpi laser printer might be good enough for your personal use, but if your publication is destined for greater things, such as full-color printing or appearing as an ad in a magazine, you might have to send it to an outside printer.

An outside printer can bring to your project expertise and specialized equipment you may lack. In particular, an outside printer will have high-resolution printers that can give your publication that final professional polish. An outside printer can also help you with color choices, and even design.

Publisher can help you prepare a publication for printing by an outside printer.

Outside Printer Setup

First, choose File, Outside Print Setup. This opens the Outside Print Setup dialog box (see Figure 18.14).

Fig. 18.14
Professional printers offer many more options for printing your publication than the typical home or office computer system.

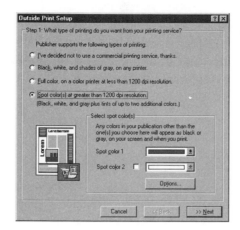

Here you're asked the question, "What type of printing do you want from your printing service?" and offered four possible answers:

- I've decided not to use a commercial printing service, thanks. So what are you doing opening this dialog box? Choose Cancel.

- Black, white, and shades of gray, on any printer. You'd choose this one if you want to print your publication at a higher resolution than is available from your desktop or office printer.

- Full color, on a color printer at less than 1,200 dpi resolution. If you don't have a color printer or have only a low-resolution color printer, you might want to send your publication out for full-color printing of this sort. Publisher doesn't support full-color printing at greater than 1,200 dpi resolution.

66 *Plain English, please!*

Printer resolution determines how sharply text and graphics will print. Resolution is measured in dpi, which stands for dots per inch. Although the letters in a laser-printed font look like they're drawn with lines, they're actually made up of tiny dots. The more dots per inch there are, the smaller the dots are, and the finer the printer's resolution. 99

- Spot color(s) at greater than 1,200 dpi resolution. Publisher *does* support the use of up to two colors, plus black and shades of gray, at greater than 1,200 dpi. Spot color can be a highly effective way to add color to your publication, and generally costs less than full color.

If you choose this option, you must select your spot colors from the two boxes that become available. Click the Options button just below the color controls to open the Spot Color Options dialog box in Figure 18.15.

Of course, if you're going to use spot color, you should design your publication with that in mind from the very beginning, using those colors on your screen in the places where you want them to print. This will give you a much clearer idea of how the finished publication will look. It's just another good reason to plan carefully *before* you begin designing.

 Plain English, please!

> The kind of full-color printing you see on the cover of this book, which faithfully reproduces everything from skin tones to the color of someone's sweater, requires four different versions of the same image, each designed to be printed in a different color (red, cyan, yellow, and black). When these four colors in varying shades are printed on top each other, they can produce any color. This kind of color printing is process color. Any other kind of color printing, which doesn't involve all those inks or (necessarily) overprinting one color on another, is spot color. Because spot color is so much easier to produce, it's also less expensive, which makes it a popular choice in publication design for those on a limited budget. **""**

Fig. 18.15
Specify how Publisher handles black objects and text overlying colored objects with these controls.

If you select Overprint black objects, black objects overlying colored objects print on top of the color, so you have black ink over colored ink on the page. If you don't select this box, no colored ink prints in areas masked by the black.

Similarly, if you select Overprint black text under, text smaller than the size specified in the box prints over colored objects. The color under text larger than that size doesn't print.

Disabling overprinting can lead to gaps on higher resolution color printers, so you should discuss the best settings for these controls with your outside printing service.

After you choose the type of outside printing you're interested in, choose Next. That moves you to the next page of the Outside Print Setup dialog box, which asks if you want to use Publisher's outside printer drivers, or select a specific printer. If you're setting up a publication for an outside printer, you'll probably want to check the first option; you can't select a specific printer unless it's installed on your system.

Click Next again (if you're preparing a black-and-white or spot-color publication) to move to the next page of the Outside Print Setup dialog box, which gives you two more options: Automatically Choose "Extra" Paper Sizes and Show All Printer Marks.

Outside printers frequently print publications on oversized paper to accommodate various printing marks and special effects, such as bleeds—colors that go right to the edge of the page. So you should usually select the Automatically Choose "Extra" Paper Sizes check box.

Selecting the Show All Printer Marks check box means that crop marks, registration marks, and information about the publication will print with the publication. Again, you should usually select this check box.

 Plain English, please!

> Crop marks are not mysterious circles that appear in farmers' fields overnight, but marks that tell the printer where to trim the page. They appear as short horizontal and vertical lines that stop just short of intersecting. Each line marks one edge of the page; the invisible intersection marks the corner.
>
> A printing press doesn't print color all at once; each color is laid down on the page separately. Registration marks (crosshairs outside the printing area of the page), are lined up to ensure that each color prints exactly where it should. Crop marks and registration marks are collectively known as printing marks.

The outside printing checklist

Dealing with printers of the human sort can be just as confusing as dealing with printers of the computer sort. Publisher offers you a helping hand in the form of the Outside Printing Checklist, which is also available on this final screen of the Outside Print Setup dialog box. Click Print Outside Printing Checklist and your printer will spit out a very thorough five-page checklist that takes you through the whole process of using an outside printer.

Part A gives you a series of questions to ask printers, which vary depending on what kind of printing you want done, and urges you to call several different printing services before settling on one.

Part B is a list of more detailed matters you need to get settled with the printing service you choose before you finalize your publication.

Follow this checklist and, even if it's the first time you've printed something anywhere but on your own desktop, you'll have the printing service thinking you're a pro.

The outside printing info sheet

Publisher also prints an information sheet that answers many of the questions an outside printer might ask, including the fonts and colors used, the resolution, what kind of printer the proof was printed on, and more. To print this sheet, choose File, Print Infosheet.

19

Paperless Publishing: Design Your Own Web Site!

In this chapter:

- **Formatting, graphics, and hyperlinks**

- **Pitfalls of Web design**

- **Previewing your Web site**

- **Turning existing publications into Web pages**

- **Publishing your site to the Web**

No need to learn a whole new program! Now you can use Publisher's familiar tools to create your own home on the World Wide Web . . . . ⊳

here's something about the World Wide Web that makes people itch to be a part of it. I put up a Web site of my own within three months of getting my Internet account a couple of years ago…but I found it a bit of a struggle, since it involved learning HTML, a programming language that, while not difficult, did bring back memories of my first encounters with computers in the late '70s, and learning to program in BASIC.

I kept looking at other programs that promised to make designing a Web site easy, and while all of them had their good points, what I really wanted was a program that would let me use my desktop publishing skills without worrying about the HTML coding at all. I never found such a program…until now.

Now, with Publisher 97, you never have to look at HTML if you don't want to. You can design your Web page just as you would any other publication (well, almost—more on the exceptions later!), and the results can be spectacular. Even better, you can turn anything you've already created in Publisher into a Web page. It's paperless publishing at its finest, courtesy of Publisher 97.

Using the Web site PageWizard

The easiest way of all to create your own Web site is to let Publisher do most of the work for you, with the Web Site PageWizard.

To access the PageWizard, choose File, New; then double-click Web Site when the list of PageWizards appears. The Web Site PageWizard Design Assistant appears (see Figure 19.1), and immediately wants to know, "What's the Web site for?"

Fig. 19.1
The Web Site Page-Wizard Design Assistant helps you no matter what kind of Web site you create.

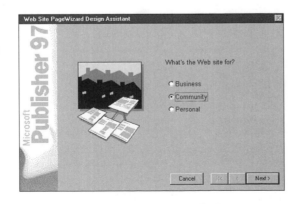

Your choices are Business, Personal, or Community. Which choice you make determines what types of pages the Web Site PageWizard offers to create for you a little later on. I've chosen to create a Community site—the sort of site you might make for a school, a church, or a club.

Whichever choice you make, you're next asked if you want to create a single-page site or a multiple-page site. Since I have far too much information to impart than I could possibly get on a single page, I select Multiple-page site, which brings up the screen in Figure 19.2.

Fig. 19.2
These choices vary, depending on which type of site you choose to create: Business, Community, or Personal.

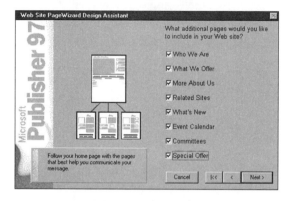

Here you're offered a selection of pages the PageWizard thinks you might want in your site. You can choose any or all of these. I've chosen all of them.

Next, you're asked what style of page you want to create (see Figure 19.3). Your choices are Basic, Bold, Classic, Jazzy, and Modern. Each thumbnail sketch gives you a hint of what they'll look like; the larger preview to the left also changes to reflect the new style as you click each one. Being a jazz fan, I've chosen Jazzy.

Fig. 19.3
Pick a style that reflects the organization or individual your Web site is about.

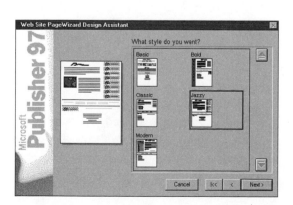

Now you're asked what sort of background you want for your site: Plain, Solid, or Texture. I like Web pages with textured backgrounds, so that's what I chose to add to mine.

Then, PageWizard asks what kind of navigation buttons you want: Text Only, Buttons and Text, or Icons and Text (see Figure 19.4). These are the links that allow you to move from page to page of your site. If you choose Text Only, the links appear only as the names of the various pages from Figure 19.2. Buttons and Text adds eye-catching buttons to the text, while Icons and Text adds larger images that give a graphical clue as to which page they point. Again, the preview changes as you click each option so you can get a better idea of what the effect will be. I chose Buttons and Text.

Fig. 19.4

How will you have visitors move from page to page of your site? Make up your mind here.

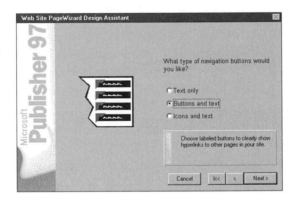

In the next few pages, Publisher asks you to name your home page, whether you want a postal or street address on your page (if you do, you're asked to enter it), and whether you want to add a phone number, fax number, and e-mail address. Once you enter all that information, click Create It and watch PageWizard do its stuff (see Figure 19.5).

TIP **Choose the name of your home page carefully; it's the name that** appears in the browser program of a visitor to your page, and the name he'll save if he likes your page so much he adds it to his file of favorite links. I learned this the hard way: the first time I created a Web site using Publisher, I left the home page labeled Home Page and learned the error of my ways in no uncertain terms from a friend who later visited the site.

Fig. 19.5
Here's my Regina Lyric
Light Opera Web site,
as created by the Web
Site PageWizard.

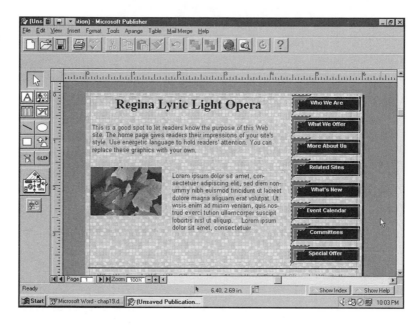

Be your own Web site wizard

Even if you use the PageWizard to begin your Web site, you have lots to do to truly make it your own. You may even decide it's easier to simply create a Web site from scratch. Publisher lets you do that, too.

To create a new Web site, choose File, New. This time, click the Blank Page tab, and select Web Page from the choices offered (see Figure 19.6).

Fig. 19.6
Don't use an ordinary
blank page to create
your Web site; use a
Web Page instead.

The standard Web Page is designed to display normally on all video monitors at VGA resolution (640×480) and higher. If for some reason you want to create a larger or smaller page, click Custom Web Page (see Figure 19.7).

Fig. 19.7
If the Standard Web Page doesn't suit you, you can change its size here.

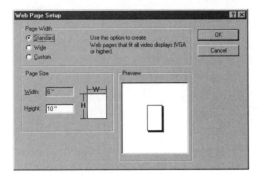

Here you have three choices: Standard [which fits all video displays from VGA (640×480) on up], Wide [which fits SVGA (800×600) displays, but may require some viewers to scroll horizontally], or Custom (whatever size you want).

TIP **Although there is a trend in Web design to optimize pages for** 800×600 displays, for the time being, I still recommend sticking with the Standard, 640×480 size if possible, so everybody can view your site easily, no matter how their equipment is set up. Web surfers, remember, are always only a mouse-click away from getting fed up and moving on to something else, so you don't want to annoy them!

Once you choose a page size, the page appears in your workspace just like any other publication's page. You can design it just as you would any other publication, adding text frames, WordArt, and pictures to your heart's content (albeit with a few caveats I'll get to in the next section).

You have a couple of new things to play with, however: hyperlinks, backgrounds, and textures.

Adding hyperlinks

Hyperlinks are what make the World Wide Web a Web: they're links that the viewer clicks to go visit some other page. That page can be posted at your site or halfway around the world; to the person doing the clicking, it's all the same (assuming the volume of traffic hasn't slowed the Internet to a crawl at the time).

 Anything on your page can be a hyperlink: text, a picture, a table, WordArt. To create a hyperlink, click the object you want to apply the link to; then click the Hyperlink button that now appears in the standard toolbar, or choose Insert, Hyperlink (or press Ctrl+K). This opens the Hyperlink dialog box in Figure 19.8.

Fig. 19.8
Point your hyperlinks in the right direction with these controls.

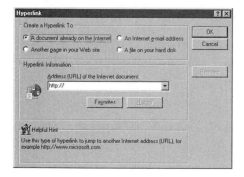

You have four choices for your hyperlink:

- **A document already on the Internet**—If you choose this, Publisher asks you to enter an address, or URL, for the Web page you want to point to. These addresses always begin with http://, so that much is entered for you; you just type in the rest.

- **Another page in your Web site**—My personal Web site (**http://www.wbm.ca/users/ewillett**) has more than 80 pages, so I have a lot of these kinds of links. Publisher asks if you want this link to point to the first (home) page, the previous page, the next page, or a specific page.

- **An Internet e-mail address**—If you choose this, a form opens whenever anyone clicks the hyperlink, inviting them to send an e-mail message to the address you specify here. You'll almost always have at least one of these types of hyperlinks, unless you really don't want people e-mailing you (always a possibility!).

- **A file on your hard disk**—If there's some file on your computer you want people to download from your Web site, enter its location here (or find it by browsing). When you publish your Web site to the Web, this file will be included.

Hyperlinks are the heart and soul of the Web, so use them freely!

Choose an attractive background and text colors

You can leave the background of your Web page blank, in which case, the viewer will see your words and pictures on whatever color background she has set as the default for her browser. But most Web pages have some sort of specific color or texture as their background.

Textured backgrounds, although they often look like one big picture of, say, burlap, are usually made up of a single smaller picture that repeats over and over. (You can have a background made up of one big picture, but it will slow down your page's loading time considerably. Actually, any textured background will slow your page's loading time a bit, so if speed is your primary concern, stick to plain or colored backgrounds.)

You access both of these functions in the same place, by choosing Format, Background and Text Colors (see Figure 19.9).

Fig. 19.9
Publisher gives you several preset combinations of backgrounds and text colors to choose from.

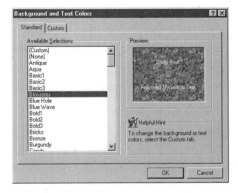

By clicking through the list at the left, you can see the various combinations of backgrounds and text colors that Publisher thinks work together well (there are many combinations of background and text colors that can render your text illegible, so you might be wise to heed Publisher's advice). If you find one you like, double-click it or choose OK, and it will be applied to the Web site you're creating.

If you'd like to create your own background/text color combination, click the Custom tab (see Figure 19.10).

Fig. 19.10
Customize your background and text colors with these controls.

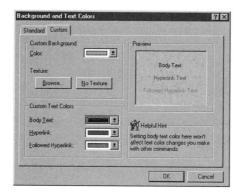

In the Custom Background area, decide if you want a texture or just a color for the background. If you just want a color, click No Texture and choose the color using the Color control.

If you do want to use a texture, click the Browse button and locate the file you want to use to create that texture on your hard drive.

TIP **You can use any picture file to create your background. You can** create a background for your business Web site, for example, by choosing a digital version of your logo, or a (rather egotistical) background for your personal Web site using a snapshot of yourself. Use your imagination to make your background reflect the personality of your Web site.

At the same time, sometimes simpler is better. As with desktop publishing on paper, the goal of publishing to the Web is to communicate. There are plenty of Web sites out there where the cleverness of the design is matched only by the illegibility of the message. A too-complicated background image can make your text, no matter what color it is, very difficult to read.

In the Custom Text Colors area, choose colors for your Body Text, Hyperlinks, and Followed Hyperlinks. The Body Text is the main text of your Web site. We discussed Hyperlinks just a couple of pages ago. Followed

Hyperlinks are links the viewer has clicked. They're usually a different color from unfollowed Hyperlinks to help the viewer keep track of where he has been.

Q&A **What if I want to make some of my body text a different color than the rest of it?**

Go right ahead. These commands don't affect any text whose color you changed using other Publisher tools.

Pitfalls of Web design

Now that I've indicated you can design a Web site just like you design any other publication in Publisher, it's time for those caveats I mentioned.

Peel away the layers

The first thing to look out for when creating your Web site is overlapping frames—especially text frames overlapping picture or WordArt frames.

When you create a publication for paper, overlapping frames are a great way to achieve certain affects. But when you create a Web site, any frames that overlap must be joined together and turned into one giant graphic region, which is saved to your Web site as a single file. These large files will slow down the loading of your pages into a viewer's computer, and just might send them on to another site without ever seeing yours at all. Any text that is in this graphic region is also saved as part of the graphic file, instead of being saved as text—which, again, will slow down the loading of your pages.

By default, Publisher warns you when you overlap frames. A bright red border momentarily appears around the elements that will be turned into a single picture file when you publish the page (see Figure 19.11). You can turn this feature off by choosing <u>T</u>ools, <u>O</u>ptions, Show <u>r</u>ectangle for text in Web graphic region, but I don't know why you'd want to.

Fig. 19.11
Here I overlapped the
text frame on the left
(with the welcoming
text) with the picture
file and smaller text
frame (with the name
of the artistic director)
at the right, and
Publisher has framed
all three to warn me
they'll become a single
picture file when the
site is published.

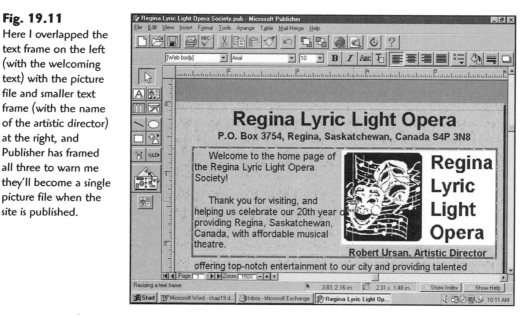

That's not to say you can't overlap frames; if that's the only way to achieve a
particular effect, and you're willing to risk a slightly longer load time for that
page. Go ahead; just don't overdo it.

Keep text simple

Keeping text simple, in the context of using Publisher for Web design, doesn't
mean using small words and short sentences; it means keeping your text
frames plain. If you add a border or BorderArt, or rotate the text, it won't
load as text into a viewer's browser; instead, again, it will load as a picture
file, and take much longer to do so. Text in unadorned text frames appear
almost instantly in the viewer's browser, and with any luck, will be so
fascinating she will stick around to wait for the graphics to load.

Also, be aware that indents don't exist in HTML. Instead, use extra spaces.

Watch the size!

It's wonderful to have the ability to easily place photographs and other
picture files on the Web; but keep an eye on the size of those photographs,
not necessarily their physical size, but their digital size. The more disk space

they take up, the longer they take to load. The largest photograph on my person Web site is 199K; most are under 50K in size. They're not high-resolution, by any means, but they're quite viewable and they load quickly.

WYSIWYG? Not!

WYSIWYG is an old computer term meaning, What-you-see-is-what-you-get. WYSIWYG applies to publications you create with Publisher for printing on paper; it doesn't necessarily apply to publications you create for the Web.

Many things influence the way your page appears when somebody calls it up over the Internet. To begin with, you can't control how your visitors have set up their own software. They may have turned off graphics altogether and are only loading text, to save time; they may have their browser set to use specific text colors, no matter what your page wants them to use; they may be using 1280×1024 resolution and your page looks like a postage stamp on their screen.

You're also facing certain limitations of HTML, which, although you didn't have to learn it, is still used to code your Publisher-designed Web site. HTML won't let you position things as precisely as you can position them for printing on paper. As a result, pictures and text that you carefully line up during your design may not line up quite the way you expect when the page converts to HTML.

There's only one way to find out exactly what your page will look like once you load it into a browser: preview it.

Previewing your Web site

 To preview your Web site, you must have World Wide Web browser software installed on your computer. In Publisher, click the Preview button, or choose File, Preview Web Site. Publisher chugs away for a moment or two, then launches your browser with your Web site loaded into it. This is your opportunity to look over each page and see exactly how it will look on the Web—and how it differs from the way it looked while you were designing it (see Figure 19.12 and Figure 19.13). You should also test all your hyperlinks and make sure they work.

Fig. 19.12
Here's a portion of my Regina Lyric Light Opera Web site as it appears in Publisher....

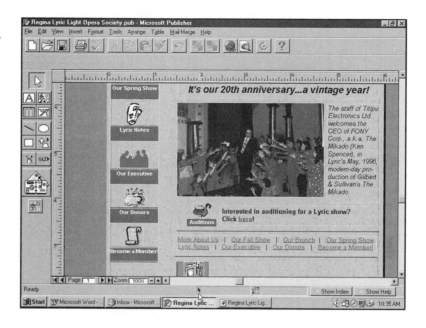

Fig. 19.13
...and here's how it appears during previewing, using Microsoft Internet Explorer 3.0.

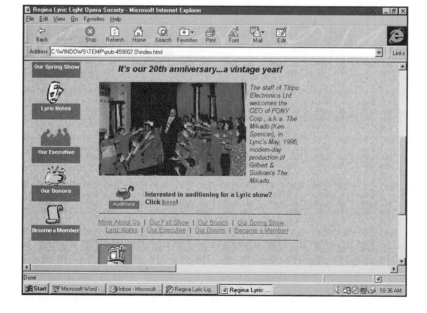

Notice the slight differences between the two figures. In Figure 19.13, there appears to be empty space to the right; that's because I designed the page to fit onto a VGA screen (640×480), but I'm personally viewing it in SVGA

(800×600). Also in Figure 19.13, the word "production" is no longer hyphenated in the photo caption, which has resulted in an extra line, which now makes the caption extend below the bottom of the picture, for a rather untidy effect. And although it's very close, things don't line up exactly the same as they do in Figure 19.12.

Things look even more different if you preview with a different browser. In Figure 19.14, I've loaded the same page into Netscape Navigator 3.0. Notice how differently the various objects are aligned.

Fig. 19.14
The various browsers each make your page look different.

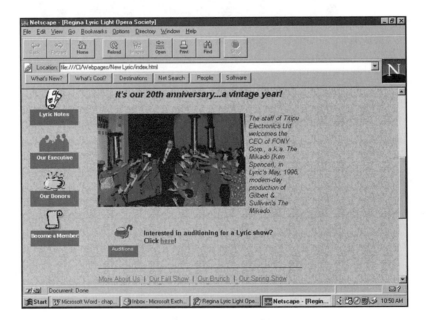

In general, then, and I guess not too surprisingly, your Publisher-designed pages look more closely like the way you intended them to look to viewers using Internet Explorer. You can minimize the differences, however, if you take time to preview your pages with other browsers, too, so you can find and simplify problem areas.

Using Preview Troubleshooter

If Preview Web site with Preview Troubleshooter is selected under Tools, Options, a special section of the Help files will open whenever you preview your Web site. If something about your preview doesn't look right, you may find an answer to your problems here.

Using Design Checker

Publisher's Design Checker, which we discussed in detail in Chapter 16, "Fine-Tuning Your Layout," can help you find problems with your Web site, too. In addition to checking for all the problems outlined in Chapter 16, it can point out any places where a text frame overlaps another frame, and is therefore in danger of being converted into a graphic. It can also warn you of large graphics that might take a while to load (see Figure 19.15). To access the Design Checker, choose Tools, Design Checker.

Fig. 19.15
If you ask it to, Publisher will warn you of large graphics that might slow the loading of your Web site.

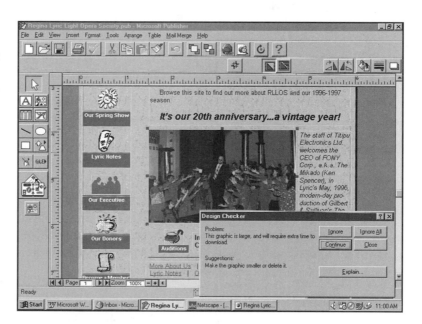

Converting existing publications to Web pages

Publisher also makes it easy to take any existing publication and turn it into a Web site. Just open the publication you want to convert, and choose File, Create Web Site from Current Publication.

Publisher closes the current publication and immediately opens a new publication, which looks exactly the same—except the new one is a Web site. It will then offer to run Design Checker to look for any layout that is inappropriate to a Web site, such as overlapping frames and large graphics.

That's all there is to it. Once you make whatever changes you want—and maybe add a few hyperlinks—our publication is ready to take its place on the Web.

Publishing to the Web

Publisher lets you publish your Web site directly to the World Wide Web, or to a folder on your hard drive. Before you do either one, choose File, Web Site Properties (see Figure 19.16).

Fig. 19.16
Before you publish your Web site, make sure this information is correct.

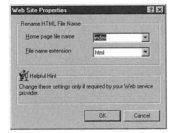

This shows you what the first, or home, page of your Web site will be called—almost always index—and what extension will be used on the pages' names: html or htm. Html is the most common, but some service providers require an htm extension. Check with whomever is hosting your Web site to make sure you've chosen the right one.

Once you're sure these settings are correct, you can choose either File, Publish to Web, or File, Publish Web Site to Folder.

If you choose Publish to Web, you get a message telling you that you need to download the Web Publishing Wizard from Microsoft's Publisher Web site (although why they didn't simply include it with the program, since they included the command for it, is beyond me). Publisher will gladly connect you right away.

The Web Publishing Wizard is software that will FTP your Web site to your Internet provider. You need to know the Internet address to which you are supposed to post your Web pages.

But you don't have to use the Web Publishing Wizard at all, if you have other FTP software and know the address to which you are supposed to post your pages. In that case, choose File, Publish Web Site to Folder. You'll be asked to select a folder (or create one) on your hard drive. Click OK, and Publisher will create your Web site in that folder. Then you can FTP it to your Internet service provider at your convenience.

 ### *Plain English, please!*

FTP stands for File Transport Protocol. It's a widely used protocol for transmitting computer files over the Internet and ensuring they arrive in one piece.

Part VI: Reference

Appendix A: **Installing Microsoft Publisher 97**

A

Installing Microsoft Publisher 97

● **In this chapter:**

● **What do I need to run Publisher on my computer?**

● **Should I install the whole thing or just bits and pieces?**

● **Thanks but no thanks; get it off my system!**

Knowing how to use Publisher is all well and good, but you can't do much of anything if you haven't installed the software. Here's how . . . . ⏵

Before you begin

The system requirements for running Microsoft Publisher 97 aren't as oner-
ous as you might think. According to Microsoft, you need:

- A personal computer with a 386DX or higher processor (486 recommended).

- Microsoft Windows 95 or Microsoft Windows NT 4.0.

- A minimum of 8M of memory for Windows 95 and 12M for Windows NT.

- A minimum of 9.5M of free space on your hard drive (maximum of 72M
  if you install from floppies; 116M if you install the typical CD Deluxe
  version. There's also 140M of additional clip art on the CD you can
  install if hard drive space is no problem).

- A 3.5-inch high-density disk drive; optionally, a CD-ROM player.

- VGA or higher-resolution video adapter and monitor (SVGA 256-color
  recommended).

- A 9,600 or higher baud modem for online features (28,800 recommended), plus World Wide Web browser software and Web access.

These are, of course, minimum requirements; and operating any software
package with just the minimum requirements is frequently an exercise in
frustration. To use Publisher to the best of its capability, you need a Pentium
computer, 16M of RAM in Windows 95, a CD-ROM player, and a fast modem.

To see what kind of system you have, click Start and choose Settings, Control
Panel, and then double-click System. Windows 95 automatically examines
your system and displays its findings. (Once you install Publisher, you can
check system information by choosing Help, About Microsoft Publisher,
System Info.)

After you know you have everything you need to run Publisher effectively,
the rest of the installation procedure is smooth sailing.

Installing Microsoft Publisher 97

Installing any software in Windows 95 is usually a reasonably painless
process; that's certainly true of installing Microsoft Publisher 97.

With Windows 95 running, click the Start button, choose Settings, Control Panel and, finally, double-click Add/Remove Programs. From the dialog box that appears, click Install. If you're installing from a CD, insert the disc in your CD-ROM drive at this point; if you're installing from floppy disks, insert the first one in your floppy disk drive; then click Next.

Windows 95 searches for the installation program SETUP.EXE. When it finds it, you need to confirm the choice by clicking Finish.

The first thing you see is a page explaining exactly what you're licensed to do with the software, plus a message urging you to close any other open applications (because Setup can't update any files that might be in use by another program).

Next, Setup asks you to enter your name and organization and then to confirm what you entered.

Then Setup asks you to enter your 10-digit CD key, a yellow sticker on the back of your CD case. You can't run Setup without this key, so don't lose your case!

Once that's done, Setup gives you a product ID number (a very long string of digits) that you might be asked for should you have to contact technical support. Write it down.

Finally, after searching your drive for previously installed components of Publisher, Setup presents you with the Setup dialog box shown in Figure A.1.

Fig. A.1
You can install all of Publisher's options or choose to install only some of them.

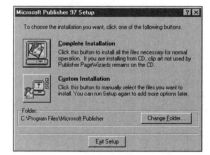

Here you can choose from two options:

- Complete Installation. This is recommended. All of Publisher's options will be available to you.

- Custom Installation. If you choose this option, you can pick and choose among Publisher's options to minimize the use of disk space. But, of course, you won't have the use of anything you don't install (see Figure A.2).

Fig. A.2
From here, you can install some or all of Publisher, which is useful if you want to conserve disk space.

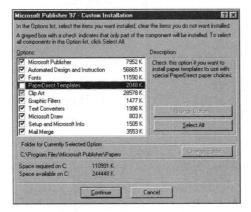

Choose your weapon

CAUTION **The following assumes that you're installing from CD-ROM.** Although the process of installation is the same, some of the details of the setup options in this section might be different if you're installing from floppies. In particular, the CD-ROM version of Publisher includes much more clip art and many more fonts.

If you choose Custom Installation, the Custom Installation dialog box in Figure A.2 opens. Here, Setup breaks Publisher into eight segments. You can choose to install any or all of the following:

- **Microsoft Publisher**—These are the essential system files for Publisher. If you install the program for the first time, you have to install these, including Clip Gallery and WordArt. Disk space required: 7,952K.

- **Automated Design and Instruction**—This is the largest segment; it includes the PageWizards and the built-in demonstrations of features. These elements are not required, but they can be extremely helpful, especially for novice users. Disk space required: 56,865K.

- **Fonts**—Publisher comes with many new fonts that can add flair to your publication, however, you don't have to install them if you don't want them. Disk space required: 11,590K.

- **PaperDirect Templates**—Publisher offers templates that help you design applications that you can print on special papers, created by the company PaperDirect, that already include various design elements. Unless you plan to buy these papers from PaperDirect, you don't need these templates, which is why I've removed the check for this option. Disk space required: 2048K.

- **Clip Art**—Publisher also includes a huge amount of clip art. The default selection is to load only previews of most of this clip art, which you can view in Clip Gallery, and leave the rest of it on the CD. There's a good reason for this: if you only load some of the clip art, and previews for the rest, you "only" use up 28,578K of space. If you load all of it (by clicking Change Options and making that choice), you need an additional (gulp!) 174,144K of disk space.

- **Graphic Filters**—When you import a graphic into Publisher, it must change that graphic into a format Publisher can read. That's the job of these filters, which are available for most of the common picture formats. If you want to install only a few graphic filters—say you only plan to import graphics in PC Paintbrush format and Windows Bitmap format—choose Graphic Filters, click Change Options and select only those filters you want to install. Disk space required for all of them: 1,477K.

- **Text Converters**—Just as Publisher has to convert pictures to a format it can use, it also has to convert text. Because most people prefer to create large documents in their favorite word processor and then insert those documents into Publisher, Publisher must recognize text generated by many different programs. To save disk space, you can install converters only for word processors you have on your system. Choose Text Converters and click the Change Options. You see the Text Converters dialog box shown in Figure A.3. Choose the converters you want to install and click OK to return to the Custom Installation dialog box. Disk space required for all converters: 1996K.

Fig. A.3

Publisher has text converters for several Microsoft word processors, as well as their chief rival, WordPerfect.

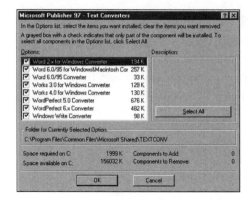

- **Microsoft Draw**—If you previously installed a Microsoft software package such as Word or Works, you may already have this basic drawing program. If not, you have to decide whether you want it, which probably depends on how likely you are to draw your own graphics when you can't find what you need. Disk space required: 803K.

- **Setup and Microsoft Info**—You don't need Setup and its support files to run Publisher, but you need them if you plan to customize your installation in the future by adding or removing components (for example, if you buy a larger disk drive and decide you want to store 170M of CD clip art on it). Microsoft Info provides detailed information about your system. Disk space required: 1,505K.

- **Mail Merge**—If you don't think you'll ever use Publisher to create mailing labels or personalize publications, you don't need Mail Merge and can save a little space by not installing it. Disk space required: 3,553K.

At the bottom of the Custom Installation dialog box, Publisher keeps track of how much space your selected options require in total, and reminds you of how much space you currently have available on the drive to which you're installing.

After you select the components you want to install (or simply click Select All), click Continue, and Setup begins installing files.

Setup prompts you for the floppy disks or CD-ROM it needs as it needs them and keeps you apprised of how the installation progresses with a bar that shows you the percentage of the installation complete.

Once installation is complete, Setup gives you the option of registering your software online. If you have a modem and World Wide Web access, all it takes is a click of a button, and in minutes, the process is done. Otherwise, you have to fill out and mail the postcard that comes with the program (just like in the old days!).

You can cancel installation at any time; Setup simply warns you that Publisher was not installed properly. You can return to Setup later.

If you do return to Setup after installing part or all of Publisher, you see a slightly different dialog box (see Figure A.4).

Fig. A.4

You can install some or all of Publisher for the first time, reinstall it (to add segments you didn't install the first time), or remove it from your hard drive altogether.

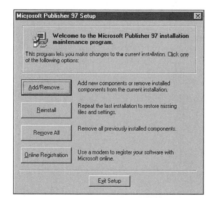

Here you can choose from four options:

- Add/Remove—If you install Publisher for the first time, or if you have previously installed Publisher but want to add or remove certain segments of it, click this button. You see a Maintenance Installation dialog box similar to the Custom Installation dialog box described earlier where you can choose which segments you want to add or remove.

- Reinstall—If you previously started to install Publisher but had to quit before you finished, or you installed Publisher but elements of it didn't install properly or have been damaged somehow, click this button to repeat installation.

- Remove All—If you previously installed Publisher and wish you hadn't, or desperately need to free up disk space (who doesn't?), click this button. Setup asks you if you're sure you want to take such drastic

action before removing all of Publisher's files. It also gives you the
option of removing any files created with Publisher.

- <u>O</u>nline Registration—Again, this gives you the option to connect to
  Microsoft's Web site and register your copy of Publisher.

CAUTION **If you already installed a working version of Publisher and cancel**
an update in midstream, you might find that your original no longer works
properly. Run Publisher Setup again and complete the new installation.

All done!

Assuming you're installing and not removing Publisher, after the process is
complete, you can close Setup and start Publisher by simply clicking Start,
choosing <u>P</u>rograms and then double-clicking the Microsoft Publisher icon
(a big purple P).

Voilà! You're off and running. (I told you it was simple!)

Index

Check out Que® Books
on the World Wide Web
http://www.quecorp.com

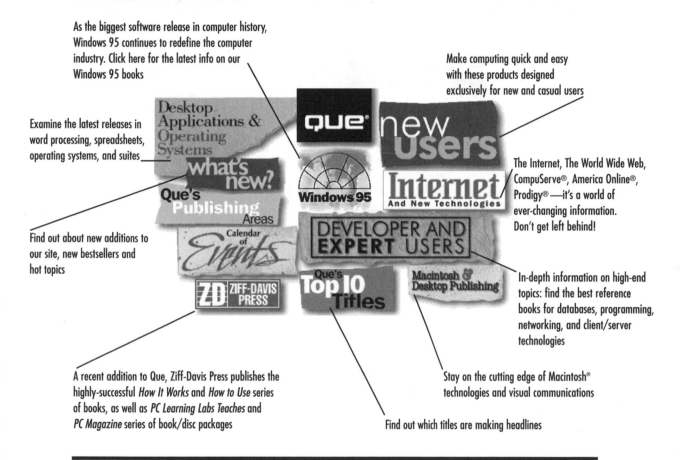

As the biggest software release in computer history, Windows 95 continues to redefine the computer industry. Click here for the latest info on our Windows 95 books

Make computing quick and easy with these products designed exclusively for new and casual users

Examine the latest releases in word processing, spreadsheets, operating systems, and suites

The Internet, The World Wide Web, CompuServe®, America Online®, Prodigy® —it's a world of ever-changing information. Don't get left behind!

Find out about new additions to our site, new bestsellers and hot topics

In-depth information on high-end topics: find the best reference books for databases, programming, networking, and client/server technologies

A recent addition to Que, Ziff-Davis Press publishes the highly-successful *How It Works* and *How to Use* series of books, as well as *PC Learning Labs Teaches* and *PC Magazine* series of book/disc packages

Stay on the cutting edge of Macintosh® technologies and visual communications

Find out which titles are making headlines

With 6 separate publishing groups, Que develops products for many specific market segments and areas of computer technology. Explore our Web Site and you'll find information on best-selling titles, newly published titles, upcoming products, authors, and much more.

- Stay informed on the latest industry trends and products available
- Visit our online bookstore for the latest information and editions
- Download software from Que's library of the best shareware and freeware

MACMILLAN COMPUTER PUBLISHING USA

A VIACOM COMPANY

Technical ---- Support:

If you need assistance with the information in this book or with a CD/Disk accompanying the book, please access the Knowledge Base on our Web site at **http://www.superlibrary.com/general/support**. Our most Frequently Asked Questions are answered there. If you do not find the answer to your questions on our Web site, you may contact Macmillan Technical Support **(317) 581-3833** or e-mail us at **support@mcp.com**.